# Juneteenth

# Juneteenth

## THE STORY BEHIND THE CELEBRATION

EDWARD T. COTHAM, JR.

# State ✦ House Press

State House Press
at Schreiner University
Kerrville, TX
325-660-1752
www.mcwhiney.org

Cataloging-in-Publication Data

Names: Cotham, Edward T, 1953-  (Edward Terrel), author.
Title: Juneteenth: the story behind the celebration / Edward T. Cotham.
Description: First edition. | Kerrville, TX: State House Press, 2021. | Includes bibliographical references and index.
Identifiers: ISBN 9781649670007 (soft cover); ISBN 9781649670021 (e-book)
Subjects: LCSH: Juneteenth. | Slaves – Emancipation – Texas – Anniversaries, etc. | African Americans – Anniversaries, etc.
Classification: LCC E185.93.T4 (print) | DCC 326.809764

First edition 2021

Cover and page design and production by Allen Griffith of Eye 4 Design.

Distributed by Texas A&M University Press Consortium
800-826-8911
www.tamupress.com

*"20 years ago the majority of the men you have seen march with high steps through the streets of the city today were permitted to make their first step out into the broad American Republic as freemen. Your mothers and sisters, together with four millions of their kinsmen, wept their thanks to the God of nations for their liberation from the damnation of slavery. We have met here today to put ourselves on record by giving expressions of our profound gratitude of what has been vouchsafed to us."*

—Oration titled "Why we celebrate the 19th of June in each year,"
Rev. Mack Henson, San Antonio, June 19, 1885

# Contents

# List of Images

*Preface*

This book project is, in some ways, an effort to trace the genealogy of a piece of paper. The paper in question is the military order commemorated every year on "Juneteenth." For those who may be unfamiliar with the event, Juneteenth is the celebration of the end of American slavery that takes place every 19th of June. Indeed, the name "Juneteenth" is a short-hand reference to June 19, 1865, the date upon which a staff officer in the headquarters of Maj. Gen. Gordon Granger in Galveston, Texas, issued an order designated "General Orders No. 3." That order stated in its famous first sentence that "all slaves are free."[1]

Because there were many numbered general orders issued during the Civil War, with confusingly similar names and numbers, the Galveston order has become more popularly known as the "Juneteenth Order." But what has made this order so popular? Why did anyone care enough to name and celebrate an order that only received a routine number when it was originally issued? The answer is that the Juneteenth Order has long been celebrated in Texas, and increasingly, across the nation, as marking the end of slavery and the arrival of "first freedom" for millions of people. On or even before the first anniversary of the order's issuance, freed slaves in Texas began celebrating their emancipation, making Juneteenth what some claim to be the oldest continuous commemoration of emancipation in America.[2] The tradition of celebrating Juneteenth continues today, and has expanded far beyond the boundaries of Texas, where the tradition originally began.

My interest in the Juneteenth Order originated more than forty years ago when I was casually skimming through a newspaper article describing that year's version of the annual Juneteenth celebration. In reviewing the newspaper account, I noted that, as usual, the article quoted only the first line of General Granger's order, which declared that "all slaves are free." Knowing that there had to be more to the Juneteenth Order than this one sentence, I became curious about the remainder of the text. When I looked up the order's full text, I learned that it read as follows:

Headquarters, District of Texas

Galveston, Texas, June 19, 1865

**General Orders, No. 3**

The people are informed that, in accordance with a proclamation from the Executive of the United States, "all slaves are free." This involves an absolute equality of personal rights and rights of property, between former masters and slaves, and the connection heretofore existing between them, becomes that between employer and hired labor. The freedmen are advised to remain at their present homes, and work for wages. They are informed that they will not be allowed to collect at military posts; and that they will not be supported in idleness either there or elsewhere.

By order of

Major-General Granger

F. W. Emery, Maj. & A.A.G[3]

I must confess that, upon reading the full text of the Juneteenth Order, my initial reaction was disappointment. Although General Granger's name was attached to it, the order was technically issued only by a staff officer who hadn't even used his full name. What was even more surprising to me was that the text of the order was not really the sweeping proclamation of emancipation I had been expecting; instead, more than half of the text was a rather patronizing admonition to the freed slaves to continue to stay put where they had been enslaved and keep doing the same work they had been doing for the same old masters. What kind of freedom was that?

The more I read General Orders No. 3, the more questions that arose. If this was the third general order, what were the first two orders about? What subjects could possibly be more important to the Union army in 1865 than announcing the coming of emancipation? I was also troubled by the use of a military order in 1865 to announce the end of slavery. After all, this was a subject that had been repeatedly addressed by President Lincoln in his 1862 and 1863 emancipation proclamations and by the U.S. Congress in a variety of legislative efforts. Why would anyone choose to celebrate a seemingly pedestrian military order issued in Texas more than two months after Confederate Gen. Robert E. Lee's surrender at Appomattox and use it as the point of origin for emancipation?

In my experience as a military historian, orders issued by generals usually had military subjects. They tended to be directed at people serving under them and mandated or prohibited specific actions. But the Juneteenth Order starts with the phrase "The people are informed." Its contents are plainly directed at civilians and only tangentially involve any discernable military subject. It would be like the modern military issuing an order on tax policy or putting out a position paper on climate change. There simply had to be more to this story.

The more I studied the text of the Juneteenth Order, the more I was bothered by the provisions in its last two sentences warning the "freedmen" against the perils of being idle.[4] For obvious reasons, many of the modern newspapers that report on Juneteenth do not quote the Juneteenth Order's final sentences in their annual coverage of the celebration. Why were these sentences originally included? Indeed, what made the military feel the need to offer public "advice" to people who were not even part of the military? And if the military felt the need to offer advice to the freedpeople, why was it phrased in such patronizing and insulting language? "You now have a job and you better stay there," the order all but directed. I began to wonder why this order and its seemingly embarrassing contents were worthy of any form of commemoration. Why would anyone give speeches and hold parades to celebrate this?

The thing that kept drawing me back to studying the Juneteenth Order as a historian was the fact that so many freed slaves had so quickly and enthusiastically gravitated to celebrating its promulgation. Out of all the proclamations, orders, and legislation made, issued, or enacted during the war, this particular order, issued in Galveston, Texas, on June 19, 1865, was chosen by a broad consensus of formerly enslaved people to mark the commemoration date of emancipation. The date had almost immediately become synonymous with freedom for a host of people who regarded it as the most important event that had taken place in their lives and collective memory. When and how did this happen?

Juneteenth is celebrated every year precisely because it does involve a subject that is of real importance. Indeed, there can be no subject worthier of celebration (and study) than human freedom. Juneteenth provides an annual opportunity to think back to a time when millions of people in America were not free and to remember the sacrifices made by those who fought and died to make their freedom a reality. It also serves to remind us of the challenges that were faced by people suddenly thrust from bondage into a new way of life with its own unforeseen and unforeseeable difficulties and opportunities.

One thing that the reader will note immediately in reviewing the contents of this book is that it starts well before June 1865 and spends a great deal of time discussing events that occurred outside the borders of Texas. The reason for this is that the author believes that the events behind the Juneteenth Order cannot be properly understood without being placed in context. To use an analogy, studying Juneteenth is like a person who pulls a sample of water out of a flowing river and then attempts to study it. Is the water cold? Is it clear or murky? What does it taste like? None of the answers to these questions involve the identity of the person who drew the water sample or even the person who owns title to the riverbank from which the sample was obtained. Instead, to really understand the water and its properties, the observer would need to go upstream and determine where and how the river originated and trace its path downstream.

The history of the Juneteenth Order fits the studied glass of water analogy rather well. The identity of the man (Gen. Gordon Granger) who is usually credited with issuing the order is not particularly important to the story. And although understanding the end of the war in Galveston helps provide some important context for the issuance of the Juneteenth Order, events before 1865 and people located outside of Galveston are even more important in shaping the order and its meaning. To really understand Juneteenth, it is necessary to travel well upstream from General Granger and Galveston.

Much of this book involves a journey upstream from the Juneteenth Order to see why the river flowing from slavery to emancipation produced that particular expression of liberation. It will also spend some time near the conclusion briefly discussing some of the events that occurred downstream. For the river that resulted in Juneteenth continues to flow and shape events to this day.

Dr. Martin Luther King, Jr., chose to close his iconic "I Have a Dream" speech at the Lincoln Memorial in 1963 with the words of an old spiritual song that is believed to have originated during the Civil War: "Free at last! Free at last! Thank God Almighty, we are free at last!"[5] Every Juneteenth, we are reminded of a time when people who had been held as slaves could first make the supremely important claim that they were finally and irrevocably "free at last." It is the purpose of this narrative to explore how and why that remarkable claim first became a celebrated reality in Texas.

**Edward T. Cotham, Jr.**
Galveston, Texas
June 19, 2020

Ulysses S. Grant (c. 1880). Library of Congress, LC-USZ62-79351.

*Introduction*

On March 23, 1880, Ulysses S. Grant returned to the United States from a business trip to Mexico. Famous as both a general and a two-term President of the United States, Grant stepped ashore in Galveston, Texas, as the biggest celebrity ever to visit the state. Traveling was nothing new for Grant. Since leaving the White House, he literally toured the world, being enthusiastically received by a host of monarchs and heads of state. Grant's arrival in Galveston was a triumphant spectacle. Huge crowds turned out to see the famous "Silent Man," as the general had been dubbed by the popular press.

This was not Grant's first visit to Texas. In fact, in 1846, at the age of twenty-four, Grant served as part of the American force that came to South Texas to fight the conflict later called the Mexican War. But Grant's 1880 visit was his first to the City of Galveston, and he eagerly looked forward to the opportunity to evaluate the commercial and civic prospects of the Island City.

On the third day following his arrival in Galveston, Grant made a very special visit to a local school. The Barnes Institute, established a few years after the end of the Civil War, became one of the first schools opened in Texas to educate former slaves and their descendants. The school children waiting to meet Grant spent days decorating their school and were feverish with excitement. The general's arrival triggered a cacophonous greeting that combined childish squeals with thunderous applause. As Grant waved and acknowledged the enthusiastic reception, he could not help but notice his picture hung prominently from the ceiling, alongside a picture of Abraham Lincoln.[1]

As Grant studied the dual portraits, a young student named Willie Whales stepped up to the stage and delivered a short speech. The eloquent young man used the occasion to explain why Grant's portrait occupied such a place of importance in his school:

> I cannot tell you fittingly all of the happiness we feel at beholding your living features and being in the presence of one whose genius did so much to make it possible for us to be here today. We have often looked with grateful emotions at your picture hanging there, where it has hung for the past ten years, but we never expected to behold your distinguished person. We rejoice that the institution of slavery has crumbled into fine dust, and though it has long retarded our growth, and doomed us to be the most disesteemed people of America, yet we hold no harsh feelings toward those who upheld it, and this they well know. With faith in God and charity for all, we trust to time and ourselves, the only builders of peoples, to elevate us. You sir, and the peoples of America, have your George Washington, but we envy you not. We too have our George Washington—Abraham Lincoln and U. S. Grant—and we would not exchange with you. Repeating our welcome, I have only to express the hope that you may rise in public esteem as long as you shall live, and that your life may be extended to the utmost limit.[2]

To modern ears it may sound strange, almost heretical, to hear Gen. U. S. Grant referred to as one of the co-founders of emancipation in America along with President Lincoln. But this ignores an important, indeed critical, part of the story that surrounded emancipation. As Willie Whales reminded his young audience in 1880, less than fifteen years after the end of slavery, the death of that institution had not been accomplished through President Lincoln's pen alone. The end of slavery had only been possible because of the deeds and sacrifice of men who fought for the cause of freedom.

Modern commemorations of emancipation celebrate the words that began the progress down the road to ending slavery—the Emancipation Proclamation—as part of Abraham Lincoln's continuing legacy. But Lincoln himself recognized that even his stirring rhetoric could not capture the full story of the sacrifices made during the war. As he reminded his audience so memorably in the Gettysburg Address, "The world will little note, nor long remember what we say here, but it can never forget what they did here."[3]

The battle to end slavery would not have been won, indeed could not have been won, without the leadership of a host of military leaders like Ulysses S. Grant. But good leaders are not enough to win wars, and the struggles and sacrifices of the men, black and white, who fought and, in some cases gave their lives as "the last full measure of devotion" to their cause, were critical elements that made that outcome possible.[4] The military's contribution to the end of slavery is justly remembered and celebrated annually in the event that today is called "Juneteenth."

For decades, celebrants have described Juneteenth as the "oldest known celebration commemorating the ending of slavery in the United States."[5] Every year, large and increasing numbers of people around the United States gather to pay tribute to an event that took place in Galveston, Texas, on June 19, 1865. On that day, later to become famous as the original "Juneteenth," a staff officer acting under the direction of Maj. Gen. Gordon Granger issued "General Orders No. 3." The first line of this order authoritatively declared that "in accordance with a proclamation from the Executive of the United States, 'all slaves are free.'"[6]

The reverberations from General Granger's "Juneteenth Order" continue to echo to this day. Many states have officially declared Juneteenth to be some form of holiday or day of remembrance, and there is also a growing momentum in Congress to recognize June 19 of each year as a holiday or "National Day of Observance." But what precisely is being observed, remembered, or commemorated on Juneteenth? For something so famous, the events of Juneteenth stay shrouded in a fog of mystery. What do historians really know about the history behind the holiday? To put the question another way, what actually happened in Galveston on June 19, 1865? Where did it happen and how did it happen?

Modern Juneteenth commemorations tend to focus on Gen. Gordon Granger, whose name a staff officer affixed to the order that Juneteenth commemorates. In some ways, however, this attention seems misguided. The historical event of Juneteenth had very little to do with General Granger. Indeed, a later section of this book argues that of all the military officials involved with the authorship and issuance of the Juneteenth Order, General Granger played one of the smallest and least essential parts.

The origin of the Juneteenth Order lay in social and military events that took place largely outside Texas and involved military officials not present in the state when the order was issued. Interestingly, the Juneteenth Order was far from unique. As the narrative that follows demonstrates, Granger's famous order was one of a series of similar orders and proclamations that began relatively early in the war and changed in tone and scope throughout the conflict. By tracing the history of these orders and their evolution the language and larger meaning of the Juneteenth Order can be fully appreciated.

The purpose of the Juneteenth Order is commonly misunderstood. When it was issued, the order was intended to do far more than proclaim the end of slavery. Although the order does indeed confirm in its first sentence that slavery had ended, it explicitly credits that result to President Lincoln's 1863 Emancipation Proclamation. As far as the authors of the Juneteenth Order were concerned, slavery had already ended in Texas. The first sentence stood as merely a public reaffirmation and proclamation of that fact—and a not very subtle reminder that the U.S. Army, now in Texas, would enforce that change in status.

If confirming the end of slavery was not the sole purpose of the Juneteenth Order, then what did military leaders intend with its issuance? The bulk of the order sounds, to modern ears at least, like patronizing instructions directing former slaves to remain at their current locations and continue to work for wages. This language was intentional. One of the primary purposes behind the military's issuance of the Juneteenth Order was to maintain order, keep laborers at work in the fields, and prevent the civil unrest that white officers and politicians feared might result from exuberant celebrations by the newly emancipated freedpeople.

Modern Juneteenth commemorations also differ from the historical events of 1865 in how the order was originally communicated to its intended audience. Modern celebrations of Juneteenth often include a reading of the order from a podium or the balcony of a prominent Galveston building. It is highly unlikely, however that any such public reading took place on or around June 19, 1865.

No contemporary historical record of such a reading has been found to date, nor would a reading of this type have been an efficient way to deliver the emancipation message either to the eager ears of former slaves or the reluctant ears of their former masters.

Historical accounts suggest that the Juneteenth Order was issued at General Granger's headquarters near the waterfront, in a building (the Osterman building) later destroyed by a storm and today a parking lot. The order was one of five, relatively routine, general orders issued for General Granger by Maj. Frederick W. Emery, one of his staff officers. Although the Juneteenth Order was indeed widely circulated, that distribution occurred not through speeches, but primarily by publication in newspapers throughout the state and specially printed handbills distributed by public officials and Union occupation troops.[7]

The many myths and mysteries surrounding the actual historical events of June 19, 1865, do not make Juneteenth unimportant. They also do not mean that celebration of Juneteenth is misguided. To the contrary, one of the central conclusions of this work is that the Juneteenth Order accompanied the actual liberation of at least 250,000 people in Texas and surrounding territories. The importance of the Juneteenth Order lies not in its language, but in its results. To appreciate the true significance of the Juneteenth Order it is necessary to understand the people and events behind its issuance, and to separate fact from fiction.

This book is subtitled "The Story behind the Celebration" because to understand the Juneteenth Order's purposes and impact it is necessary to review some of the key events of the Civil War that preceded Juneteenth. Indeed, to fully illuminate the historical events that occurred on Juneteenth it becomes necessary to shine a light in some unexpected places. It may not be at first apparent why, for example, the actions of Union generals John M. Schofield in North Carolina or Francis J. Herron in Louisiana should be integral to the story of Texas and Juneteenth. After all, the only general named in the Juneteenth Order was Gen. Gordon Granger. But Granger was not the author of any significant portion of the language in the Juneteenth Order. That honor fell in large part to Gen. Philip H. Sheridan, who based his proposed language for the order on language in Schofield's and Herron's earlier orders. Even Ulysses S. Grant, who never visited Galveston until 1880, helped set in motion the events that culminated in the Juneteenth Order. Each of these generals played important and largely unexplored parts in the drama that resulted in the Juneteenth Order.

No discussion of the events surrounding emancipation in this country would be complete without exploration of President Abraham Lincoln and the executive actions known collectively to history as the "Emancipation Proclamation." But as this book details in later chapters, Lincoln's actions with regard to emancipation were subject to important limitations, not the least of which resided in the fact that the president's proclamation, by its own terms, expressly applied only to those areas under effective Confederate control. In other words, Lincoln purported to free the slaves only in areas where he held no effective power to actually free the slaves. Lincoln himself understood his proclamation's limitations; indeed, he had deep reservations about its legal validity and feared its impact. This is almost certainly why he tenaciously fought for the passage of the Thirteenth Amendment to the United States Constitution.

In some ways, General Granger's Juneteenth Order in Galveston proves the perfect bookend event to study in conjunction with President Lincoln's Emancipation Proclamation. When Lincoln issued his Emancipation Proclamation in Washington at the beginning of 1863 it was widely viewed as an important symbolic announcement that would have very little immediate effect. Few slaves, if any, were actually freed when Lincoln signed his proclamation. A popular website called "How Things Work" asks a trivia question: "How many slaves did the Emancipation Proclamation free?" to which the correct answer offered is "Zero." By contrast, General Granger's Juneteenth Order in 1865, which did not purport to break any new ground or announce any new policy, resulted within a short period of time in freedom for hundreds of thousands of people formerly held in bondage.[8]

It should not be surprising that something as important as the end of slavery was the culmination of a series of steps and events. In fact, it is rare that a truly significant change in history is accomplished in a single document or at a single point in time. The founding of the Union that was at issue in the Civil War provides an illustration of this principle. The adoption of the Declaration of Independence on July 4, 1776, while important, did not result immediately in the creation of the United States as an independent country. In fact, the British Crown, as well as many American colonists, regarded the Declaration as merely the treasonous act of a body of rebels. It was only when the American colonies earned their freedom through force of arms and ultimately adopted a Constitution many years later that America as we know it today took form as an independent nation.

The United States celebrates its independence on July 4 because that is a convenient and appropriate date to commemorate the process that eventually resulted in independence. The same could be said about Juneteenth and emancipation. As explored in a later section of this book, there is no natural holiday date for emancipation in America. President Lincoln issued a "Preliminary" Emancipation Proclamation in September 1862 followed by what is usually called the "Final" Emancipation Proclamation effective January 1, 1863.[9] But neither of these executive actions resulted in the actual freeing of significant numbers of slaves in Confederate states. Only after federal soldiers could physically enforce the Emancipation Proclamation in the last of the Confederate States, and the Thirteenth Amendment to the Constitution was fully ratified later, did emancipation reach the status of an accomplished fact for many people in bondage. There is simply no "Fourth of July" date to conveniently point to as the natural date to commemorate actual liberation.

Kenneth C. Davis, author of a book titled *Don't Know Much about History*, stated that Juneteenth is unique in that it is "the holiday that doesn't mark a document, a battle, a birthday or a national tragedy, but the fundamental promise of America being more completely realized."[10] That is an eloquent statement, but Juneteenth actually does mark something more specific. When historians search for the place and time when federal authority finally prevailed over the last major part of the Confederacy, the search leads almost inexorably to Galveston and June 19, 1865. Galveston, Texas, was the most prominent port city in the Confederate Department of the Trans-Mississippi, that department being the last major territory to come back under Union control at the conclusion of the Civil War. As its name suggests, the Trans-Mississippi was the area west of the Mississippi River, which finally succumbed to Union control in June 1865. Large numbers of enslaved people lived in this large Confederate area. In fact, the number of people held in bondage in Texas increased significantly throughout the war as slaveholders across the South moved or "refugeed" their slaves to Texas as part of an increasingly desperate attempt to keep them away from the liberating presence of invading Union armies.[11]

Students of the Civil War are quite naturally conditioned to think of that war as a collision between two forces: the Union and Confederate armies. There was a third force suspended between and among these armies, however: the roughly four million people who started the war as slaves and ended it, after the passage of a Constitutional amendment, as free men and women. In some ways, their struggle was a revolution within a revolution. Neither military force that entered the conflict devised a coherent strategy for how to handle or interact with the slave population. As Union armies fought their way across the South, they were alternately hindered and helped by their interactions with a slave population that often outnumbered the armies in the field. Eventually, largely by virtue of necessity, the Union army began to recruit the slaves it freed and brought them into the fold of military service. Black men in uniform fittingly played a large part in the final progress and outcome of the war.[12]

The men and women freed by the Civil War spent little time debating which of President Lincoln's executive actions technically resulted in their freedom. Nor did they spend any time analyzing the various Congressional actions that, by fits and starts, eventually addressed their legal status. They were much more practical about this critical event in their lives. Interviewed many years after the fact, many of the freed slaves remembered exactly where they had been when they learned for certain that their freedom was finally secured.

In some scholarly works a distinction is drawn between "emancipation" and "actual freedom," with the former being a legal concept and the latter representing the arrival of immediate and permanent personal liberty. Juneteenth is more about the latter concept, although its arrival would not have been possible without a favorable change in legal status. It is important to acknowledge this distinction at the outset, however, because the coming of actual liberation to millions of American slaves is difficult to document and has probably not received the full historical attention it deserves.

It is impossible to overestimate how life-changing and momentous the arrival of actual freedom was to those who had lived, in many cases for generations, in bondage. When questioned about the coming of freedom years after the fact, many freed slaves recalled in great detail the day in the summer of 1865 on which the "freedom paper" was read to them announcing and confirming their freedom. This brings up a natural question. What was this paper? It was almost certainly not President Lincoln's Emancipation Proclamation. In most cases it was an order or proclamation issued by a Union general that declared the Emancipation Proclamation to be in effect in a particular territory brought back under Union control by force of arms.

Almost immediately after the end of the war, freed slaves seized on the moment the "paper" that freed them was issued as the key event in their emancipation. For many of these people, particularly those who lived in Texas, the "paper" they remembered hearing was the Juneteenth Order issued in Galveston. When the freedpeople eventually began to collectively celebrate their emancipation in increasingly formal ways, they searched for a common date to memorialize something that was by definition impossible to pin down to a particular date or location.

The date that the freed slaves in Texas and neighboring states ultimately chose to celebrate as the date of their freedom was June 19, 1865, the day that actual freedom finally arrived on Texas shores with General Granger and the Union occupation force he represented. Granger's Juneteenth Order may well have resulted in actual and relatively immediate freedom for more people than any other document issued during the Civil War.

The real facts behind the Juneteenth Order are perhaps less dramatic than the speeches from balconies that have over time become an accepted part of its legend. But in some ways, the real facts are even more remarkable. The liberation of enslaved African Americans came about not just because of speeches by politicians, but because of their own struggles and the struggles of people who fought to free them. This fundamental truth underlies the real importance of Juneteenth and gives it continuing relevance.

# Juneteenth

## Chapter 1

### SLAVERY AND TEXAS

The Census of 1860, the last census taken before the advent of the Civil War, recorded that almost four million people were held in bondage in the United States. Just under five percent of these slaves lived and worked in Texas. This number represented a little more than half the slave population in neighboring Louisiana. It was not that slavery was less popular or less profitable in Texas. The smaller slave population in the Lone Star State relative to other Southern states (Texas ranked tenth in terms of total slave population) was primarily due to the fact that slavery as an institution had gotten a late start in Texas.

When Texas declared independence from Mexico in 1836, approximately 5,000 slaves lived in the new republic. The new Anglo immigrants who flooded into Texas, however, brought large numbers of slaves with them and wasted no time in importing even more. The institution of slavery spread rapidly and, in the decades preceding the Civil War, the slave population in Texas expanded significantly faster than the white population. By 1850, more than 58,000 slaves lived in the state. By 1861, the number of slaves rose to almost 200,000.[1]

As the Civil War approached, Texas was in the process of becoming what historian Randolph B. Campbell has called a virtual "empire for slavery." The "peculiar institution," as some contemporaries referred to slavery, flourished in virtually every inhabited part of Texas. Slave ownership became an integral part of the social and economic fabric of Texas. "Far from being unimportant," Campbell confirmed, "slavery played a vital role in shaping antebellum Texas and determining its future."[2]

While uncomfortable to modern ears, "property in man," as nineteenth century legal scholars routinely referred to slaves, held several unique aspects worth noting. Slaves represented an inherently difficult type of property to own and manage. First, slaves were independently mobile and might seek to leave the person who claimed ownership. Second, slaves represented a continuing threat to the lives and wellbeing of their owner. Many slave owners in Texas and elsewhere in America, therefore, lived in virtually constant fear of their slave property either departing or committing violent acts.[3]

As the number of slaves in Texas increased, the slave owners who lived among them became increasingly concerned about their personal security. This was not a phenomenon limited to Texas. Southerners feared that some event or agitator somewhere might trigger a general slave revolt. The average white American—Northerners, Southerners, and even some of those who favored abolition of slavery—worried about the potential for bloodshed that might result from a slave revolt. Part of this concern seemed understandable, and indeed had a basis in then-recent history.[4]

In August 1791, a massive slave revolt rocked the prosperous French colony of Saint Domingue. Triggered in part by the events and rhetoric of the French Revolution, the revolt eventually spread and in 1804 led to the independence of the colony as the new republic of Haiti. The early portions of the rebellion featured reprisals by the slaves against their masters, leading to published accounts of almost unbelievable acts of violence and revenge. Lurid stories ran plentiful in American newspapers detailing atrocities committed by the rebelling slaves against their former masters. Typical of these accounts is the following history published in Ohio in 1860:

> The news ran through the island like the tremor of an earthquake—"The blacks have risen!" The appalling news was too true. . . . The insurrection now burst forth in all its terror and calamity. . . . The ranks of the rebels were increased at every step of their progress, and along their march of devastation they murdered every white who fell into their power, without distinction of age or sex, viewing with fiendish delight the agonies and groans of those whom so lately they had not dared to look in the face.[5]

Although no slave rebellion of the scale that occurred in Haiti ever took place on American soil, continuing concerns that such an event might suddenly and without warning erupt into an orgy of violence remained. From time to time, newspaper editors speculated about parties whose interests might be served by such a revolution. There was even historical precedent for such speculation. During the period preceding the American Revolution, rumors flourished that the British encouraged a slave rebellion. Indeed, one of the central causes for revolution cited in the Declaration of Independence stated that the British monarch "excited domestic insurrections amongst us."[6]

Some of the French planters who escaped from the violence of the slave rebellion in Haiti came to America, bringing with them tales of atrocities and sparking fears that a similar rebellion might break out in the new nation. These fears heightened in August 1831, when an enslaved man named Nat Turner led a rebellion known at the time as the "Southampton Insurrection." Nat Turner's Rebellion, as it eventually became known, resulted in the deaths of approximately sixty white Virginians, making it the deadliest slave revolt in American history. In retaliation, whites murdered between one and two hundred blacks, many of the deaths resulting from mob action.[7]

As the Civil War approached, rumors of slave rebellions and alleged plots by Northerners to incite them appeared frequently in Southern newspapers. Particularly frightening to planters was an all too real plot, the Harper's Ferry raid launched by John Brown in October 1859. Brown led an attempt by twenty-one men to capture the federal arsenal and obtain arms for a spontaneous and simultaneous uprising of slaves across the nation. The uprising Brown envisioned never took place, and his entire group was either killed or captured by a force commanded by Col. Robert E. Lee. Before his execution, Brown made the chilling prediction that "I, John Brown, am now quite certain that the crimes of this guilty land will never be purged away but with blood."[8]

Brown's raid convinced many Americans, particularly those living in the South, that agitators from the North were secretly organizing and aiding slave rebellions. Southerners seemed easily persuaded that the bloody purge promised by Brown lay just around the corner if steps were not taken to eliminate the threat.

Under these circumstances, little was needed to fan the sparks of fear into the flame of a full-scale panic. In the summer of 1860, just such a flame arrived on the plains of North Texas.

The summer of 1860 proved one of the hottest on record. When a fire destroyed a portion of Dallas, residents at first attributed the incident to the drought and the heat. But then fires began to mysteriously occur in Denton and other Texas towns. A Dallas newspaper editor became convinced that the fires were the result of a vast conspiracy involving slaves and abolitionists. He wasted no time in circulating a series of lurid reports to other news outlets around the state charging that prominent citizens were being marked for death or even worse fates:

> Many of our most prominent citizens were singled out for assassination whenever they made their escape from their burning homes. . . . Poisoning was to be added, and the old females to be slaughtered along with the men, and the young and handsome women to be parceled out among these infamous scoundrels. They had even gone so far as to designate their choice, and certain ladies had already been selected as the victims of these misguided monsters.[9]

These reports produced widespread and intense panic across the state, even though many of the accounts held absolutely no factual basis. As one historian who studied these events later characterized it, "a shroud of fear settled over the state"—a shroud nearly impossible to escape.[10] As the election campaign of 1860 proceeded, the Texas fires and the alleged abolitionist connection to them took front and center stage. Newspapers throughout the South warned that John Brown's raid and the fires in Texas were all part of a vast Northern conspiracy whose chief organizers were the "Black Republican" party and its nominee, Abraham Lincoln. If the Southern states refused to take prompt action to remove themselves from the Union, the papers warned, Southerners would soon find themselves the victims of a slave insurrection that would rival the legendary bloodbath in Haiti.[11]

This climate of fear in the summer of 1860 explained, at least in part, why Texas joined the Confederacy in the coming Civil War. On the surface, this decision seems puzzling. Not long before, Texas eagerly joined the Union, becoming the twenty-eighth state on December 29, 1845. Yet, on February 2, 1861, a little more than fifteen years later, Texans voted to leave the Union by a wide margin.

What caused so many Texans to change their minds? Historians have offered numerous explanations, but fears surrounding slavery certainly influenced many. While only about one in four Texans owned slaves, slavery played a key part in the Texas economy. Many Texans also feared for their personal safety, as it was generally believed white victims of a slave revolt would likely extend well beyond the slave owning class. Slaveholders also tended to be men of wealth and influence. They dominated the economic, social, and political institutions of the day. Not surprisingly, therefore, when Texas attempted to secede in 1861 the official declaration of the causes of Texas secession cited protection of slavery as the most critical reason to withdraw from the Union and join the rebellion:

> [Texas] was received as a commonwealth holding, maintaining and protecting the institution known as negro slavery—the servitude of the African to the white race within her limits—a relation that had existed from the first settlement of her wilderness by the white race, and which her people intended should exist in all future time. Her institutions and geographical position established the strongest ties between her and other slave-holding States of the confederacy.[12]

Some prominent American leaders had long foreseen the growing presence of slavery in Texas as an ominous development. John Quincy Adams, for example, delivered an "Address to the People of the Free States" as early as 1843 in which he opposed the admission of Texas to the United States and warned that it would so upset the balance between free and slave states that it would inevitably "result in a dissolution of the Union."[13] A mere eighteen years later, Adams' comments proved prescient.

The Civil War that Adams saw coming ultimately ended the institution of slavery, but no one could have predicted the winding and tortured route by which that destination was eventually reached. The end of American slavery proved to be a dramatic production that took place on many different stages at the same time, featuring a constantly changing cast of characters. Some of these characters are

Slaves standing in front of buildings on Smith's Plantation, Beaufort, South Carolina. Library of Congress, LC-USZ62-67819.

well known, while others have eluded modern scholarship. But all actors in this important drama are worthy of study.

The end of American slavery resulted from action on three, roughly parallel, tracks. The first track, the "Washington track," became the prominent theory that most Americans imagine when they hear the word "emancipation." This track featured President Lincoln acting in his time-honored role as the "Great Emancipator." It also involved a host of legislators who were eventually cajoled, coerced, and persuaded to enact the Thirteenth Amendment to the U.S. Constitution. While the "Washington track" plays a prominent role in American memory, more of the story remains.

The second, and less familiar, track that resulted in emancipation involved the actions of the enslaved people themselves. Scholars have called this path the "self-emancipation track." In recent years, historians belatedly came to a consensus and understanding that one of the critical forces that made emancipation both necessary and possible was the actions that enslaved people took, at great risk, to force the issue and free themselves. Historian David Williams wrote an excellent book, titled *I Freed Myself: African American Self-Emancipation in the Civil War Era*, which argued convincingly that the contributions of black people (free and slave) to the outcome of the war have been underappreciated. Without their resistance to the Confederate war effort and their support of the Union cause, slavery might not have ended as and when it did. Calling it a "story too long in the shadows," Williams described the "unrelenting resistance to slavery among slaves themselves that was the essential condition, the one thing without which the sectional crisis, secession, the Civil War, the Emancipation Proclamation, and the Thirteenth Amendment would not have happened."[14]

The third track that resulted in the end of slavery was the "military track." Nothing that Lincoln or other politicians said or accomplished in Washington mattered if the Union army lost the war on the battlefield. Lincoln's "Emancipation Proclamation" would have proved meaningless without the Union soldiers and sailors who came to the Southern states and forced Confederate masters to forever relinquish their positions of power over the slaves they claimed as property. "Without the United States Army," historian Gary Gallagher argued, "none of the other actors could have succeeded."[15]

Historians actively debate which of these three tracks was the most important, but the end of slavery could not have been achieved without simultaneous, and successful, progress along all three tracks. What destination lay at the end of each of the three tracks? To some extent, the answer was Juneteenth, the event representing the army's delivery of freedom to the last large group of enslaved people in the Confederacy.[16]

## *Chapter* 2

# LINCOLN AND THE APPROACHING WAR

On the afternoon of March 4, 1861, a large crowd assembled to witness Abraham Lincoln take the oath of office and officially become the sixteenth President of the United States. As the circumstances of his inauguration made clear, the position that Lincoln prepared to assume was both difficult and dangerous. Just reaching the inauguration had been an ordeal. Warned of an assassination plot, the president-elect had been smuggled into Washington, D.C., in the middle of the night. Lincoln then spent the time following his arrival dealing with one crisis after another, amid more rumors of plots and threats against his life and the lives of those around him.[1]

The security precautions taken for Lincoln's celebratory journey along Pennsylvania Avenue to the site of his inauguration were unprecedented. Riflemen stationed themselves on the roofs of the tall buildings and squads of cavalry were placed strategically at each of the intersections. Double files of cavalry surrounded the presidential carriage as it made its way to the Capitol. Some in the crowd lining the parade route cheered Lincoln, but an uncomfortably large number of spectators shouted threats and curses.[2]

As Lincoln stepped up to the inauguration platform, he moved into the protective view of a company of sharpshooters with rifles trained on the crowd from the windows of the Capitol. Although this attention to security was impressive, no president-elect ever approached inauguration with more reason to be concerned about his personal security or the security of the nation he intended

The 1861 inauguration procession passing the gate of the Capitol grounds (President-elect Lincoln and President Buchanan in carriage). *Harper's Weekly* (March 16, 1861), Library of Congress, LC-USZ62-331.

to lead. It was a nation in the process of breaking apart. Prompted by Lincoln's election, seven Southern states had already seceded and many more states talked about the possibility of joining the entity that Southerners mockingly named the "Confederate States of America." Two of the states that were seriously considering secession, Virginia and Maryland, surrounded Washington, D.C. For all Lincoln knew, his government in Washington was on the verge of becoming a small island of loyalty in the midst of a large surrounding sea of rebellion.

Even on the speaker's platform, Lincoln was not surrounded by friends. As he looked for a place to rest his hat, Lincoln found no suitable location. He finally handed it to his one-time rival and famous debate adversary Sen. Stephen A. Douglas, who held Lincoln's hat for the duration of the ceremony. Stepping forward to administer the oath of office was Roger B. Taney, the eighty-three-year-old chief justice of the U.S. Supreme Court. Lincoln had highly and publicly criticized Taney and his court for the 1857 *Dred Scott* decision, which held that no black man could ever be a citizen of the United States. Lincoln knew that one of the few things he could count on was Taney's continued resistance to the president and his policies.[3]

The president that Chief Justice Taney reluctantly helped swear into office held no strong mandate to govern. Lincoln only received about forty percent of the popular vote and had not even been on the ballot in many Southern states. As Lincoln prepared to deliver his inaugural address, many remained curious as to how the new president would handle the delicate subject of slavery. This, after

Rare photograph of inauguration of President Abraham Lincoln, March 4, 1861. Library of Congress, LC-USZ62-48090.

all, was the central issue dividing the nation. If he failed to address slavery at all, Lincoln risked angering the abolitionists and the other Republican factions who had supported and ultimately elected him. On the other hand, if Lincoln took too strong a tone on slavery, he risked further alienating the citizens of the rebellious states as well as the inhabitants of other slave-holding states that were actively considering secession.

Lincoln quickly tried to put to rest any concerns that he intended to eliminate slavery, quoting a previous speech where he said, "I have no purpose, directly or indirectly, to interfere with the institution of slavery in the States where it exists. I believe I have no right to do so, and I have no inclination to do so."[4] Lincoln went on to say that he would also honor the provision in the Constitution regarding delivery of fugitive slaves to their masters. Having done what he could to assuage the concerns of slaveholders, Lincoln then argued forcefully against the legality of secession and declared the Union still intact: "I therefore consider that, in view of the Constitution and the laws, the Union is unbroken; and to the extent of my ability, I shall take care, as the Constitution itself expressly enjoins upon me, that the laws of the Union be faithfully executed in all the States."[5]

The Abraham Lincoln who tiptoed around the issue of slavery in this speech in 1861 seems far removed from the "Great Emancipator," a title bestowed on him less than two years later. Indeed, judged by the words of his first inaugural speech alone, Lincoln seems more a moderate or even a conservative on the issue of slavery and its legal status. This comforting tone was undoubtedly Lincoln's objective and the impression he wanted to leave with his audience. This speech proved the first, but not the last, time that President Lincoln attempted to carefully walk a linguistic tightrope in addressing the contentious issue of slavery.

Why was the issue of slavery so difficult for Lincoln to address directly? Lincoln held no personal or moral confusion on the issue. As he wrote to Kentucky newspaper editor Albert Hodges in 1864, "I am naturally anti-slavery. If slavery is not wrong, nothing is wrong. I can not remember when I did not so think and feel."[6] But as Lincoln continued in the same letter, his commitment to the law would not permit him "to practically indulge my primary abstract judgment on the moral question of slavery."[7]

If Lincoln so firmly opposed slavery as an institution, why would he not begin to position his government to end the practice? In large part, Lincoln's reluctance stemmed from precedent: Americans had gone to great lengths to avoid dealing with the slavery issue since before the nation was founded. As originally drafted, the United States Constitution recognized the existence of slavery as an institution but refused to address the establishment by name. The U.S. Constitution only mentioned slavery in two places, and there solely in connection with unrelated governmental functions. The Constitution's "Three-fifths clause" (Article 1, Section 2, Clause 3), for example, provided that for purposes of apportioning Congressional representation, persons "bound to service" (the phrase indicating slaves) would count as three-fifths of a person.

Since the adoption of the Constitution, the institution of slavery had been regarded as a creature of state law. This suggested that as a legal matter it could only be abolished by state action. Since the 1860 Census estimated the value of slave property in America at three billion dollars, anything that might impact that institution represented much more than an abstract philosophical question. Lincoln and even most abolitionists believed that slavery under normal circumstances could not be eliminated except by the actions of the states whose laws authorized it. Lincoln may have considered slavery wrong as a moral matter, but he also thought that as a legal matter only the states could determine its fate. As he said in his famous 1860 Cooper Institute speech in New York City, "Wrong as we think slavery is, we can yet afford to let it alone where it is, because that much is due to the necessity arising from its actual presence in the nation."[8]

Lincoln repeatedly stated that only a state that permitted slavery under its state law could end that institution. Indeed, that point was one of the central concessions he made in his famous series of debates with Stephen A. Douglas. While acknowledging that "I have always hated slavery," Lincoln attempted to quell fears that he was a rabid abolitionist by stating: "I have said a hundred times, and I have no inclination to take it back, that I believe there is no right, and ought to be no inclination in the people of the free States to enter into the slave States, and interfere with the question of slavery at all. I have said that always. Judge Douglas has heard me say it—if not quite a hundred times, at least as good as a hundred times."[9]

Even if Lincoln had been persuaded that as president he had the legal authority to take some action to end slavery, in the early part of the Civil War he had every reason as a practical and political matter to deny that he ever intended to interfere with the institution. To understand this context, a brief examination of the geography of slavery in the United States on the eve of the Civil War proves useful. Figure 1 represents a table detailing the distribution of slaves by slave-owning state as enumerated in the 1860 Census:

**FIGURE I**

| STATE | SLAVES | SLAVES AS % OF POPULATION | SECESSION DATE |
|---|---|---|---|
| Alabama | 435,080 | 45% | January 11, 1861 |
| Arkansas | 111,115 | 26% | May 6, 1861 |
| Delaware | 1,798 | 2% | Did not secede |
| Florida | 61,745 | 44% | January 10, 1861 |
| Georgia | 462,198 | 44% | January 19, 1861 |
| Kentucky | 225,483 | 20% | Did not secede |
| Louisiana | 331,726 | 47% | January 26, 1861 |
| Maryland | 87,189 | 13% | Did not secede |
| Mississippi | 436,631 | 55% | January 9, 1861 |
| Missouri | 114,931 | 10% | Did not secede |
| North Carolina | 331,059 | 33% | May 20, 1861 |
| South Carolina | 402,406 | 57% | December 20, 1860 |
| Tennessee | 275,719 | 25% | June 8, 1861 |
| Texas | 182,566 | 30% | February 1, 1861 |
| Virginia | 490,865 | 31% | April 17, 1861 |
| Totals | 3,950,528[10] | | |

The statistics in this chart were critically important to the way that events played out in 1861 and are well worth studying in detail. First, the states with the highest slave populations felt most strongly about the fate of that institution and tended to be the states that seceded first. For example, South Carolina and Mississippi, the first two Southern states to secede, clearly possessed the largest slave population by percentage. In fact, every one of the first six states to leave the Union and join the Confederate States had a slave population exceeding more than forty percent of its inhabitants. Such a high correlation between secession and slave population confirms the common understanding that slavery was at the heart of the causes that led to secession and rebellion.

Analysis of this data also illuminates the situations of the four so-called "border states." These states (Delaware, Maryland, Kentucky, and Missouri) were perceived as a border or buffer between the soon-to-be Confederate States and the remainder of the Union. Out of the combined American slave population of approximately four million, the border states together possessed a little more than ten percent of this total. Each of these border states had a significantly smaller slave population percentage than the states that seceded. These figures do not indicate that slavery was unimportant to those states or to their inhabitants. They simply reflect the reality that the border states enjoyed more diverse financial and cultural identities that connected to both the industrial economies of the North and the agricultural economies of the South.

One entry not present on the slave population chart in Figure 1 is the District of Columbia, which was formed out of territory taken from Maryland and Virginia. Although it served as the capital of the Union, the District included a slave population of 3,185 in 1860. As events played out, the enslaved people in the District of Columbia would not be freed until April 1862, when President Lincoln signed into law the District of Columbia Emancipation Act. That law not only brought emancipation to the District's slaves, but also compensation for their owners, an act Lincoln originally proposed as early as 1849 as a member of the House of Representatives.[11]

Modern students of history tend to think of the Civil War, quite rightly, as the war that ultimately produced an end to slavery. But that was not Lincoln's original plan. As President Lincoln stepped to the podium in 1861 to deliver his first inaugural address, he was in a slave-holding jurisdiction (the District of Columbia), surrounded by other slave-holding states (Maryland and Virginia). The Capitol building at which he delivered his speech and the White House in which he was to live had both been built with the aid of slave labor. Even Lincoln's wife, Mary Todd Lincoln, came from a Kentucky family that owned slaves. Lincoln's capital, and the government over which he presided, was in the midst of an area that held long and strong connections to the institution of slavery.

Lincoln knew all too well that he owed his election in 1860 almost exclusively to the actions of voters in Northern states. He knew also that although many of these Northern states had abolished slavery, the states contained substantial numbers of citizens who either supported the institution or were not yet willing to fight a war to end it.

One group of citizens that Lincoln knew he must avoid alienating at all costs consisted of the citizens of the border states. Openly threatening the institution of slavery might tip the balance and send these states into the eager hands of the secessionists. Lincoln seemed particularly concerned with maintaining good relations with the citizens of Kentucky, fearing a domino reaction: if that state fell into the hands of the rebels, others would soon follow. As he confessed to his friend Orville Browning, "I think to lose Kentucky is nearly the same as to lose the whole game. Kentucky gone we cannot hold Missouri, nor, as I think, Maryland. These all against us, and the job on our hands is too large for us. We would as well consent to separation at once, including the surrender of this capitol."[12]

Faced with these difficulties, the Lincoln Administration adopted a stated policy of strict neutrality with respect to slavery, choosing to pretend—at least initially—that the institution was not a central factor in the war. As far as Lincoln's public pronouncements went, the war was solely about preservation of the Union and slavery was only a minor factor that might, or might not, eventually be relevant to achieving that goal. As Lincoln wrote famously in a public letter published in the newspapers in 1862: "My paramount object in this struggle is to save the Union, and is not either to save or to destroy slavery."[13]

There would come a time when Lincoln publicly proclaimed abolition of slavery as a key weapon that would help end the war and restore the Union. But in 1861, that time had not yet come. As war planners in Washington gathered to plan the military campaigns that they hoped would quickly end the rapidly escalating conflict, they recognized the possibility of a variety of contexts in which the armies would encounter slaves and their owners. But each of these contexts differed significantly, and military leaders determined that establishing general guidelines for these situations seemed impossible. In eighty-five years, the United States government had not found an easy way to deal with the subject of slavery, and as it prepared to fight a war, the Union army found this task just as difficult.

One factor that loomed potentially large in the military calculations of both sides was the reaction of slaves to the coming war. In the period leading up to war, many Northerners speculated that in the event of war, Southern slaves might simply cease their work and rise up as part of a vast servile insurrection. There would be no need for a John Brown this time, they asserted, simply furnish some arms and ammunition and the slaves would spontaneously throw off their bonds and revolt. As one abolitionist newspaper gleefully predicted:

> Help the negroes to fight their way to freedom and settle their own accounts with their present masters; they will make excellent bargains with their owners in their own way. . . . Unless the government controls their movement, they will act for themselves, and be very likely to perpetrate an indiscriminate massacre of the whites in every servile insurrection. This course will save thousands of lives, and a mint of money, and settle a pestilent question forever.[14]

It was not just the radical abolitionists who believed that slaves would revolt if given the opportunity. William H. Seward, who eventually served as Lincoln's Secretary of State, warned his Southern colleagues on the floor of the Senate in January 1861 that in the event of war, millions of slaves would rise up and deal harshly with their former masters.[15]

Some Southern partisans, on the other hand, played down these fears, confidently predicting that slaves would remain docile and loyal, even helping their masters to fight off their Northern aggressors if it came to war. A British reporter asked Confederate Gen. Braxton Bragg's orderly if he was comfortable leaving his wife home alone with the slaves and but a single overseer, to which the man responded: "They're ignorant poor creatures to be sure, but as yet they're faithful. Anyway, I put my trust in God and I know He'll watch over the house while I am away fighting for this good cause."[16]

Agitators on both sides of the conflict used the threat of a slave rebellion to motivate their audiences to choose sides in the coming war. But nobody on either side, from Jefferson Davis to Abraham Lincoln, really knew what the slaves would do in the event of a serious military conflict. They were about to find out. On April 12, 1861, only thirty-nine days following Lincoln's inauguration, Confederate forces launched an attack on Fort Sumter near Charleston, South Carolina. The Civil War had at last begun.

## Chapter 3

## SLAVERY AND THE ARMY

One of the greatest sources of confusion and frustration for Union army commanders during the early part of the Civil War involved the status of slaves and the claims of their owners. This was in large part a reflection of the dilemma in which Washington policymakers continued to find themselves. President Lincoln contended publicly that the army's mission was solely to preserve the Union and denied any intention to put an end to slavery. One reason Lincoln remained reluctant to turn slavery into a war aim centered around the unwillingness of many Northerners, including many commanders serving in his armies, to support a policy ending slavery. Caught between the abolitionists who favored immediate emancipation and more moderate elements who argued that slavery remained a property issue governed by state law, the Lincoln administration and the military high command chose initially to address the subject as lightly, and as little, as possible.

Washington might be tempted to avoid the issue of slaves and their status, but commanders in the field had no such luxury. While bureaucrats in Washington tried to sweep slavery under the rug, military commanders found slavery impossible to avoid. Slaves were an ever-present feature of the battlefields and every road leading to and from combat areas. With roughly four million slaves in the Southern states and a Union force that eventually numbered more than two million men, it was inevitable that these two populations would interact. As it turned out, when confrontations started to occur, neither population knew quite what to expect from the other.

Even before the war officially started, runaway slaves sought sanctuary with the Union troops serving as garrisons in forts in the hope that such a move provided a pathway to freedom. They quickly discovered that this was not yet the case. As one artillery officer at Fort Pickens, Florida, reported in March 1861:

> On the morning of the 12th instant four negroes (runaways) came to the fort, entertaining the idea that we were placed here to protect them and grant them their freedom. I did what I could to teach them the contrary. In the afternoon I took them to Pensacola and delivered them to the city marshal, to be returned to their owners. That same night four more made their appearance. They were also turned over to the authorities next morning.[1]

With the firing on Fort Sumter, a scramble by both sides ensued to seize control of the key coastal fortifications along the Southern coast. In places where the Union army successfully maintained control of a coastal fort (e.g., Fort Monroe in Virginia or Fort Pickens in Florida), the Confederates typically either built or reinforced their own fortifications facing the Union fort in an attempt to isolate the enemy. Most of these new Confederate fortifications rose rapidly with the aid of slave labor. As the Confederates learned, however, using slave labor so close to enemy lines placed slaves near potential avenues for escape. Small groups of slaves soon took advantage of this proximity and escaped to Union forts, hoping that the Northerners brought liberation as well as armies.

Union officers in these situations were initially unprepared for the exodus that confronted them. In the absence of formal instructions from Washington, the response to these escape attempts during the early months of the war depended very much on the personal inclinations of the commander. Some commanders, like the officer at Fort Pickens previously quoted, simply sent the slaves back to local masters or authorities. Others elected to hold on to the slaves and await further instructions. As one colonel admitted, "I shall not send the negroes back, as I will never be voluntarily instrumental in returning a poor wretch to slavery, but will hold them subject to orders."[2]

Guidance regarding the proper handling of escaped slaves was not soon in coming. Orders on the subject would set policy, and at that time, Washington authorities felt uncomfortable announcing any policy regarding slavery. But try as they might, Union military officials could not ignore the issue forever, and before long the army high command had to address the subject. In May 1861, three enslaved men (Shepard Mallory, Frank Baker, and James Townsend) escaped from working on a Confederate battery and rowed over to Fort Monroe, Virginia, in a small boat. That short voyage had profound and lasting implications for slaves across the South anxiously waiting to secure their freedom.[3]

Maj. Gen. Benjamin F. Butler arrived at Fort Monroe and assumed command only the day before the three fugitives reached the garrison. Butler's decision regarding the fate of these men would be his first important decision as commander. Having little military experience, Butler spent his life before the war as a prominent lawyer and politician in Massachusetts. Later to become infamous to Southerners as "Beast Butler" for his controversial policies as commander in New Orleans, many forget that Butler had been a Democrat before the war. Indeed, he cast fifty-seven consecutive votes to nominate Jefferson Davis for president at the Democratic convention in 1860.[4]

Maj. Gen. Benjamin F. Butler. Library of Congress, LC-DIG-ppmsca-35233.

As later events proved, General Butler lacked much as a military commander, but he was an able lawyer, probably one of the outstanding attorneys of his day. Butler interviewed the three escaped slaves and learned that their owner was a Confederate officer. Tired of building Confederate fortifications and believing that their owner intended to send them out of state to keep them away from federal troops, the men chose to escape to federal lines when the opportunity presented itself. Butler ordered the refugees to be fed and put to work while he considered the merits of their case.[5]

It proved fortunate that the escaped slaves ended up in a fort commanded by General Butler. Butler was reluctant to return the men to his enemy, so he sought any, even remotely credible, justification for not doing so. He began using his legal skills to craft an argument that might convince Washington to approve his decision. When a Confederate officer named John B. Cary came under a flag of truce to inquire about the return of the escapees, Butler stood ready with an excuse and some intellectual sparring. Near the end of their meeting, Major Cary got to the real point of his visit:

> "What do you mean to do with those negroes?"
>
> "I intend to hold them," said [Butler].
>
> "Do you mean, then, to set aside your constitutional obligation to return them?"
>
> "I mean to take Virginia at her word, as declared in the ordinance of secession passed yesterday. I am under no obligations to a foreign country, which Virginia now claims to be."
>
> "But you say we cannot secede," he answered, "and so you cannot consistently detain the negroes."
>
> "But you say you have seceded, so you cannot consistently claim them. I shall hold these negroes as contraband of war, since they are engaged in the construction of your battery and are claimed as your property. The question is whether they shall be used for or against the Government of the United States."[6]

Sensing his opponent's floundering, Butler made a cunning offer: if Colonel Mallory (the alleged owner of the slaves) came to the fort in person and took the oath of allegiance to the United States, Butler would surrender the fugitive slaves to him and then immediately hire the men back to work at the federal fortress. Butler understood that Colonel Mallory would not take the oath—so did Major Cary. As they courteously parted, both men must have known that this encounter was not the last time this rather confusing subject would be addressed.[7]

Modern historians have tended to praise Butler for his creative use of the legal doctrine of "contraband" as a justification for not returning the escaped slaves, but as a legal matter the claim was highly suspect. To begin with, the concept of seizing goods as "contraband" arose out of maritime law and usually involved one nation seizing goods at sea that a belligerent power used to conduct war. In this case, however, slaves were not goods (according to Northern abolitionists), the men were not seized (either on land or on the high seas), and they were not directly employed by a foreign nation to make war upon the United States. Butler raised the issue of contraband status purely as part of his witty banter; he was probably as surprised as anyone to see it thereafter become the centerpiece for a War Department strategy on slavery.[8]

Almost as soon as his meeting with Cary ended, Butler prepared a dispatch to Lt. Gen. Winfield Scott in Washington seeking approval for his position. As an experienced trial lawyer, Butler made his case sound as strong as possible. Butler presented the following key facts to Scott: (1) the escaped slaves in question were being actively used in the service of the Confederate war effort; (2) they were about to be taken out of state, leaving their wives and families behind; and (3) they were needed for the Union war effort.[9] Butler recalled in his memoirs that he referred to the men in question during his conversation with Major Cary as "contrabands" of war, a legal term that might justify their retention. But his letter to General Scott used the word "property" to refer to the men, not "contraband," making it possible that the term was not actually used by Butler until some later date.[10]

Long after the war, a controversy arose as to whether Butler was the first to use the doctrine of contraband as a legal justification for confiscation and emancipation of slaves. Butler believed that he deserved credit for this line of reasoning. In 1891, Butler secured a letter from Major Cary confirming that he used the term "contraband" at their first meeting. Cary agreed that Butler utilized the word, noting that the instance became the first time he heard it used in that particular context. President Lincoln was said to be amused by Butler's legal creativity in employing the doctrine, later referring to it as "Butler's fugitive slave law."[11]

Several days following Butler's dispatch to General Scott, the situation got more complicated. By this time, word had spread throughout the local slave community that escape to the Union fort might mean emancipation. Lured by the potential of freedom, more slaves escaped to Fort Monroe and promised Butler that others would soon follow. Some of these new escapees had not actively worked for the Confederate war effort, however, while others brought their wives and children. As Butler quickly realized, the people in this new fugitive popula-tion did not meet the criteria that he originally used to justify his retention of the first three escapees.

Butler believed that he helped shape the debate surrounding army policy on escaped slaves. As he saw the situation, only Washington could take the next step in clarifying military policy. In an updated report to his superiors, Butler acknowledged that the new refugees fell outside the parameters of his original communication. Nevertheless, Butler proposed to keep all of the runaways at the fort, promising to put them to work and keep a careful record of the value of their work and expenses in the event that some compensation later needed to be arranged with their former owners. The "question in regard to slave property is becoming one of very serious magnitude," Butler noted, and made a formal request for guidance on the issue.[12]

The military authorities in Washington who received Butler's guidance requests knew that they operated in treacherous waters. Any policy change could possibly offend influential people. There seemed no way to avoid creating a significant controversy. They determined to take the course of least resistance and followed General Butler's lead on the issue with as little fanfare as possible. In a very short dispatch dated May 30, 1861, Secretary of War Simon Cameron advised Butler that his "action in respect to the negroes who came in your lines from the service of the rebels is approved."[13] Emphasizing that this approval only applied to slaves who came into federal lines, and stressing that it primarily applied to slaves who worked towards the Union war effort, Cameron also approved Butler's commitment to keep good accounting records relating to the fugitives. Cameron's May 30 dispatch, which eventually circulated throughout the Union army, concluded with the admonition that the question of the "final disposition" of escaped slaves "will be reserved for future determination."[14]

As General Butler attempted to prod officials in Washington closer to issuing guidance on escaped slaves on the coast of Virginia, other commanders in the Union army took a very different approach to similar issues. Maj. Gen. George B. McClellan, in command of the Department of the Ohio, encamped near Cincinnati and carefully monitored the situation in the western part of Virginia. That portion of Virginia was not only an area with relatively strong Union sentiment, it contained important railroad connections linking Washington to the rest of the country.

As General McClellan prepared his advance into Virginia, he reluctantly contemplated what to do with the slaves he would encounter. To avoid any controversy, McClellan issued a proclamation titled "To the Union Men of West Virginia" on May 26, 1861. This proclamation, coming at almost the same time as Butler's dispatches across the state of Virginia, struck a very different tone. McClellan wrote: "Notwithstanding all that has been said by the traitors to induce you to believe that our advent among you will be signalized by interference with your slaves understand one thing clearly—not only will we abstain from all such interference but we will on the contrary with an iron hand crush any attempt at insurrection on their part."[15] Reinforcing this commitment, McClellan issued orders the same day to his troops in Virginia: "See that the rights and property of the people are respected and repress all attempts at negro insurrection."[16]

As these examples demonstrate, military authorities at this early point in the war tried to carefully handle what became widely known in the army as the "Negro question." While going out of their way to publicly avoid interference with the institution of slavery as it existed in loyal states like Maryland or loyal portions of states (like the future West Virginia), the military nevertheless took commonsense steps where possible to deprive the Confederates of the benefits of a ready supply of slave labor. Military officials were also afraid that their actions might inadvertently trigger a slave rebellion, leading to a loss of order and bloodshed for which they would be blamed. All of these concerns led to a cautious and somewhat confusing mix of policies.

On July 9, 1861, the U.S. House of Representatives, now missing its Southern contingent, passed a resolution declaring that "in the judgment of this House it is no part of the duty of the soldiers of the United States to capture and return fugitive slaves."[17] President Lincoln was receiving reports on almost a daily basis from slaveholders in loyal states complaining of army units that sheltered fugitive slaves. At the same time, he received complaints from abolitionists about officers who returned fugitive slaves to their owners. In an attempt to avoid the controversy, the army's Department of Washington issued General Orders No. 33 directing the expulsion of fugitive slaves from all camps and preventing them from joining the troops when they moved.[18]

To add to the confusion, on August 6, 1861, Congress enacted, and President Lincoln reluctantly signed into law, a bill that became known as the "First Confiscation Act." Following the "contraband" legal theory offered originally by General Butler, the new law expressly authorized the confiscation of property used to support the insurrection. This included a provision terminating ownership claims for any slave (referred to as a "person claimed to be held to labor or service" in the statute) used in the Confederate war effort.[19] Of questionable legality, the law proved effectively unenforceable because it required a formal determination of confiscation by a local court. Since no court in a Confederate state would issue any such declaration, the First Confiscation Act became a frustrating exercise in futility.[20]

Gen. Benjamin Butler, still in command at Fort Monroe, soon learned that he had opened a Pandora's Box by shielding the first batch of escaped slaves. A flood of runaway slaves poured into Butler's lines and the general rapidly lost control of the situation. Secretary of War Simon Cameron used the passage of the First Confiscation Act as support for a slightly revised and expanded interpretation of Butler's authority to deal with refugees. In essence, Cameron instructed Butler not to honor any demands by slaveholders. This policy fell well outside the boundaries and mechanics of the Confiscation Act itself, but Secretary Cameron used the unstable military situation as a reason to let commanders like Butler step in and effectively substitute their judgment for the local judicial authorities contemplated by the new law. Butler was warned to continue to keep good records about the service and costs for all the refugees and report in twice a month. Of particular importance, Butler was instructed again to avoid doing anything that might lure or entice slaves to come within Union lines.[21]

Over in the West, things became more chaotic. Missouri, which failed to secede from the Union, quickly descended into its own internal civil war. Since Missouri was technically a loyal state where slavery was still legal, it was difficult for military authorities to apply General Butler's "contraband of war" rubric to seize and free slaves. That did not stop Maj. Gen. John C. Fremont, in command of the Western Department of Missouri, from making a bold attempt to do so.

Following a Confederate victory at the Battle of Wilson's Creek on August 10, 1861, General Fremont decided to implement some desperate measures to try and restore order in Missouri. In a proclamation issued on August 30, 1861, in St. Louis, Fremont declared martial law throughout the State of Missouri. Announcing that all enemies found armed inside the lines of occupation would be shot, Fremont further ordered that all real and personal property of rebels would be seized. One clause in the confiscation provision soon proved immensely controversial. In describing the property subject to confiscation, Fremont proclaimed "[the

Maj. Gen. John C. Fremont. Library of Congress, LC-USZ62-100092.

rebels'] slaves if any they have are hereby declared free men."[22] This went well beyond Fremont's apparent authority and seemed to be at odds with the judicial enforcement provisions of the First Confiscation Act.

When President Lincoln received news of General Fremont's proclamation, he was both surprised and concerned. Fearing that the Confederates might now begin shooting Unionists in retaliation, Lincoln quickly dashed off a letter instructing Fremont not to shoot anyone without receiving his prior approval. He then brought Fremont's attention to the language in his proclamation about freeing slaves and requested him to voluntarily withdraw that provision. Noting that it might "alarm our Southern Union friends and turn them against us, perhaps ruin our fair prospect for Kentucky," Lincoln observed that Fremont's proclamation was also inconsistent with the recently enacted Confiscation Act.[23] Fremont refused to act on Lincoln's suggestion and Lincoln eventually modified the slavery provision of Fremont's proclamation to conform to the Confiscation Act. As Lincoln feared and predicted, representatives of the slave-owning border states lost no time in complaining about the slave emancipation portions of Fremont's proclamation.[24]

Frustrations ran high throughout the Union army regarding implementation of the military's increasingly ill-defined policy on fugitive slaves. In border states like Missouri, where slavery was legal and soldiers were charged with returning escaped slaves, many soldiers bitterly resented this service. An example of this frustration is illustrated by the intemperate reply made by former Congressman James Henry Lane, the commander of the Kansas Brigade, in response to orders directing his men to assist in returning fugitive slaves:

> I am here in obedience to an order from Maj Gen. John C. Fremont to co-operate with you in ferreting out and fighting the enemy. Kindly and promptly do I desire to obey that order. My brigade is not here for the purpose of interfering in anywise with the institution of slavery. They shall not become negro thieves nor shall they be prostituted into negro-catchers. The institution of slavery must take care of itself.[25]

With officers like Lane openly questioning the validity of their orders regarding slaves, fugitive slave policy in the West led to dissension and turmoil. Meanwhile, in the East, Maj. Gen. John Wool replaced Benjamin Butler as commander of Fort

Monroe. At the time of Wool's arrival, a large number of runaway slaves, many women and children, filled the fort and the number grew even larger daily. Wool, irascible at the age of seventy-seven, tired of the difficulties of providing for the multitudes of unwanted persons and made his views quite clear to Washington. Writing sarcastically to the Secretary of War, Wool asked:

> I would be much gratified if you would tell me what I am to do with the negro slaves that are almost daily arriving at this post from the interior. Am I to find food and shelter for the women and children who can do nothing for themselves? . . . It appears to me some positive instructions should be given in regard to what shall be done for the number that will be accumulated in and about this post during the approaching winter. I hope that you will give me instructions on this very important subject. Humanity requires that they should be taken care of.[26]

Wool would have no better luck than Butler in obtaining actionable guidance and assistance from Washington. The only response Wool received was a short note permitting him to send some of the excess men and their families to General McClellan in Washington. Faced with constant controversies about employment of the fugitives and their families, Wool decided to take matters into his own hands and issued regulations spelling out in detail an elaborate scheme of compensation for each specified class of labor.[27]

As the time for commencement of large-scale military operations across the South approached, everyone in a position of authority within the Union understood that the issues surrounding fugitive slaves were not, and probably could not be, satisfactorily resolved. Between the need to placate slaveholders in loyal Union states and the need to avoid offending influential abolitionists demanding immediate emancipation, military officials in Washington found it virtually impossible to give clear and consistent direction to commanders in the field regarding the slaves they were certain to encounter. One thing seemed clear, however: a widening war would only make the problems surrounding fugitive slaves even larger and more complicated.

## Chapter 4

# PORT ROYAL AND THE FIRST GENERAL ORDER

In Fall 1861, Union military officials launched a bold plan to seize the Sea Islands off South Carolina and gain control of Port Royal Sound. The justification behind this plan was partly punitive and partly strategic. Taking the war to the Palmetto State, the first Confederate state to secede, held important symbolic value. Union leaders hoped that by occupying key parts of the South Carolina coast the stain on Union honor left by the capture of Fort Sumter at Charleston might partially be removed. From a strategic standpoint, the capture of the City of Port Royal would also give the Union navy an important base along the Atlantic coast to support the expanding blockade of Confederate ports. The "Port Royal Expedition," as it became known, turned out to be a striking military success for both the Union army and navy. The campaign also resulted in the issuance of a general order that is in some ways perhaps the first direct ancestor of the Juneteenth Order.

Because its targets included forts along the South Carolina coast, the Port Royal Expedition included both a significant naval force and a large body of infantry. Gen. Thomas West Sherman commanded the land troops. No relation to William Tecumseh Sherman, with whom he is sometimes confused, Gen. Thomas Sherman was a forty-one-year-old career soldier from Rhode Island. After graduating from West Point in 1836, Sherman spent a significant amount of time fighting in the Second Seminole War. He also assisted in the removal and relocation of the Cherokee to the Indian Territory. Sherman served successfully in the Mexican War, where he received the brevet rank of major for gallantry.[1]

The Port Royal Expedition was the first important command of the Civil War for Sherman, who had been elevated to the rank of brigadier general shortly before the campaign's start. Military planners in Washington knew they were sending Sherman into a theater of war where he would encounter plantations with large numbers of slave laborers. To equip Sherman for his new command, Secretary of War Simon Cameron provided him with copies of the two dispatches previously furnished to Benjamin Butler, as well as the following directions:

Brig. Gen. Thomas W. Sherman. Library of Congress, LC-DIG-cwpb-05370.

You will, however, in general avail yourself of the services of any persons whether fugitives from labor or not who may offer them to the National Government; you will employ such persons in such services as they may be fitted for either as ordinary employees or if special circumstances seem to require it in any other capacity with such organization in squads, companies or otherwise as you deem most beneficial to the service. This, however, [is] not to mean a general arming of them for military service. You will assure all loyal masters that Congress will provide just compensation to them for the loss of the services of the persons so employed.[2]

After a short series of engagements between the Union navy and the Confederate forts, on November 11, 1861, Union forces established firm federal control over the Port Royal Sound area. Sherman and his infantry force moved ashore and spread out to take control of key military objectives. The results of these Union movements into enemy territory proved entirely predictable. As soon as the infantry went ashore at Port Royal, large numbers of slaves attempting to free themselves by entering Union lines greeted the Union field commanders. This raised real problems for the army, which only brought along enough supplies for themselves. As quartermaster Rufus Saxton worried, "Contraband negroes are coming in in great numbers. In two days 150 have come in, mostly able-bodied men, and it will soon be necessary to furnish them with coarse clothing."[3]

Slave quarters on a plantation, Port Royal, South Carolina.
Library of Congress, LC-DIG-ppmsca-10964.

Union troops soon learned that they had more in common with the slaves than they expected. One after another, a host of black men arrived at the army camps to sell the chickens, turkeys, and other livestock they liberated from their former plantations. Although the traders' Gullah dialect caused some initial communication difficulties, the soldiers discovered a common language, music, which made communication between the liberators and those they liberated possible. In the evening, large "sings" were held, featuring spirituals with lyrics that spoke of freedom and an end to slavery.[4]

As the former slaves sang proudly of the "many thousands" of their number that would soon escape to freedom, Secretary of War Simon Cameron worried about how to handle just such an influx. If he sent the refugees back to their masters, Cameron knew, they might be used for military purposes by the Confederates or put to work producing supplies for the Confederate armies. "They constitute a military resource," Cameron concluded, "and being such that they should not be turned over to the enemy is too plain to discuss."[5]

The question for Cameron and other Union officials became how to make the most effective use of this new "military resource." It was during this time that General Sherman encountered a problem that caused continuing friction between the military and freedpeople throughout the war. The freedpeople, quite understandably, believed that with the advent of their freedom they could do as they wished. The military, on the other hand, believed that as long as the freedpeople stayed within Union lines, the army could, and indeed had an obligation to, direct the people to work and keep them from being idle.

As his instructions to General Sherman reflected, Secretary of War Cameron believed that the primary answer to the fugitive slave problem involved putting the fugitive slaves to work at various tasks around army camps. But such a policy produced severe limitations. The former slaves, given a taste of freedom, showed reluctance or unwillingness to submit to discipline from the white men in blue uniforms, men who, to the former enslaved people, seemed to have replaced their white masters. To make matters worse, the soldiers chosen to supervise these workers possessed no experience directing this kind of labor force. The result was chaos.[6]

General Sherman landed at Port Royal with the expectation of using large numbers of freed slaves as essentially free and willing labor to erect fortifications and build the infrastructure necessary for a future, major Union base of operations. But one month after landing, Sherman found these particular expectations entirely unjustified.

Employing freed slave labor in South Carolina proved "almost a failure," General Sherman reported to Washington. Why was this the case? Unsurprisingly, Sherman rooted many of his reasons for the turmoil in the prevailing racist views of the era: "They [former slaves] are naturally slothful and indolent and have always been accustomed to the lash, an aid we do not make use of."[7] Second, offered Sherman, "they appear to be so overjoyed with the change in their condition that their minds are unsettled to any plan."[8] The result, concluded Sherman, was that "a sudden change of condition from servitude to apparent freedom is more than their intellects can stand, and this circumstance alone renders it a very serious question what is to be done with the negroes who will hereafter be found on conquered soil."[9]

One circumstance that General Sherman encountered in South Carolina, which General Butler had not faced in Virginia, involved abandoned plantations. Confronted with a sudden invasion of federal troops, large numbers of South Carolina plantation owners simply fled to the interior, leaving behind what they viewed as their least valuable slaves on otherwise deserted farms and plantations. This left General Sherman in a difficult position. Secretary of War Cameron told Sherman to anticipate the arrival of many freed slaves anxious to volunteer their service in support of the Union cause. But one month after his arrival, only about 320 of the "hordes of negroes left on the plantations" had offered their services. Of these 320, several then ran away, forcing Sherman to report only "sixty able-bodied male hands, the rest being decrepit women and children."[10] These people are not an asset, Sherman reported; unfortunately they are a major liability.[11]

As disgusted as Sherman seemed regarding the conditions on the abandoned plantations surrounding him, he knew the situation could not endure long. Sherman realized that some sort of central and organized direction of the labor force was needed to make the farms and plantations productive. In the absence of such direction, the general worried, starvation and social strife would eventually prevail. Sherman contemplated his position and settled on a bold solution: if the freed slaves left on the plantations would not come to him, Sherman would go to them. From his headquarters at Hilton Head, South Carolina, Sherman issued General Orders No. 9 on February 9, 1862. Declaring that "hordes of totally uneducated, ignorant and improvident blacks have been abandoned by their constitutional guardians," Sherman divided the occupied country into districts and appointed agents for each district to manage the plantations and instruct the former slaves on moral matters.[12]

Although Sherman may have been motivated by genuine concern for the wellbeing of the freedpeople and their families, the provisions of his General Orders No. 9 sound to modern ears unbelievably paternalistic. Sherman's experience prior to the Civil War, however, lay with military situations regarding native peoples, and his tone in General Orders No. 9 aligned with the ways the federal government handled native affairs before the war. The heart of his order involved blacks working the plantations under the supervision of a white agent appointed by Sherman:

> For each of these districts a suitable agent will be appointed to superintend the management of the plantations by the blacks, to enroll and organize the willing blacks into working parties, to see that they are well fed, clad and paid a proper remuneration for their labor, to take charge of all property on the plantations whether found there, provided by the Government or raised from the soil, and to perform all other administrative duties connected with the plantations that may be required by the Government.[13]

Sherman quickly forwarded his order to Washington, explaining that its bold scope was necessary to prevent a looming disaster. In the general's mind, "The imperative necessity of putting the blacks in the way of avoiding starvation before the planting season expires without a draw on the commissariat to an extent that would cripple the service" justified his extraordinary action.[14] Sherman estimated that the "number of blacks on land in possession of our forces to be at least 9,000, which is probably a low estimate."[15] When Northern forces stormed ashore, they made free use of the abandoned plantation food stores they found, treating the items as captured booty. Sherman belatedly realized this action was a colossal mistake, a mistake that led Union commanders to make an urgent call on Northern charities for food and clothing to assist desperate black refugees.[16]

Sherman's General Orders No. 9 commenced a bold experiment eventually known as the "Port Royal Experiment." As a means of preparing former slaves for land ownership and administration, it seemed innovative and creative, but the plan failed as a lasting model of general applicability. Missionaries continued the experiment with mixed success after the military abandoned the project. Sherman himself was later transferred to another command. Rufus Saxton, the quartermaster who earlier worried that freed slaves might deplete his supplies, later viewed those men in a different light. Promoted to the rank of brigadier general in 1863, Saxton returned to South Carolina and trained some of the freedpeople in the Port Royal area to become some of the first black troops in the Union army.[17]

At the White House, President Lincoln possessed his own ideas regarding the flood of fugitive slaves that fled to the Union army on a daily basis. At this point in the war, Lincoln viewed freedpeople primarily as an obstacle, to either be removed or neutralized as to not cause him political problems or hinder planned military operations. On December 3, 1861, in his annual message to Congress, Lincoln noted that many slaves found liberation by virtue of the Confiscation Acts or through abandonment by their former masters. The people thus liberated, the president observed, "are already dependent on the United States and must be provided for in some way."[18] Lincoln believed the solution might be to colonize these people along with any freed black people who wanted to join them "at some place or places in a climate congenial to them."[19]

Neither Lincoln's colonization plan nor Thomas Sherman's plantation confiscation plan at Port Royal proved a lasting solution to the problems surrounding the transition between slavery and freedom. But Sherman's concept of dealing with freed slaves in the broader context of a general order tailored to the problems of the local region set a precedent that other Union commanders in other contexts experimented with throughout the course of the war.

Some commanders carried their experiments too far and found themselves severely chastised. In Spring 1862, Maj. Gen. David Hunter was transferred to command the military Department of the South, a department comprised of

Maj. Gen. David Hunter. Library of Congress, LC-DIG-cwpb-04526.

Georgia, Florida, and South Carolina. Only a small part of this department, the Sea Islands of South Carolina, was actually under Union control at this early stage in the war. But Hunter, a friend of President Lincoln, was determined to make a name for himself. The son of a Presbyterian minister, Hunter went to war determined to use his military authority to put a quick end to slavery whenever and wherever possible. Hunter started small, issuing a general order on April 13, 1862, that confiscated and freed "[a]ll persons of color lately held to involuntary service by enemies of the United States in Fort Pulaski and on Cockspur Island, Ga."[20]

Hunter's order freeing the slaves at Fort Pulaski was not too controversial and was arguably within the authority granted him by the Confiscation Act and previous War Department instructions. Receiving no objection from Washington, Hunter decided to go ahead with the next step in his plan to test the full limits of his authority. On April 25, Hunter placed the entire territory of the three states in his Department of the South under martial law, once again another understandable and relatively uncontroversial act given the limited Union control over this region. Then, on May 9, 1862, Hunter played his full hand and issued General Orders No. 11. Using martial law as a justification, Hunter extended the emancipation order from Fort Pulaski and its environs to his entire department: "Slavery and martial law in a free country are altogether incompatible; the persons in these three States—Georgia, Florida and South Carolina—heretofore held as slaves are therefore declared forever free."[21]

When news of Hunter's emancipation order reached the North, it resulted in an explosion of anger and blame. The House of Representatives launched an immediate investigation and President Lincoln, blindsided by Hunter's action, was quickly bombarded with objections from the many politicians and businessmen not yet ready for a general policy of emancipation. "This act has done us more harm than a loss of two battles," one correspondent warned the president.[22] Lincoln was caught completely by surprise by Hunter's proclamation, and he at first questioned its authenticity. Something needed to be done quickly to contain the damage and regain control of the situation.[23]

Noting too much "excitement and misunderstanding," President Lincoln issued a declaration stating that Hunter's emancipation order was unauthorized and void, stating: "[N]either General Hunter nor any other commander or person has been authorized by the Government of the United States to make proclamations declaring the slaves of any State free."[24] Using the occasion to lay some of the groundwork for emancipation, Lincoln said that if military necessity might ultimately make it necessary to free slaves, it would be accomplished in a more deliberate fashion: "[T]o exercise such supposed power [emancipation] are questions which under my responsibility I reserve to myself and which I cannot feel justified in leaving to the decision of commanders in the field."[25]

*Chapter 5*

## BUTLER AND LOUISIANA

On May 1, 1862, Gen. Benjamin Butler arrived in the City of New Orleans to begin the Union military occupation of the most important city in the South. One reason behind this important assignment probably involved the skill with which Butler handled the politically charged escaped slave issues at Fort Monroe. New Orleans, however, was an entirely different command, and Butler soon learned that the Crescent City presented its own unique set of controversies and challenges.

Having been told many loyal citizens lived in New Orleans, Butler immediately issued a declaration announcing that the property of New Orleans residents who took the oath of allegiance to the United States would be safeguarded. Presumably, this assurance extended to their slaves, although Butler neglected to say so explicitly. This lack of specificity became a significant problem for Butler and his new "Department of the Gulf."[1]

New Orleans was never intended to be the stopping point of Butler's expedition; his orders were to gradually spread his forces out and continue the conquest of Louisiana and its rich agricultural regions, particularly those bordering on the Mississippi River and its tributaries. Butler soon learned, however, that operations in Louisiana involved many complications, including dealing with the huge numbers of slaves his men encountered whenever and wherever they marched.

Gen? Butler Holding the Mob in Check at New Orleans.

Cartoon by Charles Stanley Reinhart labeled "General Butler holding the mob in check at New Orleans." Library of Congress, LC-USZ62-130292.

James Parton, author of one of the earliest histories of the Department of the Gulf, described Butler's challenge in handling the horde of noncombatants in a chapter that he titled simply "The Negro Question—First Difficulties:"

> [W]hen the Union troops landed at New Orleans, there was one slave in the state to every white person. Many of the parishes contain twice as many slaves as whites; some, three times as many; a few, four times as many; one has nine hundred white inhabitants to nearly nine thousand slaves. The marching of a Union column into one of those sugar parishes, was like thrusting a walking-stick into an ant-hill—the negroes swarmed about the troops, every soldier's gun and knapsack carried by a black man, exulting in the service. For, in some way, this great multitude of bondmen had derived the impression that part of the errand of these troops was to set them free.[2]

At this point in the war, General Butler possessed no instructions to set any slaves in Louisiana free. In fact, he knew that Generals Hunter and Fremont had been officially reprimanded for even attempting to emancipate slaves in their departments. If he could not emancipate them, what could he do with all the slaves flocking to his lines in ever-increasing numbers? Butler tried all the standard alternatives previously sanctioned by the War Department. He employed as many of the able-bodied men as he could reasonably justify. He returned slaves to owners who seemed to be loyal Unionists. He even directed that all of those not employed be driven outside of his lines, providing just enough rations and supplies to keep them alive. But in the end, the numbers proved too overwhelming. Unable to devise any clever solution as he had at Fort Monroe, an exasperated Butler wrote to Washington, describing his actions and asking, "Now, what am I to do?"[3]

As in the past, Union war planners gave no easy answer to this question. Drawn by the lure of freedom, masses of black men and their families quite understandably sought shelter in places close to the protection of Union armies. Some of these people were not even fugitive slaves, as their masters intentionally abandoned them in an effort to strain the resources of Northern troops. In June 1862, for example, an officer reported to Butler the arrival of "a large number of negroes, of both sexes and all ages, who are lying near our pickets, with bag and baggage, as if they had already commenced an exodus."⁴ Butler learned that a nearby sugar plantation owner drove his slaves from his land, stating "the Yankees are king here now, and that they must go to their king for food and shelter."⁵

If Butler was viewed as the "King" of the Yankees in Louisiana, he seemed to be a ruler with little control over his princes in the field, particularly a general named John Wolcott Phelps. Phelps was a particularly interesting character. A West Point trained soldier from Vermont, Phelps hated slavery and slaveholders with a passion bordering on obsession. As one European war correspondent described him, Phelps was "a tall, saturnine, gloomy, angry-eyed, sallow man, soldier-like too, and one who places old John Brown on a level with the great martyrs of the Christian world."⁶

Butler thought Phelps a good enough soldier, but privately characterized him as a "crank" on the issue of slavery, and Phelps certainly held an intense personal focus on that issue. On the voyage down to the Gulf of Mexico, Phelps wrote an abolitionist manifesto, later referred to as the "Phelps Emancipation

Brig. Gen. John Wolcott Phelps. Found in Francis T. Miller, ed.,
*The Photographic History of the Civil War*, vol. 10 (1911).

Proclamation," that he insisted on reading to the ship's passengers and officers after the vessel arrived at Ship Island, Mississippi. The document had been ignored by everyone except the Southern press, which used a leaked copy of the writing to stoke Southerners' fears that the Yankees had arrived with the intention of fomenting a slave insurrection.[7]

Once landed in Louisiana, Phelps was assigned to service at Camp Parapet, a fort near New Orleans. Fugitive slaves congregated near the camp, and Butler received a series of complaints that Phelps and his soldiers visited local plantations and encouraged the workers to run away and stay near them. Capt. Edward Page, Jr., wrote General Butler and complained that he found it difficult to hire and retain the workers he needed for a critically important levee repair project. The problem arose because Page had been using "rented" or "hired" slaves. Whenever Page tried to punish a slave worker, however, Phelps sent men to liberate the slave and bring him to the growing "contraband camp" near Camp Parapet. The result, Page claimed, was that "it is utterly impossible to call upon the negroes for any labor, as they have only to go to the fort to be free and are therefore very insolent to their masters."[8]

Butler feared that Phelps' actions would alienate the supposedly loyal landowners of the area and precipitate a humanitarian crisis by gathering fugitive slaves that the army could not support. He sent orders to Phelps directing him to expel all unemployed persons, black or white, from his lines. Hearing reports that Phelps was not complying with this order as fast and completely as he desired, Butler sent another officer to inspect Camp Parapet and report on matters there.[9]

As the report received by Butler confirmed, Phelps avoided returning fugitive slaves to their masters. Phelps held an almost religious conviction that the best policy for dealing with slaves was to emancipate them immediately and provide temporary sustenance until they could transition to an independent lifestyle. Butler viewed Phelps' belief as interesting, but understood it fell outside of President Lincoln's policy at the time. More importantly, Phelps held no authority to grant any form of emancipation. On June 16, 1862, the short-tempered Phelps reached his breaking point. Writing a lengthy defense of his actions and a plea that the president act to end the crisis by declaring immediate emancipation, Phelps demanded that his highly unusual report be forwarded directly to President Lincoln.[10]

Butler promptly forwarded the entire communication to Secretary of War Stanton, noting that Butler wished to "leave the whole question with the President, with perhaps the needless assurance that his wishes shall be loyally followed even if not in accordance with my own, as I have no right to have any upon the subject."[11] One might wonder why Butler forwarded such an unconventional and, in some ways, insubordinate communication all the way up through the chain of command. The answer was almost certainly that Butler shared Phelps' desire for urgent action on the emancipation issue but feared acting himself because of the risk of presidential condemnation. Butler could not afford to do anything that would further tarnish his rapidly worsening reputation as military commander in New Orleans.[12]

Butler sent the Phelps communication off to Washington and both men waited anxiously for a response. After no communication in six weeks, Phelps decided that silence amounted to consent and moved on to the next element in his personal crusade to end slavery. On July 30, 1862, Phelps submitted requisitions for arms and equipment for three black regiments, claiming that he intended to create the regiments by making fugitive slaves into soldiers. Arguing that "the best way of preventing the African from becoming instrumental in a general state of anarchy is to enlist him," Phelps declared dramatically that it was "for the interests of the South as well as for the North that the African should be permitted to offer his block for the Temple of Freedom."[13]

Phelps may have been ready for the African to offer his block, but his superior, General Butler, was caught completely by surprise by Phelps' announcement. As Butler wrote to his wife, "Phelps has gone crazy. He is organizing the negroes into regiments and wants me to arm them."[14] This was a step that Butler was not prepared to take, absent express authorization from Washington. He tried to find a middle ground, directing Phelps to use his new black "regiments" to cut down trees and do military work around the camp. Phelps could call them soldiers, if he wanted, but they would not be allowed to associate with other troops or fight.[15]

Once again, Butler used semantics in an effort to achieve the result he wanted. Phelps, however, rejected Butler's offer. Angrily declaring that he was a soldier and not a slave driver, Phelps tried to tender his resignation. Butler hoped that Phelps would calm down and refused to accept his resignation for a time. The men reached an impasse, with Phelps arguing that Butler's order to employ the black men as laborers was equivalent to a form of slavery. Faced with numerous other difficulties, an exasperated Butler forwarded the whole correspondence with Phelps to Washington and again requested instructions.[16]

The answer from Washington appeared both cryptic and unhelpful. The army decided simply to accept General Phelps' resignation without comment. As for Butler's request for clarification, Secretary of War Stanton advised the general to find answers to his questions in the confiscation laws and the president's previous orders relating to them.[17]

Not all Union soldiers in the area supported Phelps' efforts to attract black refugees to their camps and train them as soldiers. One Vermont soldier recorded that at the height of the Phelps controversy, "They [fugitive slaves] are coming into camp by the hundred and are a costly curse. They should be kept out or set at work, or freed or colonized, or sunk or something."[18]

Butler may have thought Phelps a "crank," but he hated to lose his services. Phelps possessed a reputation as a good military commander and his soldiers loved and respected him. He also refused to compromise on principles in which he firmly believed. The Union army eventually enlisted black men into black regiments, but not formally until the end of 1862. As one biographical entry on General Phelps accurately observed, the general "seems to have made a career of espousing either the right cause at the wrong time or vice versa."[19]

Ironically, one of the first Union commanders to formally enlist black soldiers was Gen. Benjamin Butler, who began his effort shortly after General Phelps' resignation. After a Confederate attack at Baton Rouge, Butler became concerned about a similar attack against New Orleans. Butler wrote a letter to Secretary of War Stanton describing his difficulty obtaining troops and suggesting that if matters made it necessary, "I shall call on Africa to intervene and I do not think I shall call in vain."[20]

Soon thereafter, Butler issued his "call on Africa" for troops. Desperate for soldiers, Butler hit upon the idea of enlisting the "Native Guard," a New Orleans militia company originally composed of free black men who had offered to fight for the Confederacy at the beginning of the war. Butler talked to the officers of the company, who assured him that the offer to fight for the South was only a matter of expediency, and they were eager and willing to join the Union army and fight for the end of slavery. On August 22, 1862, Butler issued Order No. 426, praising the Native Guard for their proud tradition of service (soldiers from the Native Guard fought under Andrew Jackson at the Battle of New Orleans), and formally welcomed them into the Union army. The Native Guard thus became the first official all-black regiment in the Union army.[21]

Why did Butler choose to enlist the Native Guard as the first all-black regiment instead of forming a regiment from newly emancipated slaves as General Phelps attempted? Butler knew that the first commander to utilize armed black troops would face criticism in both the North and South. Starting the process with the Native Guard, however, offered two advantages from a political standpoint. First, the unit had technically been mustered into Confederate service early in the

Pickets of the First Louisiana "Native Guard" guarding the New Orleans, Opelousas, and Great Western Railroad." *Frank Leslie's Illustrated Newspaper* (March 7, 1863). Library of Congress, LC-USZ62-105562.

war. Butler believed that enlisting a unit of Union troops that the Confederates attempted to utilize previously would garner less condemnation. Secondly, the core of the Native Guard consisted of free black men, many of whom were of mixed-race parentage. In justifying his action to the War Department in Washington, Butler later claimed that the men were unobjectionable because the darkest member of the guard was "about the complexion of the late Mr. [Daniel] Webster."[22]

The regiment that Butler mustered into Union service was formally called the "First Louisiana Native Guard." Despite Butler's representations to his superiors in Washington, only about 108 of the men in that regiment were actually free at the time the war commenced. The rest of the regiment consisted of escaped slaves who represented themselves as free in order to fight for the end of slavery. By this point in the war, Butler was not really too particular about the nature or the identity of the troops willing to fight for him.[23]

Watching them drill in the hot Louisiana sun, Butler praised his new black soldiers:

> Better soldiers never shouldered a musket. They were intelligent, obedient, highly appreciative of their position and fully maintained its dignity. They easily learned the school of the soldier . . . They learned to handle arms and to march more readily than the most intelligent white men. My drillmaster could teach a regiment of negroes that much of the art of war sooner than he could have taught the same number of students from Harvard or Yale.[24]

Butler conceived that the black troops learned the art of war so quickly because they were acclimated to the weather, used to taking orders, and often imitated their masters in the course of completing repetitive actions. There may be some small element of truth to Butler's theory, but a more likely explanation is that former slaves proved the most motivated and personally committed soldiers to the new cause of freedom. As Frederick Douglass argued, former slaves "have a deeper interest in the defeat and humiliation of the rebels than all others."[25]

## Chapter 6

# LINCOLN AND THE EMANCIPATION PROCLAMATION

As Summer 1862 approached, it appeared that the war might soon be settled in the North's favor. Union Gen. George B. McClellan landed at Fort Monroe, Virginia, with an army that grew to more than a hundred thousand men. His army began a painfully slow approach up the peninsula towards the Confederate capital of Richmond. With McClellan's strength in numbers, it seemed just a matter of time before the Confederate capital fell into Union hands. But as the days went by, momentum shifted. Confederate troops forced McClellan's grand army back from the gates of Richmond in a series of humiliating engagements that became collectively known as the "Seven Days' Battles."[1]

As McClellan retreated from Richmond, almost losing large portions of his army on some occasions, Lincoln became concerned about the general's lack of effective leadership. In early July, Lincoln decided to meet with McClellan in the field to learn the reasons for the general's withdrawal and discuss the available military options. As soon as the president arrived in Virginia, however, McClellan handed him an extraordinary document. Known today as the "Harrison's Landing Letter" because of the location Lincoln received the paper, McClellan's letter ignored the military situation almost entirely and focused exclusively on political considerations. Arguing that forcible abolition of slavery should not "be contemplated for a moment," McClellan advised Lincoln that "Military power should not be allowed to interfere with the relations of servitude, either by supporting or impairing the authority of the master."[2]

Stunned by this unsolicited lecture, Lincoln returned to Washington with even more concerns about General McClellan's loyalty and ability. From Lincoln's perspective, McClellan lacked any clear military strategy for dealing with the enemy in front of him and seemed preoccupied with a host of political considerations outside the responsibilities of an army commander. McClellan's letter appeared to reinforce the rumors making the circles in Washington that the general held political aspirations and might be making plans for a military coup. There may have been something to these rumors, as evidenced by the fact that McClellan ran against Lincoln in the 1864 presidential election.[3]

Lincoln returned to Washington with no faith in General McClellan and great concern about the timid and inept way his military commanders used their armies to fight the war. The president also gained a new perspective on the way the enemy's slaves impacted the progress of the war. When he talked with his field commanders in Virginia, Lincoln heard time and again about the strong defensive lines the rebels constructed with the aid of slave labor. Some reports, difficult to corroborate, proposed that the Confederates used slaves as sharpshooters or to serve in artillery crews. Other reports, widely believed at the time, suggested that some blacks actively fought against Union troops while wearing Confederate uniforms. Enough was enough, Lincoln's critics argued; the time had come to take slaves out of the enemy's service and put them to work supporting the Union cause. Although Lincoln had long resisted these arguments, the president changed his mind, and soon thereafter began to steer a new course that led to emancipation.[4]

President Lincoln's momentous decision to issue the Emancipation Proclamation came in the midst of a year of immense personal tragedy for the Lincoln family. Early in the year, both of Lincoln's sons became very sick with a disease that is today thought to be Typhoid fever. Although Tad eventually recovered, Willie passed away in February, leaving the president and his wife, Mary, devastated with grief. Although Lincoln eventually recovered to the point where he could continue his public duties, Mary was profoundly affected by the death of their son and was never the same following this tragic event.[5]

In their grief over Willie's death, the Lincolns sought a more private place of refuge. They found their retreat in a house that became known as "Lincoln's Cottage." This home, more substantial than its name implies, was located at the

Soldier's Home, a short ride outside Washington. The Lincolns escaped to the cottage beginning in June 1862 and continued to reside there for most of the next five months. The president most likely drafted the Emancipation Proclamation, which he later considered the most important work of his life, during this time at the cottage.[6]

Lincoln never wanted emancipation to arrive by way of a presidential proclamation. Indeed, he went to great lengths to avoid association with anything of the kind. He long believed that the end of slavery should come by a deliberate and gradual process that included compensation for the affected slaveholders. Most importantly, Lincoln maintained that broad acceptance of emancipation was impossible unless accomplished by a vote of the people or their elected representatives. If slaveholders saw emancipation as something forced upon them by a government autocrat with questionable legal power, he thought it would only provoke more fighting and bitterness. This was in large part why Lincoln declined to go along with the emancipation declarations issued by Generals Fremont and Hunter.[7]

President Abraham Lincoln's "Cottage" at the Soldiers' Home in Washington, D.C. (c. 1863). Library of Congress, LC-USZ62-87597.

Even before his visit to General McClellan in Virginia, Lincoln began to see the merits of a presidential proclamation declaring emancipation. Perhaps his mental shift came after his proposals to the border states to implement voluntary and gradual emancipation failed to gain momentum. Perhaps he grew weary of responding to Northern abolitionists and the radical elements of his own party demanding that he embrace emancipation as a tool to harness the power of the freed slaves to support the Union war effort. Whatever his motivation, Lincoln began secretly working on an emancipation decree sometime in the late spring or early summer of 1862.

Hannibal Hamlin, Lincoln's vice president, later claimed that Lincoln showed him a draft of the Emancipation Proclamation in the upstairs library of the cottage at the Soldier's Home in mid-June. Many historians doubt this story, which surfaced many years after the event. Another story, also of doubtful pedigree, claimed Lincoln started to work on the proclamation while waiting for military news in the War Department telegraph office.[8]

The earliest credible and contemporaneous reference to Lincoln's proclamation is found in a diary entry of Secretary of the Navy Gideon Welles dated July 13, 1862. Welles recorded a conversation with Lincoln and William Seward that took place during a carriage ride to attend the funeral of Edwin Stanton's infant child. According to Welles, Lincoln "dwelt earnestly on the gravity, importance and delicacy of the movement, said he had given it much thought and had about come to the conclusion that it was a military necessity absolutely essential for the salvation of the Union, that we must free the slaves or be ourselves subdued."[9]

Surprised by Lincoln's decision, Welles noted, "until this time, in all our previous interviews, whenever the question of emancipation or the mitigation of slavery had been in any way alluded to, [Lincoln] had been prompt and emphatic in denouncing any interference by the General Government with that subject."[10] Until that moment, Welles believed, and thought every member of Lincoln's cabinet agreed, that slavery "was a local, domestic question appertaining to the States respectively, who had never parted with their authority over it."[11]

What changed? Welles believed that recent events of the war caused Lincoln to despair:

[T]he reverses before Richmond [during the Seven Days Campaign], and the formidable power and dimensions of the insurrection, which extended through all the Slave States, and had combined most of them in a confederacy to destroy the Union, impelled the Administration to adopt extraordinary measures to preserve the national existence. The slaves, if not armed and disciplined, were in the service of those who were, not only as field laborers and producers, but thousands of them were in attendance upon the armies in the field, employed as waiters and teamsters, and the fortifications and intrenchments [sic] were constructed by them.[12]

Events moved relatively quickly after the July 13 carriage ride. On July 17, Congress passed the Second Confiscation Act. This law purported to free the slaves of all rebels, regardless of whether the slaves were directly employed in the Confederate war effort. But since the act's enforcement relied on a court declaration that a slaveholder was a rebel, the Second Confiscation Act proved of limited practical use. Lincoln also possessed lingering concerns about the act's constitutionality, saying that "it is startling to say that congress can free a slave within a state."[13] To Lincoln, the Second Confiscation Act, like the first such law, did not represent a major breakthrough on resolving the issue of slavery. Perhaps because he was preoccupied with his own, still secret, emancipation vehicle, Lincoln signed the bill as well as sending over to Congress a potential veto message identifying a list of problems with the bill's language.[14]

One of the reasons that Lincoln seemed so concerned about the potential constitutional deficiencies of the Second Confiscation Act stemmed from similar issues he encountered in creating his own presidential proclamation. Lincoln publicly stated on many occasions that, in his legal judgment, the federal government lacked the legal power to abolish slavery in Southern states. Indeed, Lincoln held so little doubt about this point that he supported a constitutional amendment in 1861 (the so-called "Corwin Amendment") that expressly prohibited Congress from interfering with slavery in the slaveholding states. If, as Lincoln said about the Confiscation Act, it was "startling to say that Congress can free a slave within a state," he believed it even more far-fetched to think that a president could do so on his own.[15] Despite his misgivings, that proved precisely the course of action that Lincoln then privately committed himself to attempt.

Lincoln had long heard and considered all of the arguments about his ability to free slaves under the so-called "war powers" of the president. He wanted to believe that, in his role as commander-in-chief, he held a wide range of powers to deal with the military situation. The scope of these powers remained unclear and untested, however. If he proceeded, Lincoln knew his legal justification for emancipation must rely on a claim of "military necessity." Emancipation based on such a controversial justification would certainly face a court test in a forum he had reason to fear. Lincoln knew his old adversary, Roger B. Taney, still oversaw the Supreme Court as chief justice. Taney, who had ruled against the Lincoln administration's use of emergency military powers in a previous case, would undoubtedly provide an unsympathetic and exacting review of Lincoln's actions. One historian accurately called the courts "the ghost at the emancipation banquet."[16] It was a ghost that clearly haunted Lincoln as he considered his options.

Lincoln held strong concerns regarding the Supreme Court's views because of his private lack of conviction that an executive could legally decree large-scale emancipation based on a claim of military necessity. In Lincoln's mind, emancipating a slave who worked for the enemy's cause differed greatly from issuing a broad proclamation of freedom for enslaved persons in the rebellious states. Declaring a large group of slaves "forever free" and extending the freedom for a period after the end of the war particularly troubled Lincoln. In a confidential letter to his friend Orville Browning in 1861, Lincoln wrote about General Fremont's attempt to issue such a proclamation:

> Genl. Fremont's proclamation, as to confiscation of property, and the liberation of slaves, is purely political, and not within the range of military law, or necessity. If a commanding General finds a necessity to seize the farm of a private owner, for a pasture, an encampment, or a fortification, he has the right to do so, and to so hold it, as long as the necessity lasts; and this is within military law, because within military necessity. But to say the farm shall no longer belong to the owner, or his heirs forever; and this as well when the farm is not needed for military purposes as when it is, is purely political, without the savor of military law about it. And the same is true of slaves. If the General needs them, he can seize them; but when the need is past, it is not for him to fix their

President Abraham Lincoln. Library of Congress, LC-DIG-pga-00352.

permanent condition. That must be settled according to laws made by law-makers, and not by military proclamations.[17]

Lincoln told Browning that freeing slaves forever by means of a proclamation was nothing more than a disguised "dictatorship." The president knew that such an action might be popular with some "thoughtless people," but said he could not see his own way clear to adopt any such "reckless position." To do so, Lincoln warned, would surrender the proper role of a government: "Can it be pretended that it is any longer the government of the U.S.—any government of Constitution and laws—wherein a General, or a President, may make permanent rules of property by proclamation?"[18]

Despite Lincoln's deeply held reservations about the legality of such an order, by Summer 1862 the president felt that moving forward with some form of emancipation was a chance he (and the Union cause) needed to take. As Lincoln later recalled, "we had reached the end of the rope on the plan of operations we had been pursuing; that we had about played our last card, and must change our tactics, or lose the game!"[19]

Lincoln understood that any emancipation proclamation he issued would be challenged as a matter of constitutional law. Accordingly, he proceeded to draft his proclamation as carefully as possible. Here, Lincoln showed his true genius as a lawyer. To maximize his order's chance of surviving judicial review, Lincoln needed to firmly anchor it in military necessity and so strictly limit its provisions to permissible military goals and objectives that its military purpose and connection could not be denied.

The proclamation needed to look like a military act and every word of its short text needed to convey that impression. This writing would not include the rhetorical flourishes for which Lincoln was noted; instead, as one modern critic derisively commented, the work had the "moral grandeur of a bill of lading."[20] If simple language was needed to deliver the goods on emancipation, however, Lincoln would write just such a bill.

The exact number of drafts of the Emancipation Proclamation are unknown. Given its importance and the likelihood of a judicial test, however, Lincoln probably drafted and redrafted the proclamation's language many times. No other

American president had spent as much time in the courtroom as Lincoln, and many of his most important cases involved interpretation of the text of contracts, statutes, or other documents. If there was one thing Lincoln knew well, it was the way that language took on a meaning of its own in the confines of a courtroom full of skillful lawyers. Lincoln intended to draft the language of his proclamation with more care than any other document he ever authored.[21]

Key to the document's success lay in how the proclamation could be written to look like a military action designed to weaken the enemy and shorten the war. Lincoln came up with two, very clever, ideas. First, the proclamation contained geographical limitations; it would apply only to slaves in territory under the actual control of the rebels. Border states and all areas already under Union control fell outside the document's reach. Lincoln designed his proclamation to apply only to slaves located in enemy territory. The second clever idea that Lincoln incorporated into his proclamation was to delay its effective date for a period of time in order to give the rebel states one last chance to submit to federal authority and avoid emancipation of their slaves. By limiting his proclamation geographically and delaying its effective date, Lincoln made it harder for his critics to attack it on constitutional grounds. The rebels could avoid the effect of the proclamation entirely, Lincoln could point out, simply by laying down their arms. Lincoln's proclamation only emancipated slaves in territory actively controlled by the enemy, and only then if the enemy had not submitted to Union control by January 1, 1863. Lincoln still held doubts about the legality of such a proclamation but felt that his wording stood a reasonable chance of surviving judicial review given the narrow scope of its provisions.

On July 22, 1862, Lincoln convened what may well be the most famous cabinet meeting in American history. On the surface, the meeting was merely the continuation of the previous day's meeting. At the end of the July 21 meeting, Treasury Secretary Salmon P. Chase urged the adoption of a policy that not only authorized enlistment of blacks in the military, but also armed them for use in combat. Lincoln started the July 22 meeting by saying that he was not ready to authorize black enlistments yet but used Chase's proposal as an opportunity to address what he revealed as the real purpose behind the day's cabinet meeting: emancipation.[22]

The first reading of the Emancipation Proclamation before the cabinet based on a painting by Francis Bicknell Carpenter. Library of Congress, LC-DIG-pga-02502.

Lincoln began the discussion by saying that he wanted to issue a proclamation declaring emancipation of slaves as a war measure. While the cabinet members still recovered from the shock of this news, the president emphasized that the declaration was his personal decision and, while he welcomed discussion of the language and procedures surrounding its implementation, his decision to issue the proclamation was firm and irrevocable. As Lincoln later recalled, "I said to the Cabinet that I had resolved upon this step, and had not called them together to ask their advice, but to lay the subject-matter of a proclamation before them; suggestions as to which would be in order, after they had heard it read."[23]

Lincoln then proceeded to read to the cabinet his draft order declaring emancipation of slaves. Interestingly, the document that Lincoln read, a forerunner of the Emancipation Proclamation, was not labeled a "Proclamation;" indeed, the draft now in the Library of Congress has no title of any kind. This omission was probably no accident. At the time of its reading, Lincoln still searched for the best way to characterize his action in order to invoke military necessity and enhance its chances of surviving judicial review.

The document that Lincoln read began with a formalistic reference to the language of Section 6 of the recently enacted Second Confiscation Act, which required the president to issue a formal notice warning rebels that after sixty days he could proceed with confiscation of their assets. So far, Lincoln's language was on safe ground and merely followed his clear statutory responsibility.

The second paragraph of the proposed order was also relatively uncontroversial, merely notifying the public that Lincoln intended to once again urge the next Congress to enact legislation that would provide financial aid to any state adopting a policy that led to the gradual, compensated emancipation of slaves. The purpose of this policy, Lincoln specified, was "to practically restore, thenceforward to be maintain[ed], the constitutional relation between the general government and each and all the states . . ."[24]

As Lincoln turned to the second page of his draft, the cabinet ministers must have wondered what all of the fuss was about. Clerks routinely drafted and communicated this type of document; the first page seemed hardly worth a special cabinet meeting and a presidential reading. But then, Lincoln read the concluding eighty-five-word sentence:

> And, as a fit and necessary military measure for effecting this object, I, as Commander-in-Chief of the Army and Navy of the United States, do order and declare that on the first day of January in the year of Our Lord one thousand, eight hundred and sixty-three, all persons held as slaves within any state or states, wherein the constitutional authority of the United States shall not then be practically recognized, submitted to, and maintained, shall then, thenceforward, and forever, be free.[25]

With these words, some of the most important words ever uttered by an American president, Lincoln escalated the issue of emancipation to a serious possibility. The president's proposal must have hit the assembled cabinet members like a bombshell. A few minor comments were presented and then Secretary of State William Seward offered a suggestion about timing. As Lincoln later recalled the discussion:

> Nothing [in the way of suggestions] was offered that I had not already fully anticipated and settled in my own mind, until Secretary Seward spoke. He said in substance: "Mr. President, I approve of the proclamation, but I question the expediency of its issue at this juncture. The depression of the public mind, consequent upon our repeated reverses, is so great that I fear the effect of so important a step. It may be viewed as the last measure of an exhausted government, a cry for help."[26]

Seward recommended that the president delay issuing his proclamation until it could accompany an important Union military victory. Lincoln had been so focused on the language of the proclamation and its reception by the courts that he had, quite uncharacteristically, failed to consider the political implications of its timing. Seward's suggestion made immediate sense to Lincoln. As he later told artist Francis Bicknell Carpenter, who painted a famous portrait of the cabinet meeting, "[t]he wisdom of the view of the Secretary of State struck me with very great force. It was an aspect of the case that, in all my thought upon the subject, I had entirely overlooked. The result was that I put the draft of the proclamation aside, as you do your sketch for a picture, waiting for a victory."[27]

Lincoln eagerly waited for the victory that would trigger the issuance of his proclamation. On August 20, 1862, Horace Greeley, the influential publisher of the *New-York Tribune* published a public appeal for emancipation he called "The Prayer of Twenty Millions." Lincoln responded with a famous public letter released two days later that probably left many of its readers puzzled:

> My paramount object in this struggle is to save the Union and is not either to save or to destroy slavery. If I could save the Union without freeing any slave I would do it, and if I could save it by freeing all the slaves I would do it; and if I could save it by freeing some and leaving others alone I would also do that. What I do about slavery, and the colored race, I do because I believe it helps to save the Union; and what I forbear, I forbear because I do not believe it would help to save the Union. I shall do less whenever I shall believe what I am doing hurts the cause, and I shall do more whenever I shall believe doing more will help the cause. I shall try to correct errors when shown to be errors; and I shall adopt new views so fast as they shall appear to be true views.[28]

Secretary of State William H. Seward. Library of Congress, LC-DIG-cwpb-04948.

In hindsight, Lincoln was obviously hinting to the public that he had changed his position and that his solution would involve freeing some slaves (those in Confederate states) and leaving others alone for the time being. Both friends and foes of emancipation found Lincoln's response to Greeley confusing: did the president support emancipation or not? The question seemed particularly legitimate, as days after his response to Greeley was printed, Lincoln invited a group of prominent black men to the White House and then used the occasion to lecture his guests about the need to keep the races separate, urging them to support a scheme to colonize freed slaves outside the United States.[29]

On September 13, Lincoln received a delegation of clergymen from Chicago who presented an impassioned plea for an emancipation proclamation. Even though the president possessed just such a proclamation in his desk drawer, Lincoln pretended to be uncertain of the wisdom or necessity of such an action, stating "What good would a proclamation of emancipation from me do, especially as we are now situated?"[30] Lincoln then proceeded to address the subject of the logistical nightmare that might accompany emancipation, saying "And suppose [the slaves] could be induced by a proclamation of freedom from me to throw themselves upon us, what should we do with them? How can we feed and care for such a multitude?"[31] The question Lincoln posed was a good one and its resolution would soon become of paramount importance.

Although Lincoln was not yet ready to reveal his decision on emancipation, he went on record in support of his legal authority to issue such a proclamation:

> Now, then, tell me, if you please, what possible result of good would follow the issuing of such a proclamation as you desire? Understand, I raise no objections against it on legal or constitutional grounds; for, as commander-in-chief of the army and navy, in time of war, I suppose I have a right to take any measure which may best subdue the enemy. Nor do I urge objections of a moral nature, in view of possible consequences of insurrection and massacre at the South. I view the matter as a practical war measure, to be decided upon according to the advantages or disadvantages it may offer to the suppression of the rebellion.[32]

After his July 22 cabinet meeting, Lincoln reluctantly agreed to put away his draft proclamation until a Union victory provided the appropriate timing for its release. Unfortunately, the president was forced to postpone emancipation for a longer period than he had hoped. In late August, Robert E. Lee and his Army of Northern Virginia inflicted an embarrassing defeat on the Union army at the Battle of Second Manassas and prepared for an invasion of the North. Union forces eventually stopped this invasion near Antietam Creek in Maryland on September 17, 1862. Tactically, the Battle of Antietam was a draw, but Lee's invasion failed, and the Confederate army was subsequently forced to retreat.

Antietam was close enough to a victory for Lincoln's purposes, and he hurried to use the battle's result as an opportunity to issue his Emancipation Proclamation. As he later told his cabinet:

> I think the time [to issue the proclamation] has come now. I wish it were a better time. I wish that we were in a better condition. The action of the army against the rebels has not been quite what I should have best liked. But they have been driven out of Maryland, and Pennsylvania is no longer in danger of invasion. When the rebel army was at Frederick, I determined, as soon as it should be driven out of Maryland, to issue a Proclamation of Emancipation such as I thought most likely to be useful. I said nothing to anyone; but I made the promise to myself, and (hesitating a little) to my Maker. The rebel army is now driven out, and I am going to fulfil that promise.[33]

On Monday, September 22, 1862, President Lincoln convened another meeting of his cabinet to discuss emancipation. Perhaps to lighten the mood, Lincoln started the meeting by reading a chapter from a book by one of his favorite humorists, Artemis Ward. Notes of the meeting suggest that everyone except Secretary of War Edwin Stanton laughed and enjoyed the reading. With that lightening of spirits, Lincoln proceeded to address the subject of emancipation. As he did at the July 22 cabinet meeting, Lincoln prefaced the reading of his proposed proclamation by saying that he was again not asking the cabinet for their thoughts on whether the proclamation should be issued, but only solicited their suggestions for minor improvements to its language.[34]

Between the July and September cabinet meetings, Lincoln made several important changes to his proclamation draft. To begin with, the September order that Lincoln presented to his cabinet was much longer than the July 22 version, incorporating portions of the two confiscation acts concerning fugitive slaves and their status. Lincoln literally cut out portions of these acts and pasted the language in his draft in order to make certain that he got the language exactly right. Some historians have suggested, probably correctly, that by quoting these provisions, Lincoln hoped to characterize his action as mere implementation of prior congressional action and make it sound less radical.[35]

Unlike the July draft, the September order addressed emancipation earlier in the document. The new draft proclamation boldly declared in its third paragraph that on January 1, 1863, one hundred days in the future, the slaves in all states then in rebellion "shall be then, thenceforward and forever free."[36] The language that followed this declaration contained important, long-term repercussions for the military. After declaring the slaves freed, the order provided that "the executive government of the United States will, during the continuance in office of the present incumbent, recognize such persons as being free and will do no act or acts to repress such persons, or any of them, in any efforts they may make for their actual freedom."[37]

After Lincoln finished reading this provision, Secretary Seward suggested that the emancipation language be changed to both "recognize and maintain" the freedom of the slaves rather than simply to "recognize" it. In addition, Seward urged Lincoln to expand the reference to "executive government" to expressly include "the military and naval authority thereof." Under the new language, not only the president, but also the military was firmly committed to pursue a policy of emancipation. Finally, Seward proposed elimination of a provision that appeared to limit the scope of action to the period "during the continuance in office of the present incumbent."[38] Seward objected that this language could potentially be used to support an argument that the freedpeople might lose their freedom and become slaves again after Lincoln left office. Each of these changes, viewed as relatively minor at the time, were accepted and incorporated into the proclamation.[39]

None of Seward's changes proved as innocuous as they seemed at the time. By eliminating the reference to the term of office of the incumbent, the proclamation committed the full authority of Lincoln as commander-in-chief and the military forces he commanded to assure freedom in perpetuity for the slaves affected by the proclamation. As Lincoln warned in the past, freedom forever (i.e., beyond the period that could reasonably be justified as a matter of military necessity) was potentially difficult to support as an exercise of the executive's war powers. Lincoln previously told a group of clergymen that he would not promise anything he could not deliver, saying "I do not want to issue a document that the whole world will see must necessarily be inoperative, like the Pope's bull against the comet!"[40]

Enlargement of a portion of the second page of President Lincoln's draft Emancipation Proclamation showing the inserted language. New York State Library.

Delivering on a promise of freedom forever would be difficult, but that was exactly what the final draft of the declaration purported to accomplish. Seward's modification eliminated the last bit of language that could potentially excuse emancipation as a temporary military expedient. The die was cast. The final draft of the proclamation boldly declared that on January 1, 1863, all slaves in Confederate territories were "then, thenceforward, and forever free."[41] Keeping this promise turned out to be a responsibility that weighed heavily on Lincoln, who continued to worry about its legality privately while bravely declaring that he "would rather die than take back a word of the Proclamation of Freedom."[42]

The other language changes suggested by Seward also proved much more substantive than they seemed at the time. As amended by Seward, the proclamation now represented a commitment by the president and the military to "recognize *and maintain*" the freedom of the emancipated slaves.[43] The draft of the proclamation in Lincoln's hand, which now resides in the collection of the New York State Library, shows this insertion as though it was a mere clarification of little importance. But it was no such thing. As historian Allen C. Guelzo observed, "no one thought long enough about Seward's proposed *recognize and maintain* to realize that the phrase might be the most shocking in the Proclamation."[44]

Recognizing a former slave's freedom seemed fairly straightforward, but how did Lincoln (or Seward) actually mean to "maintain" that freedom? How was such a commitment possibly to be fulfilled? Lincoln later indicated that the "maintain" language suggested by Seward was something that he had considered and rejected in the original drafting of his proclamation "because it was not my way to promise what I was not entirely sure that I could perform, and I was not prepared to say that I thought we were exactly able to 'maintain' this."[45] When Seward insisted on the addition, however, Lincoln agreed to make the change and the language became a permanent part of the proclamation and its mandate.

In the end, adding the word "maintain" proved an important change. By definition, the first encounter that most slaves affected by the proclamation would have with U.S. authorities would be with the military forces invading Confederate territories. After fighting the enemy and liberating slaves, could the Union army then pause in the middle of operations to "maintain" the freedom of each of the freedpeople? The effect of the proclamation approved by Lincoln and his cabinet put the U.S. military on a collision course with the needs and demands of millions of slaves eager to free themselves from bondage, causing enormous stress and difficulties for all the actors in this drama.

Although Lincoln welcomed discussion on the wording of the proclamation, he made it clear that he intended to issue the order without further delay. Resorting, uncharacteristically, to an invocation of divine will, Lincoln declared that the outcome of the Battle of Antietam showed him that God favored immediate emancipation. As Secretary of the Navy Gideon Welles recalled Lincoln's comments, "God had decided this question in favor of the slaves."[46]

God may have decided the question in favor of the slaves, as Lincoln apparently said he believed, but many did not share this opinion. Every member of Lincoln's cabinet appreciated the risks that attended issuance of the Emancipation Proclamation. In normal times, such an action would not have been considered, let alone attempted. But these were far from normal times. Only one cabinet member—Postmaster General Montgomery Blair—went on record opposing issuance of the proclamation. The rest apparently believed, as expressed by Gideon Welles, that the order was necessary as "an arbitrary and despotic measure in the cause of freedom."[47]

The preliminary Emancipation Proclamation, as the September 22 proclamation came to be called, was issued immediately following the cabinet meeting at which it was revised and approved. The term "preliminary" was applied because the emancipation provision in the proclamation would, by its terms, only become effective on January 1, 1863, precisely one hundred days from the date of issuance of the preliminary proclamation. In order to further attest to its status as an exercise of the president's "war powers," the entire proclamation was promptly issued to the army as General Orders No. 139.[48]

As Lincoln expected, abolitionists in the North warmly greeted the proclamation's issuance, while it became the subject of bitter condemnation from those who supported the institution of slavery. More moderate factions also opposed the proclamation, maintaining that emancipation in general was good policy but opposing its pursuit now as a distraction from the country's more important immediate goals of achieving military success and restoring the Union. Lincoln was prepared for all of these reactions, admitting privately that "while I hope something from the proclamation, my expectations are not as sanguine as are those of some friends."[49]

One aspect of the public's immediate reaction to the proclamation surprised and bothered Lincoln. He had hoped that financial markets and military enlistments might both climb as an enthusiastic reaction to the new emancipation initiative, but just the opposite occurred. As Lincoln confessed to his vice president:

[The proclamation] is six days old, and while commendation in newspapers and by distinguished individuals is all that a vain man could wish, the stocks have declined, and troops come forward more slowly than ever. This, looked soberly in the face, is not very satisfactory. We have fewer troops in the field at the end of six days than we had at the beginning—the attrition among the old outnumbering the addition by the new. The North responds to the proclamation sufficiently in breath; but breath alone kills no rebels.[50]

In acknowledging that "breath alone kills no rebels," Lincoln made the obvious point that only the military could supply the force necessary to restore the Union and give effect to his emancipation decree. By its terms, the emancipation provisions of the preliminary proclamation would not come into being until January 1, 1863, when the president defined exactly which states or portions of states were still in rebellion. Several parts of the proclamation, however, were final immediately and required no further action by the president. In particular, the proclamation directed the military to strictly enforce congressional actions that prohibited returning fugitive slaves. Union troops were also ordered to presume free status for all slaves escaping into another state or the District of Columbia.

The intent of these provisions was to remove the military from the business of slave catching, in some ways simplifying the uneasy tension that existed since the beginning of the war between military commanders and escaped slaves. After receiving news of General Orders No. 139, however, military commanders knew that, on pain of court-martial, they were prohibited from returning fugitive slaves. Instead, they were to presume that such individuals were free men and women and "recognize and maintain" that freedom. But the order failed to address what the generals were supposed to do with such people. Was the Union army required to feed, employ, or protect them? These logistical problems became ever more difficult as Union armies approached operations that would take them through the heartland of the South. Nothing about this situation would be simple to resolve, and nothing any of the commanders had learned at a military academy prepared them for the challenges they soon faced in the course of liberating millions of enslaved people.

## Chapter 7

# INTO THE HEART OF THE CONFEDERACY

On one occasion during a world tour in 1877, former General and President Ulysses S. Grant met with Prince Otto von Bismarck. As the old soldiers compared military experiences, Bismarck remarked that the American Civil War would have been much shorter if America had followed the European model and maintained a large standing army. Grant observed that Bismarck's opinion might be correct, but it assumed that such a standing army would have stood and fought with the North, which Grant wryly suggested might not have been the case.

Grant also made a subtler point that reflected his years of thinking about the events of the war. He told Bismarck, "as soon as slavery fired upon the flag it was felt, we all felt, even those who did not object to slaves, that slavery must be destroyed."[1] In hindsight, Grant believed a quick war would not have served America's long-term interests because it "would have saved slavery, perhaps, and slavery meant the germs of new rebellion. There had to be an end of slavery."[2] To Grant, the need for a war that completely ended slavery "seemed odd at the time, but which now seem Providential."[3]

Although Grant in 1877 had come to terms with the war, in large part because of the death sentence it imposed on slavery, in the early years of the war he advocated against addressing the issue. Grant's position at the outset of the war aligned with that of President Lincoln. Grant opposed slavery on moral grounds (freeing his one slave in 1859) but felt that making abolition a war objective seemed unwise. Winning a war was difficult enough, Grant thought, without mixing in a thorny political and social issue like slavery. "My inclination," as Grant told his father in 1861, "is to whip the rebellion preserving all constitutional rights [including the right to own slaves]."⁴ He then continued, "[i]f it is necessary that slavery should fall that the Republic may continue its existence, let slavery go."⁵

By Fall 1862, Grant wanted to "let slavery go." After enduring a battle at Shiloh that almost destroyed his army, the general prepared to launch an invasion into the Confederate heartland from his base along the Tennessee-Mississippi border. The ultimate goal of Grant's expedition: the Confederate citadel at Vicksburg. While preparing for his campaign, Grant received word of Lincoln's preliminary Emancipation Proclamation.

Lt. Gen. Ulysses S. Grant in the field. Library of Congress, LC-DIG-cwpb-04407.

Grant's thinking on emancipation, like that of President Lincoln, had undergone a substantial transformation since the early days of the war. In May 1861, Grant wrote to his father that he expected the war to be "of short duration."[6] Early in the war, Grant thought the conflict might lead Southern slaves to "revolt and cause more destruction than any Northern man, except it be the ultra-abolitionist, wants to see."[7] As Grant's predictions of a short war accompanied by a quick slave revolt proved inaccurate, he began to reconsider how ending the institution of slavery might be an attractive addition to the North's military strategy.[8]

As a soldier, Grant saw the issue in strictly military terms; emancipation removed slave labor from the enemy's resources. After it became obvious that the war would last an extended period, he even considered endorsing emancipation as a stated war aim. While Grant approved of emancipation in principle, the Emancipation Proclamation itself greatly hindered his army in the field. With emancipation on the horizon, Grant and his Army of the Tennessee found themselves surrounded by an army: not an army of Confederates, but instead, an army of slaves seeking the promise of freedom.

One myth surrounding emancipation is the belief that Union troops physically travelled throughout the South, bringing news of emancipation to each person held in bondage. The evidence available suggests, however, that this type of uninformed isolation proved relatively rare. Instead, news of possible emancipation circulated widely through slave networks and informal methods of communication. Only six days after Lincoln issued his proclamation, the *New York Times* reported: "there is much more understanding among [the slaves] of the questions at issue in this war, and a far more rapid and secret diffusing of intelligence and news through the plantations than was ever dreamed of at the North."[9] This certainly rang true in Texas, where many slaves heard and passed along the war news received by their masters.[10]

As he would demonstrate throughout the war, Grant led best when dealing with unexpected obstacles. One of his strengths as a commander lay in his ability to choose subordinates who helped him deal with difficult situations and implement his policies. One evening in November 1862, Chaplain John Eaton received a completely unexpected order from General Grant. The order directed him to immediately put aside his duties as chaplain of the Twenty-Seventh Ohio

Infantry Volunteers and to take charge of all the nearby fugitive slaves, see to their welfare, and set them to work picking the cotton that lay unharvested in the fields. Eaton, who had never met Grant, was appalled to read the description of the job the general had assigned to him. Seeing no way to honorably decline the general's request, however, Eaton apprehensively went to report in person to his commanding general and receive further instructions.[11]

Arriving at Grant's headquarters in La Grange, Tennessee, Eaton entered the general's office and announced his identity. Grant said, "Oh, you are the man who has all these darkies on his shoulders" and directed the chaplain to sit down

Chaplain (and later Brigadier General of Volunteers) John Eaton.
Library of Congress, LC-DIG-cwpbh-00608.

for what Eaton later called a "long and intensely interesting talk on the Negro problem."[12] Eaton quickly realized that Grant was not looking for a convenient target to blame for the approaching crisis in army-slave relations. According to Eaton, Grant had carefully considered the issues surrounding emancipation and was prepared to lend his personal support to make the transition from slavery to freedom as successful as practically possible given the limitations of the available resources.[13]

The "Negro problem," as Eaton characterized it, arose because the Emancipation Proclamation put officers like Grant and his subordinates in a terrible practical dilemma. As the proclamation made clear, the president and the military were now irrevocably committed to a policy that required them to "recognize and maintain" the freedom of every escaped slave who entered Union lines. The proclamation even quoted legislation making it a court-martial offense to deliver any escaped slaves back into the hands of their former captors.

Grant realized he must take charge of the fugitive slaves and keep them out of the hands of their former masters, but he still had no direction from Washington on what exactly to do with them. The initial fugitive slave return policy announced in Washington in May 1861 was designed to deal with a situation like that faced by General Butler on the East Coast, typically involving a relatively small and manageable population of slaves who escaped into Union lines. Grant and Eaton dealt with much more than a few dozen, or even a few hundred, fugitive slaves who stumbled into camp. Grant's army found themselves in the midst of a mass of thousands of slaves, many of whom had left their homes in a state of desperate need.

As Eaton looked at his new charges, he saw a body of people with no resources to care for themselves. He later wrote:

> Imagine, if you will, a slave population . . . coming garbed in rags or in silks, with feet shod or bleeding, individually or in families and larger groups—an army of slaves and fugitives pushing its way irresistibly toward an army of fighting men, perpetually on the defensive and perpetually ready to attack. The arrival among us of these hordes was like the oncoming of cities. There was no plan in this exodus, no Moses to lead it. . . . Often the slaves met prejudices against their color more bitter than any they had left behind. But

their own interests were identical, they felt, with the objects of our armies: a blind terror stung them, an equally blind hope allured them, and to us they came. Their condition was appalling. There were men, women, and children in every stage of disease or decrepitude, often nearly naked, with flesh torn by the terrible experiences of their escapes.[14]

For authorities in Washington, recognizing and maintaining the freedom of emancipated slaves seemed possible, but the reality of doing so in the context of ongoing military operations would be difficult if not impossible. Eaton and Grant both knew the situation would only worsen as the army "advanced into the heart of the great slave population."[15]

Grant put the army's challenge to Chaplain Eaton in stark terms:

Orders of the government prohibited the expulsion of the negroes from the protection of the army, when they came in voluntarily. Humanity forbade allowing them to starve. With such an army of them, of all ages and both sexes, as had congregated about Grand Junction, amounting to many thousands, it was impossible to advance. There was no special authority for feeding them unless they were employed as teamsters, cooks and pioneers with the army; but only able-bodied young men were suitable for such work. This labor would support but a very limited percentage of them.[16]

Even though the general wanted to help each of the escaped slaves that surrounded him, Grant possessed neither the time nor the resources to do so. His army's supply line was stretched so thin that he could barely feed and clothe his own men. Some of his soldiers slept without shelter, and his transportation needs exceeded his available wagons. Grant would have trouble moving his own army during the upcoming campaign; trying to move the equivalent of a city of escaped slaves along with his army seemed unthinkable. Gen. William T. Sherman wrote to his brother from Memphis, Tennessee, that "if we are to take along & feed the negroes who flee to us for refuge, it will be an impossible task."[17] He warned: "You cannot solve this negro question in a day."[18] When Grant requested guidance from Washington on how to handle the situation, Union leaders instructed the general to subsist both his army and the fugitive slaves as far as possible on the resources taken from the rebel inhabitants of Mississippi. Since many of these residents had fled, taking their belongings with them, this instruction proved not at all helpful.[19]

If Grant possessed no resources to bring the army of former slaves with him on the upcoming campaign, he needed to find some way to "recognize and maintain" their freedom before his departure. Together, Chaplain Eaton and General Grant began to sketch out a bold plan "by which the army of blacks might be transformed from a menace into a positive assistance to the Union forces."[20]

The first step of Grant and Eaton's plan was to systematically employ as many able-bodied freedpeople as possible in activities that supported the army behind the lines. These activities included jobs like handling supplies for the quartermaster and engineering projects like building roads and earthworks. Able-bodied women would work in the camp kitchens and as nurses in the hospitals. That still left large numbers of former slaves who needed employment, both for their own good and for the good of the army.[21]

The next part of the plan took advantage of the surrounding area. Near Grand Junction, Tennessee, where the largest concentration of escaped slaves was located, many plantations and homes had been abandoned by their Confederate owners as the Union army approached. Grant decided to establish a "Contraband Camp" near Grand Junction, housing a large number of black families in the abandoned structures.

It remains unclear if General Grant and Chaplain Eaton knew about the Port Royal Experiment with free black labor on the East Coast, but certain aspects of the plan they jointly implemented in Fall 1862 seem similar. Under Eaton's supervision, the "Contrabands" (Eaton refused to refer to the former slaves as "freedmen" just yet because he saw their freedom as tenuous at best) would continue to pick cotton and other crops in the fields of the abandoned plantations. These crops would then be sold by the quartermaster's department and the sales proceeds turned over to the U.S. Treasury. From the proceeds, the laborers would receive credit for wages at a set rate, initially twelve and a half cents per pound for picking cotton.[22]

Not all of the plantations in the area had been abandoned by their owners, however. The remaining planters needed laborers to pick their crops as well.

Grant agreed to allow the former slaves to work for these landowners as hired labor, but only on the same terms established by the government for working on the abandoned plantations. Thus, black families around Grant's army began the transition from slaves to free and independent laborers working for wages. "At once the freedmen became self-sustaining," Grant later recalled, claiming that this instance planted the seed for the future "Freedmen's Bureau."[23]

Other generals experimented with creative ways of providing for the flood of fugitive slaves threatening to engulf the Union armies as they moved through the South. In Louisiana, General Butler implemented his own plan using an abandoned sugar plantation near the Mississippi River. Butler appointed an overseer to requisition labor from a nearby contraband camp to harvest the crops for the benefit of the United States. Butler believed former slaves could meet this labor need, given the "large number of negroes [who] have come and are coming within the lines of the Army who need employment."[24]

Butler gradually expanded his experiment to other plantations, other crops, and even to other locales. In November 1862, Butler wrote to Gen. Godfrey Weitzel, commander of the District of the Teche, instructing him to aggressively pursue a policy of seizing underutilized plantations and putting the former slaves to work. Butler recognized the inherent contradiction in ordering supposedly free people to a particular location to engage in a specified type of work. He warned Weitzel to "leave force enough to take care of any rising of the negroes."[25] In addition, Butler advised Weitzel to try and head off any objections in advance, noting "I think you had better see the more intelligent of the negroes in person, and assure them that all acts of Congress and laws in their favor will be carried out to them with the same effect if they remain on the plantations and the work, as if they came into camp. And caution them that there must be no violence to unarmed and quiet persons."[26]

Word of Butler's experiment reached President Lincoln, who requested more details. Butler proudly responded, sending Lincoln a barrel of what he claimed to be the "first sugar ever made by free black labor in Louisiana, and the fact that it will have no flavor of the degrading whip will not, I know, render it less sweet to your taste."[27] Butler told President Lincoln of the ten thousand fugitive slaves he must feed besides those at work on the plantations. He worried that certain disloyal planters intended to skip next season's crop, forcing the government to take on the responsibility of providing for the workers. "We shall have to meet this as best we may," Butler stated, noting that "It cannot be supposed that this great change in a social and political system can be made without shock, and I am only surprised that possibility opens up to me that it can be made at all."[28]

Butler closed his letter to Lincoln by expressing his strong belief that slavery "is doomed," noting that "while it would have been better could this emancipation of slaves be gradual, yet it is quite feasible even under this great change as a governmental proposition to organize, control and work the negro with profit and safety to the white, but that this can best be done when under military supervision."[29] Butler hastened to add that although he saw definite advantages to military supervision of the freedpeople, "I do not desire the charge."[30]

Other generals looked for work opportunities to employ residents at nearby "contraband camps." In time, many such camps existed, emerging as Union forces spread throughout the South. The eastern-most camps tended to be permanent, as Union armies established them in locations never relinquished to Confederate

Contraband Camp near Harper's Ferry, Virginia.
Library of Congress, LC-DIG-stereo-1s04358.

control. Union forces located western camps near rivers, and these proved more temporary than their eastern counterparts as they came in and out of prominence depending on the movements of the armies. Historian Chandra Manning, author of a remarkably detailed book on these camps, estimated that by the war's end more than 400,000 escaped slaves (twelve to fifteen percent of the slave population) took refuge within federal lines, most in contraband camps.[31]

Fugitive slaves who reached a contraband camp, some of which sheltered as many as ten thousand people, found no assurance of safety or comfort. Food and water often ran in short supply, and disease killed large numbers of people. Union work details recruited men from the camps to labor on projects more difficult than the work performed on plantations. As the army took black men for work, the percentage of women and children in the camps grew higher and higher. Countless numbers of former slaves in the camps had been abandoned by slaveholders because they were sick or elderly. Living conditions were often terrible by any measure, and many must have wondered whether the freedom they had escaped to was worth the cost.[32]

## Chapter 8

# THE HUNDRED DAYS AND LINCOLN'S FINAL
# EMANCIPATION PROCLAMATION

In April 1862, Lincoln signed the District of Columbia Compensated Emancipation Act into law, which freed approximately 3,100 slaves in the District. As the beginning of 1863 approached, however, only the promises outlined in the president's preliminary Emancipation Proclamation provided hope for future emancipation in other areas. And Lincoln was all too aware that his proclamation had important and possibly fatal issues surrounding its scope and application.[1]

By its terms, the emancipation provisions of the preliminary Emancipation Proclamation would become effective on January 1, 1863, exactly one hundred days after the issuance of the preliminary proclamation. The areas directly affected by Lincoln's order included only "any state, or designated part of a state, the people whereof shall then [on January 1, 1863] be in rebellion against the United States."[2] To give meaning to his preliminary proclamation, the president needed to designate the areas in rebellion on January 1, 1863. Without another proclamation defining the affected areas, Lincoln's Emancipation Proclamation was ineffective.[3]

As 1863 approached, many speculated about the practical application of Lincoln's two-stage process for emancipation, and some questioned whether Lincoln would follow through on the promised emancipation. On December 13, 1862, Robert E. Lee inflicted a crushing defeat on Union Gen. Ambrose Burnside's Army of the Potomac at the Battle of Fredericksburg in Virginia, arguably one of the most significant Confederate victories of the war. When asked about the military situation by some nurses with the Sanitary Commission, Lincoln confessed that he had no words of encouragement to give, stating "The military situation is far from bright; and the country knows it as well as I do."[4] The president used a Union victory at Antietam as the precipitating cause for his original proclamation, and many wondered if Lincoln would cancel or at least postpone emancipation on the heels of the disheartening defeat at Fredericksburg. Publicly, Lincoln held firm to his declaration of emancipation. Privately, however, Lincoln almost certainly had second thoughts.[5]

Although Northern abolitionists enthusiastically greeted Lincoln's original proclamation, it received equally strong condemnation from more moderate factions. Lincoln expected this pushback. The opponents included prominent politicians from the loyal border states, where slavery was still legal. Some abolitionists feared that Lincoln would bow before this pressure and allow his emancipation initiative simply to disappear without implementation. Lincoln never publicly wavered on the issue. On the contrary, on November 21, 1862, the president met with a delegation of Union Kentuckians. They reported that Lincoln told them, "he would rather die than take back a word of the Proclamation of Freedom."[6]

Despite his public stance, Lincoln privately worried over the timing of his proclamation. Bad news on the war front and reports that he and his party suffered substantial political damage because of Lincoln's proclamation clearly depressed the president. He confessed confidentially to friends that he feared he had lost the support of the people and might have made the biggest political mistake of his life in issuing the proclamation as a means of ending slavery.[7]

Toward the end of December, Lincoln seemed to regain confidence in the wisdom, or at least the necessity, of following through and implementing his emancipation strategy. The *New York Times* reported that when challenged on the issue of emancipation by a group of congressmen from the border states, the president snapped back, "that he was an Anti-Slavery man, and considered Slavery to be the right arm of the rebellion, and that it must be lopped off."[8] On another occasion, he told a legal colleague that he could not change his mind, even if he wanted to, because, "if he should refuse to issue his proclamation there would be a rebellion in the north, and that a dictator would be placed over his head within the week."[9] In these instances, Lincoln seemed less sure of his role as the "Great Emancipator." Instead, he sounded increasingly like a man who feared he had unwisely backed himself into a corner.

Lincoln committed himself to issue some form of additional proclamation on January 1, 1863, but was troubled about doing so. He still harbored doubts about the legality of his actions, and was increasingly uncomfortable with the form that emancipation under his order had to take. When Lincoln issued his preliminary Emancipation Proclamation in September, he justified it entirely on the basis of his war powers as commander-in-chief under the Constitution. That characterization meant two key things about the proclamation's form and substance.

First, as an exercise of his war powers, emancipation had to be directed at areas where the rebels were in control, leaving the institution of slavery intact in regions where the rebels were not in control. Slavery would legally continue in some states and not in others. Even worse, slavery would be legal in parts of some states (where the Union had already achieved a measure of control) and not in other sections of the same state. Ironically, after Lincoln's order, slavery still existed (at least technically) in New Orleans, the South's largest city, but not in much of the rest of Louisiana.

Lincoln famously argued in his 1858 debates with Senator Douglas that a "house divided against itself cannot stand," noting that a government could not function properly where part of its territory was free and the remainder allowed slavery.[10] He urged that the United States must become "all one thing or all the other."[11] Yet, under Lincoln's Emancipation Proclamation, the nation remained a patchwork quilt where slavery continued to be legal in some areas but not others. Lincoln understood this was an absurd and unsustainable result.[12]

Second, Lincoln worried about how technical and legalistic emancipation would become under his order. The president intentionally wrote the preliminary Emancipation Proclamation to read like a military directive, devoid of any rhetorical flourish or literary art. This struck Lincoln, as it does many today, as highly inappropriate. If ever an order deserved to be written for the ages, an order ending slavery seemed to fit the bill.

As much as Lincoln longed to use language of art and importance, his instincts as a lawyer kept him from doing so in the final proclamation. Lincoln also knew that others with similar goals understood the importance of maintaining the "military necessity" stance. Henry J. Raymond, one of the founders of the *New York Times*, wrote Lincoln in late November offering his suggestion that the January 1 proclamation be kept very simple, taking "the form of a military order."[13] If Lincoln used his order as a literary podium to make abolition the central goal of the war, Raymond argued, it would "revolt the Border States, divide the North and West, invigorate and make triumphant the opposition party, and thus defeat *itself* as well as destroy the Union."[14] On the other hand, if Lincoln followed his initial approach and made his order look like a military command to deprive the rebels of their slave labor, Raymond expressed his belief that the policy would be "sustained by the whole loyal country, Border States and all."[15]

Lincoln knew that Raymond was right. The president decided to stick to his original plan and keep the January 1 proclamation simple and strictly of a military character. Instead, he found a different venue to express his feelings regarding the end of slavery. On December 1, 1862, Lincoln delivered his "Annual Message to Congress." The message contained the text of a proposed constitutional amendment that provided for compensation for any state that abolished slavery by the year 1900. The proposed amendment also provided for the perpetual freedom of all slaves who enjoyed actual freedom at any time before the end of the rebellion.[16]

Lincoln's proposed constitutional amendment was destined for obscurity as neither side of the slavery controversy viewed it as a way forward on the issue. Lincoln must have known that at the time he delivered his message to Congress. By raising the issue in this form, however, Lincoln added momentum to the growing movement to solve the slavery issue in a comprehensive fashion through a constitutional amendment. This movement eventually resulted in the adoption and ratification of the Thirteenth Amendment.

The conclusion of Lincoln's message to Congress also offered a vehicle for the president to express his feelings in powerful language about the end of slavery and the necessity of cooperative action to achieve that goal:

> Fellow-citizens, *we* cannot escape history. We of this Congress and this Administration will be remembered in spite of ourselves. No personal significance or insignificance can

spare one or another of us. The fiery trial through which we pass will light us down in honor or dishonor to the latest generation. We *say* we are for the Union. The world will not forget that we say this. We know how to save the Union. The world knows we do know how to save it. We, even *we here*, hold the power and bear the responsibility. In *giving* freedom to the *slave* we assure freedom to the *free*—honorable alike in what we give and what we preserve. We shall nobly save or meanly lose the last best hope of earth. Other means may succeed; this could not fail. The way is plain, peaceful, generous, just—a way which if followed the world will forever applaud and God must forever bless.[17]

Having delivered his stirring message on the necessity of ending slavery, Lincoln proceeded to do his part to achieve that end. On December 30, Lincoln read a draft of the final Emancipation Proclamation to his cabinet and asked for suggestions. Technically, all the final proclamation needed was to list the places still in rebellion. In those areas, as the earlier preliminary proclamation had promised, slaves were to be declared "forever free."

Substantial debate ensued about the list of affected geography. President Lincoln's draft of the final Emancipation Proclamation listed each of the Confederate States and included language to exempt from emancipation those slaves in the loyal state of Tennessee, as well as the Union-occupied portions of Louisiana and Virginia. Lincoln's draft left the exempted portions of other states blank so that they could be filled in using the military's most updated information. Secretary Chase and others urged the president to merely list the states where slaves were freed and let emancipation apply to the entire states. As Chase pointed out, slaves in the exempt areas owned by disloyal owners were already emancipated, at least in theory, by virtue of the Confiscation Acts. To exempt counties and parishes from the effect of the Emancipation Proclamation served no real purpose, while "[s]uch exceptions will impair, in public estimation, the moral effect of the proclamation."[18]

Lincoln ultimately decided to follow his original plan and exempt the occupied portions of Louisiana and Virginia from the effects of his proclamation. If the legal justification for emancipation was military necessity, Lincoln believed that justification would be materially weakened if his emancipation provisions extended to areas where the Confederates were no longer in control. The president was determined not to give his enemies any legal ammunition to overturn the proclamation.

A similar consideration affected another proposed change to the draft proclamation. One key new addition to the language of the final proclamation was a provision declaring that freed slaves would be accepted into the United States military to "garrison and defend forts, positions, stations, and other places, and to man vessels of all sorts in said service."[19] Secretary Chase and others believed that this language was unnecessary and should be omitted. Other members of the cabinet felt the wording should have been included all along. Lincoln ultimately decided to keep the language in his draft, reasoning that providing expressly for the immediate employment of the freed slaves in the military further added to the military necessity and character of his action.[20]

Another new provision in the final version of the proclamation would have substantial, probably unanticipated, ramifications for the role of the military in the emancipation process. The new addition arose out of an attempt to fix a perceived flaw in the original preliminary proclamation. One of the principal objections to the preliminary proclamation centered around the belief that emancipation would lead to some form of slave rebellion in the affected states. The language of the preliminary order provided that the military would, "do no act or acts to repress [slaves], or any of them, in any efforts they may make for their actual freedom."[21] To some, this phrasing sounded as if the military was being ordered to stand by and watch the coming of a slave rebellion, an act not to be tolerated.

To combat the perception that he encouraged any form of violent insurrection, Lincoln's draft of the final proclamation added the word "suitable" to clarify that the military would only be obligated to support "suitable efforts" enslaved people might make to secure their actual freedom. The president's draft also followed up this language with an additional sentence that would later turn out to be important: "And I hereby appeal to the people so declared to be free, to abstain from all disorder, tumult, and violence, unless in necessary self defence [sic]; and in all cases, when allowed, to labor faithfully for wages."[22]

Secretary Seward suggested that the word "appeal" in Lincoln's draft lacked strength. The president needed to do more than just appeal to the freed slaves to refrain from violence and continue to work. Lincoln took the suggestion. The language of the final version of the proclamation stated: "And I hereby *enjoin upon* the people so declared to be free, to abstain from all disorder, tumult, and violence, unless in necessary self defence [sic]; and I recommend to them that, in all cases, when allowed, to labor faithfully, for reasonable wages."[23]

The language of the emancipation provisions in Lincoln's proclamation evolved significantly over the course of a relatively short period of time. Lincoln's first draft of July 22 included no language regarding the military's interaction with the freed slaves. By the time Lincoln issued his preliminary proclamation on September 22, the military was formally instructed to "recognize and maintain the freedom of such persons [freed slaves]."[24] With the issuance of the final Emancipation Proclamation on January 1, 1863, the military took on the responsibility not only of respecting and maintaining the freedom of the slaves, but also enforcing a presidential injunction that the slaves remain peaceful and continue to labor for wages. To make matters even more complicated, Lincoln's proclamation, by design, only applied to areas under the enemy's control. The language that seemed, at least initially, so felicitous as a matter of law and politics would cause the military enormous difficulties when it came time to implement it in the Confederacy.

Secretary Chase felt the president should issue the final Emancipation Proclamation with an acknowledgement of God and an express invocation of his blessing in support of the historic act. Lincoln seemed somewhat reluctant to do this, recognizing that such an addition might detract from his argument that the proclamation was merely an exercise of his military authority as commander-in-chief. In the end, however, Lincoln succumbed and included a formal conclusion that invoked both God and military necessity: "And upon this act, sincerely believed to be an act of justice, warranted by the Constitution, upon military necessity, I invoke the considerate judgment of mankind, and the gracious favor of Almighty God."[25]

Lincoln still held reservations about the legality of his proclamation. Perhaps his doubts pushed him to make one highly mysterious change in the language of the final proclamation. Lincoln's preliminary proclamation in September stated that as of January 1, 1863, the slaves would "be then, thenceforward, and forever free."[26] In his draft of December 30, 1862, Lincoln slightly altered the language to declare that the affected slaves "are, and henceforward forever shall be free."[27] But in the final version issued on January 1, 1863, Lincoln omitted the word "forever," providing merely that the affected slaves "are, and henceforward shall be

President Abraham Lincoln signing the Emancipation Proclamation, based on a painting by W. E. Winner. Library of Congress, LC-DIG-pga-08283.

free."[28] Scholars have speculated about this change, but Lincoln's intent regarding the omission will never be wholly known. Lincoln went to bed on the night of December 31, 1862, however, believing he had done his best to further the cause of emancipation.

After enduring a sleepless night, Lincoln began 1863 by running a social gauntlet. Tradition at the time had the president formally receive visitors at the White House on January 1 of each year. After three hours of shaking hands as part of this tiring ritual, Lincoln returned to his office to sign the final Emancipation Proclamation. Lincoln later said his hand shook as he signed the document, not because he second-guessed the wisdom of his actions, but because of the handshaking gauntlet associated with the New Year's reception. Given the circumstances, it is a wonder that Lincoln could write at all.[29]

## *Chapter 9*

## IMPLEMENTING EMANCIPATION

While President Lincoln prepared to issue his final version of the Emancipation Proclamation, Gen. Nathaniel Banks tried to navigate the difficult issues surrounding command of the Union army in Louisiana and Texas. In December 1862, Banks replaced Benjamin Butler as commander of the Army of the Gulf in New Orleans. The timing could hardly have been worse. On January 1, 1863, the triumphant day that Lincoln issued his final Emancipation Proclamation in Washington, Banks received word that a Confederate force attacked a Union outpost in Texas and recaptured the important port of Galveston. Two other disasters along the Texas coast followed, leaving the state entirely free of Union troops.[1]

While Banks sorted through the various disasters in Texas, he received instructions from Washington to implement the Emancipation Proclamation in Louisiana as soon as possible. Since Louisiana contained Union-occupied portions that were exempted from the emancipation provisions of the order, Banks decided that the best way to handle the situation was to issue Lincoln's proclamation as an attachment to his own order, General Orders No. 12, which clarified and explained the situation to his subordinates.

Banks began his order by advising his commanders not to pay too much attention to the geographic limitations of the proclamation. After all, other laws such as the Confiscation Acts already prohibited officers from returning slaves to their owners or to decide any claims of this kind. If a slaveholder in an exempted part of Louisiana felt wronged by the army's handling of slaves, it could be chalked

Maj. Gen. Nathaniel P. Banks. Library of Congress, LC-USZ62-122438.

up to "the inevitable conditions of a state of war."[2] Slavery might not be legally prohibited in New Orleans and other exempted areas, but as far as Banks was concerned, the institution of slavery in the exempted parts existed in name only. He explained: "Officers and soldiers will not encourage or assist slaves to leave their employers, but they cannot compel or otherwise authorize their return by force."[3]

General Banks' disinterest in helping slaveholders did not mean he was ignoring the president's proclamation. To the contrary, General Banks was absolutely determined to enforce the "law and order" portions of the proclamation where President Lincoln "recommended" to the freed slaves that they continue laboring for wages. Banks issued the following notice emphasizing that he expected freedpeople to continue working:

> The public interest peremptorily demands that all persons, without other means of support, be required to maintain themselves by labor. Negroes are not exempt from this law. Those who leave their employers will be compelled to support themselves and

families by labor upon the public works. Under no circumstances whatever can they be maintained in idleness, or allowed to wander through the parishes and cities of the State without employment. Vagrancy and crime will be suppressed by an enforced and constant occupation and employment.[4]

General Banks' order requiring freed slaves to continue working possessed a much firmer tone than the recommendation that President Lincoln included in his Emancipation Proclamation. The reaction in the Northern press to this provision was extremely positive. The *New York Times* declared:

The principle asserted [by General Banks] is eminently just, and capable of a much wider application. There is a general idea afloat that in setting the slaves free, we turn them over to idleness and starvation. Much of the apprehension to which the Proclamation has given rise, seems based upon this impression. It should be distinctly understood that the emancipation is from slavery—not from work. No community can safely have any portion of its dependent population unemployed. No State does so. Every State has its laws concerning vagrants,—compelling them to work for the public if they depend on the public for support, or punishing their refusal to do so as a crime.[5]

General Banks, like General Butler before him, believed that the answer to dealing with freed slaves involved requiring them to continue to work as agricultural laborers, but this time for wages. As Banks saw matters, laborers were entitled to "some equitable proportion of the crops" they produced.[6] The dilemma lay in setting the "equitable proportion" low enough so that the plantation owners could survive. To help define this compensation, Banks appointed a "sequestration commission" to meet with planters and government agents and come up with a "yearly system of negro labor, which shall provide for the food, clothing, proper treatment, and just compensation for the negroes, at fixed rates or an equitable proportion of the yearly crop, as may be deemed advisable."[7] Banks soon learned that such a system, in effect a government-imposed form of "sharecropping," was virtually impossible to design and even more impossible to enforce.

The labor system devised by General Banks granted black people some of the rights of free people while continuing to strictly regulate their travel and behavior.

Historian Peyton McCrary accurately termed this system something of "a halfway house between slavery and freedom."[8] While General Banks experimented with setting wages for freed slaves in Louisiana, General Grant tried to develop his own solution in Mississippi. Despite Chaplain Eaton's work, black families seeking freedom continued to flock to Grant's army, threatening to overwhelm it. "What will I do with surplus negroes?" an exasperated Grant wrote to General Halleck.[9]

Grant tried everything he could think of to solve the problem. He sent some of the black refugees off with a Northern philanthropist who offered to resettle them somewhere safe. He also encouraged Chaplain Eaton to redouble his efforts to find plantations in the area where they could live and work. One of the primary outlets for able-bodied black workers, however, continued to be a very unusual engineering project. In the summer of 1862, Grant ordered his engineers to dig a canal that would channel the Mississippi River away from the Confederate guns at Vicksburg. Although the initial work proved unsuccessful, Grant resumed the project in January 1863, making use of hundreds of black workers.[10]

Although Grant could have employed many more freedpeople in building the unsuccessful project that ultimately became known as "Grant's Canal," much of the available labor was not the type that the canal construction work required. Many planters in the area deserted their plantations, leaving only the very old or the very young slaves behind. Grant eventually prohibited any additional refugees from entering his lines, telling officials in Washington that "Humanity dictates this policy" because of the army's inability to provide for the people after active military operations resumed.[11]

When it became clear that the administration wanted to aggressively enlist black soldiers and use them in combat, Grant opened his lines to black male recruits. Some of those recruits were present at the Battle of Milliken's Bend on June 7, 1863, when a division of Texas Confederates attacked a force of black soldiers just out of training. The black soldiers fought hard and gave a good account of themselves.[12]

On July 4, 1863, Vicksburg surrendered to Grant's army. In the aftermath, the general once again faced the problem of what to do with all of the displaced freedpeople who approached his army for support. Grant finally decided that the best way to handle the situation was to clearly set out his position in a series of general orders. This demonstration would show Washington that he was doing what he could to honor the president's policies in the midst of very difficult operating conditions. Accordingly, on August 1, Grant issued General Orders No. 50. Section II of the order was addressed to the people of Mississippi and encouraged them to continue to pursue their peaceful avocations in conformity with U.S. laws. One of those laws, he reminded them, was President Lincoln's Emancipation Proclamation, which Grant indicated in gentle language that he intended to enforce: "It is earnestly recommended that the freedom of the negroes be acknowledged, and that, instead of compulsory labor, contracts upon fair terms be entered into between the former masters and servants, or between the latter and such other persons as may be willing to give them employment."[13]

Ten days later, Grant's headquarters in Vicksburg issued General Orders No. 51, one of the most comprehensive general orders of the war relating to freed slaves. This order incorporated many of the concepts that would find their way eventually into orders like the Juneteenth Order. In particular, General Orders No. 51 started by stating that camps would be set up for "such freed people of color as are out of employment."[14] The order required every able-bodied person to work, either for himself, an outside employer, or the army "so as to avoid them becoming a burthen on the Government."[15] Recognizing that small farmers in the area could not afford to pay cash wages to their new black employees, the order authorized payment in kind, declaring that the payment could not be less than five percent of the commercial value of the resulting crops. The arrangements between the former slaves and their new employers were required to be reported to the army, which would monitor the transactions to ensure the "kind treatment and proper care of those employed."[16]

Despite the seemingly comprehensive nature of these orders, Grant continued to have problems with crowds of freedpeople hindering the operations of his army. In many cases, these situations were the fault of his own officers, who continued to informally hire a legion of men and women to act as their personal cooks, valets, and servants. The people in these positions could not move with the army, so Grant decided to limit such activities as much as possible. He issued General Orders No. 53 to specify the jobs that black workers could and could not do. It also limited the number of personal servants each officer could hire. The order then instituted a system of employment "certificates" and ordered that "negroes will not be allowed in or about the camps of white troops, except such as are properly employed and controlled."[17]

While General Grant finalized the surrender and occupation of Vicksburg, he sent Chaplain Eaton to see President Lincoln in Washington so Eaton could explain the challenges and issues associated with the freedpeople. Telling Lincoln in a letter of introduction that Eaton's position as general superintendent of contrabands had been "trying," Grant stressed that Eaton's efforts had been "unremitting and skillful." Eaton had two cordial meetings with the president, who expressed interest in learning what the freed slaves could be expected to do for themselves and where they would require assistance. Eaton was pleased to report back to Grant that Lincoln seemed satisfied with the course of action they were pursuing. Eaton also warned Grant that he should stop referring to the freedpeople as "contrabands," since that term was no longer considered acceptable in Washington.[18]

On August 30, 1863, Grant paused from his labors long enough to respond to a letter from Congressman Elihu B. Washburne, an old friend of Grant's from Galena, Illinois. In a letter, Washburne passed along some Washington gossip and some compliments regarding Grant's handling of the issues surrounding the freedpeople. Sending back his "kind regards to the citizens of Galena," Grant took the opportunity to set forth his evolving feelings about the war and slavery:

> I never was an abolitionist, not even what could be called anti-slavery, but I try to judge fairly and honestly and it became patent to my mind early in the rebellion that the North & South could never live at peace with each other except as one nation, and that without slavery. As anxious as I am to see peace reestablished, I would not therefore be willing to see any settlement until this question is forever settled.[19]

Settling this question forever would require almost two more years of fighting, but after the fall of Vicksburg, the end of the war seemed much closer to becoming a reality.

## Chapter 10

# THE BEGINNING OF THE END

On May 4, 1864, the Army of the Potomac crossed the Rapidan River into the heart of the Virginia wilderness, commencing a bloody military campaign known as the "Overland Campaign" that would do much to decide the outcome of the war. Between Gen. Ulysses Grant's army in Northern Virginia and the Confederate capital in Richmond lay Robert E. Lee and his Army of Northern Virginia. Both commanders instinctively knew that this campaign represented more than casualty figures from any one battle—it was about the life and death of armies.

Union commander Ulysses S. Grant's strategic plan for victory was fairly simple. His army, coordinating with other Union armies, would march south toward Richmond, forcing Lee's army to interpose itself between Grant and the Confederate capital. Once his army pinned the Confederates in position, Grant intended to use his superior numbers to attack the Confederates and take Lee's army out of the war. To accomplish this objective, Grant was prepared for his army to endure casualties so horrific that some members of the press later called him a "butcher." Grant knew that this price must ultimately be paid for the war to be brought to a successful conclusion. On May 11, Grant wrote to his superiors in Washington, confidently declaring that "I propose to fight it out on this line if it takes all summer."[1]

Confederate Gen. Robert E. Lee, Grant's opponent, knew that his army held a series of strong defensive works in Northern Virginia. These fortifications would help him delay Grant's advance and make the enemy pay dearly for every foot of contested ground they conquered. In the end, however, Lee feared it would not be enough. "We must destroy this army of Grant's before he gets to [the] James River," Lee told his chaplain.[2] He continued, "If he gets there, it will become a siege, and then it will be a mere question of time."[3]

Lee's apprehension about the course of the campaign proved accurate. By the middle of June, Grant's army crossed the James River and besieged Lee's army in Petersburg. The Overland Campaign cost Grant nearly 55,000 men as casualties, but he had Lee just where he wanted him. Fixed in position, the Southern general could no longer use his legendary skills for maneuver to attack Union armies where they least expected it. As Lee feared, the siege of Petersburg meant that, at least for his army, it was just a matter of time. A subtle but important shift in the morale of the opposing armies began to take shape. As Grant observed in his memoirs: "The Army of Northern Virginia became despondent and saw the end. It did not please them. The National army saw the same thing, and were encouraged by it."[4]

Although the military commanders in the field on both sides saw the end of the war coming, both Grant and Lee understood that the war-weary people of the North might yet lack the patience to see it through. Abraham Lincoln ran for reelection in 1864 and his electoral prospects in the summer of 1864 were far from bright. One New York advisor told Lincoln flatly that his reelection was an "impossibility."[5] On August 23, Lincoln asked his cabinet members to sign a sealed document as witnesses. When opened in November, after Lincoln's reelection, the contents of what became known as Lincoln's "blind memorandum" were revealed as follows:

> This morning, as for some days past, it seems exceedingly probable that this Administration will not be re-elected. Then it will be my duty to so co-operate with the President elect, as to save the Union between the election and the inauguration; as he will have secured his election on such ground that he can not possibly save it afterwards.[6]

One reason Lincoln became so pessimistic about the policies of his potential replacement centered around his distrust of the candidate. In August 1864, the Democratic national convention met in Chicago and nominated former Union

Gen. George McClellan for president, adopting a platform that called for peace to be restored on terms that did not include emancipation. If any doubts surrounded the convention regarding the issues, the anti-war atmosphere dispelled them. The convention's band even played the Southern anthem, "Dixie," which the attendees cheered loudly.[7]

McClellan's peace platform would, in time, turn out to be a huge political albatross hung around his neck. The people of the North were certainly tired of the war, but they stood firm in their resolve to not render meaningless the enormous sacrifices made during three long years of fighting, particularly if the war could still be won. They mainly wanted results, to be assured that Lincoln and his commanders were finally on a path to victory. It was the army's turn to deliver results to keep the commander-in-chief in his job—this they soon did.

While Grant fought his way south toward Richmond, Gen. William Tecumseh Sherman maneuvered his army southeast from Chattanooga, Tennessee, toward Atlanta, Georgia. Capturing Atlanta, a key Confederate supply and railroad hub, became a high priority for the Union military and Sherman and Grant both knew that the favorable publicity surrounding its occupation might help swing the election in Lincoln's favor.

Like the strategy General Lee followed in Virginia, Confederate Gen. Joseph E. Johnston fought a brilliant delaying action in Georgia, buying the Confederacy the time it needed to mount a final defense of Atlanta. On July 19, 1864, Confederate President Jefferson Davis made a poor decision and replaced Johnston with John Bell Hood, a more aggressive commander who wasted no time in moving his army out of the entrenchments and launching a series of ill-planned and even worse-executed offensive operations. By September 3, 1864, the fight for Atlanta had ended. Sherman triumphantly entered Atlanta, telegraphing Washington: "So Atlanta is ours, and fairly won."[8]

While Sherman maneuvered his army toward Atlanta, another of Grant's favorite commanders, Union Gen. Philip H. Sheridan, led a different operation. Since early in the war, the Confederates had used the Shenandoah Valley of Virginia repeatedly as a source for food and supplies. The "Breadbasket of the Confederacy," as the Shenandoah became known, had proven to be a convenient route of approach for Confederate armies seeking to invade the North. Grant decided to end this threat once and for all and assigned Sheridan as the commander of a new army, the Army of the Shenandoah, named for the valley it intended to remove from Confederate hands.

In early August 1864, Grant ordered Sheridan to take on Confederate forces in the Shenandoah Valley and render useless everything in the valley that might possibly be of service to the Confederate cause. By the middle of October, Sheridan had largely accomplished his objectives, in the process making him one of the most famous Union commanders of the war. The success of Sheridan's Shenandoah campaign, coming on the heels of Sherman's capture of Atlanta, stopped the downward trajectory of President Lincoln's popularity and made his reelection possible. As General Grant later wrote in his memoirs, "these two campaigns probably had more effect in settling the election of the following November than all the speeches, all the bonfires, and all the parading with banners and bands of music in the North."[9]

## Chapter 11

## SHERMAN'S MARCH TO THE SEA

Only a week after Lincoln's reelection, Union Gen. William T. Sherman left Atlanta with an army of 62,000 men destined for the Atlantic coast. This movement, which became known as Sherman's famous "March to the Sea," was more about the journey than the destination. Traveling in four, roughly parallel, lines, Sherman intended to use his army to cut a sixty-mile-wide swath of destruction that would convince the Southern population that further resistance was not only futile, but would inevitably lead to the complete destruction of their economy and way of life. As Sherman told Grant, "I can make the march, and make Georgia howl."[1]

Part of Sherman's plan to make Georgia howl involved allowing his troops to support themselves by taking supplies from the communities through which they passed. "The army will forage liberally on the country during the march," he ordered, directing that foraging parties be sent out by each brigade "at any distance from the road traveled" to gather supplies.[2] A pioneer battalion, "composed if possible of negroes," marched in advance of the army.[3] Sherman worried that a large body of freedpeople flocking to the army would slow its movement. "Negroes who are able-bodied and can be of service to the several columns may be taken along," Sherman allowed, "but each army commander will bear in mind that the question of supplies is a very important one, and that his first duty is to see to those who bear arms."[4]

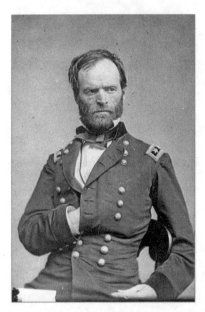

Maj. Gen. William T. Sherman. Library of Congress, LC-DIG-cwpb-07136.

Slaves in Georgia had long hoped that the presence of successful Union armies might result in the end of their captivity. In every town through which Sherman's army marched, the reaction was similar. As Sherman recalled, "The white people came out of their houses to behold the sight, [in] spite of their deep hatred of the invaders, and the negroes were simply frantic with joy."[5] To many of the black onlookers, the arrival of the Union army proved nothing less than the fulfillment of biblical prophecy, with General Sherman acting as a modern-day Moses, destined to lead the slaves out of bondage to a new land of freedom.[6]

Although many thousands of former slaves took the opportunity to march to the coast with Sherman, their newly proclaimed Moses discouraged them from doing so. Sherman personally beseeched the freedpeople to stay put. On one occasion, the general talked to an elderly black man who he thought might have influence with the surrounding slave community. Sherman explained that he "wanted the slaves to remain where they were, and not to load us down with useless mouths, which would eat up the food needed for our fighting-men; that our success was their assured freedom; that we could receive a few of their young, hearty men as pioneers; but that, if they followed us in swarms of old and young, feeble and helpless, it would simply load us down and cripple us in our great task."[7] Sherman said later in his memoirs that he believed the conversation helped the overall situation, lowering the numbers of former slaves that followed and hindered his army.[8]

Notwithstanding General Sherman's warning, the sight of large armies of blue-clad soldiers marching through the heart of Georgia's plantation country became simply too much of a temptation for many black men and women to resist. One old man came to see the general and stared at him silently and intently for a long time. When Sherman questioned this curious behavior, the man said that he wanted to make sure Sherman was really a Yankee officer, not some type of cruel trick by the Confederate plantation owners. Eventually, the man looked at the large numbers of soldiers and campfires and became satisfied that his deliverance had truly come. He then shared a drink of whiskey with some of his new saviors.[9]

Thousands of freed slaves ignored the general's instruction and attempted to follow Sherman's army to freedom, with varying degrees of success. As Gen. Henry Slocum reported about the slaves his wing encountered:

> Negro men, women, and children joined the column at every mile of our march; many of them bringing horses and mules, which they cheerfully turned over to the officers of the quartermaster's department. I think at least 14,000 of these people joined the two columns at different points on the march, but many of them were too old and infirm, and others too young, to endure the fatigues of the march, and were therefore left in rear. More than one-half of the above number, however, reached the coast with us.[10]

Although General Slocum proudly reported that many black families followed his army to freedom, many other former slaves fell behind or suffered an even worse fate. On December 9, 1864, a Union general with the unfortunate name of Jefferson C. Davis led his troops across a pontoon bridge that crossed Ebenezer Creek. Davis gave orders that the bridge be taken up as soon as his troops crossed, leaving hundreds of black men, women, and children stranded on the other side of the creek. Reports stated that some of the stranded people drowned while attempting to swim the creek; others were killed or captured by pursuing

Depiction titled "Contrabands accompanying the line of Sherman's march through Georgia" that appeared in *Frank Leslie's Illustrated Newspaper* (March 18, 1865). Library of Congress, LC-USZ62-112169.

Confederate cavalrymen. When the Northern press later blamed Davis for this atrocity, Sherman defended him, saying that Davis was "strictly a soldier, and doubtless hated to have his wagons and columns encumbered by these poor negroes, for whom we all felt sympathy."[11]

On December 21, 1864, Sherman rode triumphantly with his army into Savannah, Georgia. The next day he proudly sent what would become another famous telegram to President Lincoln: "I beg to present you, as a Christmas gift, the City of Savannah, with one hundred and fifty guns and plenty of ammunition, also about twenty-five thousand bales of cotton."[12] Sherman became the hero of the hour, receiving the thanks of Congress and cementing his reputation as one of the most successful Union commanders of the war.[13]

Soon after his exultant arrival in Savannah, Sherman learned that some in Washington criticized him for not bringing more freed slaves to the sea with him. Gen. Henry Halleck wrote a confidential letter to Sherman on December 30, noting that some men influential with Lincoln claimed that Sherman conducted his campaign in a fashion that reflected an "almost critical dislike to the negro."[14] Instead of taking fifty thousand former slaves to Savannah, these unnamed men charged, "you drove them from your ranks, prevented them from following you by cutting the bridges in your rear," and left them to drown or be massacred by Confederate cavalry.[15]

One of these unnamed men of influence was almost certainly Treasury Secretary Salmon Chase, who wrote Sherman a letter on January 2 noting what he described as the "apparent harshness of your action toward the blacks."[16] In a December 13 report to Secretary Stanton, Sherman noted that he arrived in Savannah with a large supply of "negroes, mules, horses, etc." and that his first duty would be to "clear the army of surplus negroes, mules, and horses."[17] This language struck Chase as inappropriate, making it sound as though Sherman classified black people as nothing more than surplus livestock.

Chase told Sherman that he believed "negroes as men have the same natural rights as other men," and favored allowing them the full benefits of citizenship, including the right to vote.[18] Chase correctly assumed that Sherman held a different view. Sherman responded to Chase that, in his view, "the negro should be a free race, but not put on an equality with the whites."[19] Far from expanding the number of men entitled to vote, Sherman said the number should instead be further restricted.[20]

Sherman bristled at the very suggestion that he should have brought more black families to freedom with him on his march to Savannah. He cautioned Chase: "If you can understand the nature of a military column in an enemy's country, with its long train of wagons you will see at once that a crowd of negroes, men women and children, old & young, are a dangerous impediment."[21] As Sherman pointed out, "[o]n approaching Savannah I had at least 20,000 negroes, clogging my roads, and eating up our subsistence."[22] Sherman believed he acted within his orders. He held that doing more for the former slaves at that time fell outside of his responsibilities and would have placed his army in peril. He stated to Chase, "Now you know that military success is what the nation wants, and it is risked by the crowds of helpless negroes that flock after our armies."[23]

The accusations regarding Sherman's insensitive treatment of blacks seemed serious enough that Secretary of War Stanton went to Savannah to meet with Sherman and formally investigate the allegations. At Stanton's request, Sherman arranged an extraordinary meeting with twenty black leaders, consisting primarily of Baptist and

Secretary of War Edwin M. Stanton. Library of Congress, LC-B8172-2208.

Methodist clergymen. In a series of transcribed questions and answers, Stanton asked the leaders about a wide range of subjects, ranging from their understanding of emancipation to the best ways to encourage black men to enlist in the military services. At the conclusion of the meeting, Stanton directed Sherman to leave the room while the secretary asked the men about their interactions with the general. "His conduct and deportment toward us characterized him as a friend and gentleman," they said.[24] The black leaders continued, "We have confidence in General Sherman and think what concerns us could not be in better hands."[25]

Satisfied with the results of his investigation, Stanton came away from the encounter convinced that Sherman had not deliberately hindered the slaves seeking to escape from bondage. The effect of the inquiry on Sherman and other generals, however, was immediate and long lasting. After Stanton's visit to Savannah, every Union general understood that Washington officials would judge his actions not only on military merit, but also on how the actions impacted the freed slaves in the vicinity. "It certainly was a strange fact," Sherman recorded, "that the great War Secretary should have catechized negroes concerning the character of a general who had commanded a hundred thousand men in battle, had captured cities, conducted sixty-five thousand men successfully across four hundred miles of hostile territory, and had just brought tens of thousands of freedmen to a place of security; but because I had not loaded down my army by other hundreds of thousands of poor negroes, I was construed by others as hostile to the black race."[26]

After Stanton's visit, both men faced a problem with military and political ramifications. Despite the skepticism of Northern abolitionists, large numbers of freed slaves had indeed followed Sherman to the Georgia coast, and more escaped into Union lines every day. The army needed to figure out how to help these people, particularly since Sherman contemplated leaving Savannah to launch another bold invasion into enemy controlled territory. "We agreed perfectly," Sherman later told President Andrew Johnson, "that the young and able-bodied men should be enlisted as soldiers, or employed by the Quarter Master in the necessary work of unloading ships and for other Army purposes. But this left on our hands the old and feeble, the women and children, who had necessarily to be fed by the United States."[27]

What could be done to help keep the thousands of remaining escaped slaves out of Confederate hands and yet enable them to provide for themselves? The solution that Sherman and Stanton devised made use of the coastal land around the army, much of which previous residents had earlier vacated under threat from Union armies and warships. After meeting with black leaders, Sherman and Stanton felt assured that "the negroes could with some little aid from us, by means of the abandoned Plantations on the Sea Islands, and along the navigable waters, take care of themselves."[28]

Five days following Stanton's meeting with black community leaders, after a marathon of drafting and redrafting sessions, Sherman issued Special Field Orders No. 15. Declaring that "by the laws of war, and orders of the President of the United States, the negro is free, and must be dealt with as such," the order set aside certain coastal islands and farming areas adjoining the navigable rivers for the settlement of freedpeople.[29] Under the terms of Sherman's order, and with Secretary Stanton's express approval, each black family residing on the vacated land could apply for a "possessory title" covering up to forty acres of tillable ground. There, the order directed, "the exclusive management of affairs will be left to the freedmen themselves, subject only to the United States military authority, and the acts of Congress."[30]

This order, which later became one of the principal sources for reparation claims of "forty acres and a mule," left out verbiage regarding a mule. As to the provision purporting to grant title to real estate, which in many ways turned out to be nothing more than a cruel hoax, Sherman later pointed to the order's use of the phrase "possessory title" and attempted to justify his action as nothing more than a temporary measure. "Of course," Sherman wrote in his memoirs, "the military authorities at that day, when war prevailed, had a perfect right to grant the possession of any vacant land to which they could extend military protection, but we did not undertake to give a fee-simple title; and all that was designed by these special field orders was to make temporary provisions for the freedmen and their families during the rest of the war, or until Congress should take action in the premises."[31] The freed slaves, lured by Sherman's order into working what was eventually determined to be someone else's land, found Sherman's land ownership distinction outrageous and unpersuasive, nothing more than a failed promise. Many of their modern descendants agree.

The vision that Stanton and Sherman jointly shared of creating a place where freedpeople and their families owned and farmed their own land would not last long. Within a few months, John Wilkes Booth assassinated President Lincoln, promoting to that office a Southerner, Andrew Johnson, who discontinued the land redistribution experiment. By July 1866, Congress and the president had pardoned the original Confederate landowners and eliminated forever the claims of freedpeople to what became known as the "Sherman lands." In a special irony, one of the key documents that led to this result was a communication from General Sherman to President Johnson assuring the president that Special Field Orders No. 15 had never been intended to provide land titles beyond the conclusion of the war.[32]

*Chapter 12*

## THE HAMPTON ROADS PEACE CONFERENCE

With the reelection of President Lincoln in November 1864, two critically important issues seemed decided: first, George McClellan and his supporters would not take power and revoke Lincoln's Emancipation Proclamation; and second, the North would continue to prosecute the war. Even with the end of the war in sight, the form the conclusion of the war would take remained unclear. Wars in the nineteenth century typically ended in a treaty, a surrender, or a negotiated settlement between the warring parties. But the Union did not consider the Confederacy to be a separate nation; this stance seemed to preclude any conventional peace treaty or settlement to end the rebellion. Leaders in both the North and the South worked to find some other, creative but fair, way to bring the war to a swift, negotiated, conclusion and begin the process of binding the nation's wounds.

With the encouragement of influential newspaper editor Horace Greeley, Francis Preston Blair, Sr., an influential politician and former slaveholder with many important Southern connections, volunteered to go south and visit with Jefferson Davis about the prospect of ending the war. Lincoln permitted this expedition but did not authorize Blair to do anything other than discuss the subject of ending the war with Davis. Blair made his visit and returned with a note from Davis saying he would be glad to "renew the effort to enter into conference with a view to secure peace to the two countries."[1] Noting the last two words,

Lincoln sent Blair back with his own note (addressed to Blair to avoid giving the impression that Lincoln was willing to treat directly with Davis as a head of state) responding that Lincoln would be willing to receive an agent "with the view of securing peace to the people of our one common country."[2]

The question of whether one country would become reunited or two countries would sign a settlement proved more than a semantic quibble, and the parties pondering the language of the two notes were all too aware of the divide between the two sides as 1864 came to an end. Nevertheless, Jefferson Davis decided that increasingly gloomy military developments made it necessary to send a delegation north to meet with Lincoln. Confederate Vice President Alexander H. Stephens, the head of the three-member Southern delegation, had been a friend and former political ally of Lincoln's, and Davis hoped that Stephens could quickly and diplomatically determine if there was any practical basis for a compromise.

As Lincoln made final arrangements to meet secretly with Stephens and his delegation of hopeful Confederates, a different drama played out publicly in Washington. The Thirteenth Amendment to the Constitution, designed to finally and forever end the institution of slavery in America, passed the Senate in early 1864, but failed to secure the necessary two-thirds vote required in the House of Representatives. In January 1865, the House was reconsidering the amendment, and Lincoln used every ounce of political capital and influence he could wield to secure its passage. If the amendment became law, Lincoln's concern that his Emancipation Proclamation might be rendered ineffective by the courts would disappear. But passage by the requisite two-thirds majority in the House still seemed in doubt.

Lincoln still held profound reservations about the legality of his Emancipation Proclamation, a concern shared by many observers. One journal in January 1864 wrote: "That the Supreme Court will sustain the freedom of slaves under the proclamation, unless they have become free in fact before the conclusion of the war, we suppose nobody expects. For ourselves, we do not believe a single person can sustain his freedom in the courts under that proclamation."[3]

On January 18, 1865, Lincoln received a note from Republican Rep. James Ashley, who led the effort to pass the Thirteenth Amendment in the House, inquiring if press reports of Confederate peace commissioners in Washington were accurate. "If it is true," Ashley noted, "I fear we shall lose the bill. Please allow me to contradict it, if not true."[4] Lincoln lost no time in responding "So far as I know, there are no peace commissioners in the city, or likely to be in it."[5]

Lincoln's response was technically true, but only because the Confederate peace delegation was not destined for the City of Washington. Knowing the difficulty of hiding negotiations with an enemy delegation in the capital, Lincoln planned to travel to Union-controlled territory in Virginia and there secretly meet with the Southern commissioners aboard a Union warship. Lincoln delayed his departure from Washington long enough to see the House pass the Thirteenth Amendment on January 31, 1865, whereupon the amendment was formally proposed to the states for ratification. In his excitement, President Lincoln signed the resolution submitting the amendment to the states, something that the Senate eventually protested as unnecessary and inappropriate in the case of an amendment to the Constitution.[6]

Although the Thirteenth Amendment passed by the requisite margins in Congress, lawmakers wondered how, in the midst of a Civil War, three-quarters of the state legislatures could be convened and convinced to approve an amendment abolishing slavery. Lincoln's home state of Illinois became the first state to do so on February 1. That night, an exultant crowd gathered outside the White House to serenade Lincoln and celebrate the events of the day. A newspaper recorded the president's reaction to the serenade. Lincoln's brief remarks to the crowd represent the president's most spontaneous and unfiltered comments on the path to ending slavery.

Lincoln told the crowd that he viewed the amendment as "a very fitting if not an indispensable adjunct to the winding up of the great difficulty."[7] Although he believed in the Emancipation Proclamation, Lincoln candidly admitted to the crowd his concern that his proclamation had limitations and was subject to legal attack:

> [The Emancipation Proclamation] falls far short of what the [Thirteenth Amendment] will be when fully consummated. A question might be raised whether the proclamation was legally valid. It might be added that it only aided those who came into our lines and that it was inoperative as to those who did not give themselves up, or that it would have no

effect upon the children of the slaves born hereafter. In fact, it would be urged that it did not meet the evil. But this amendment is a King's cure for all the evils. [Applause] It winds the whole thing up.[8]

While making his jubilant comments to those gathered at the White House, Lincoln was undoubtedly rehearsing his words for the Confederate peace commissioners waiting to meet with him. It remained unclear what exactly Jefferson Davis empowered the commissioners to negotiate, but, largely at General Grant's urging, Lincoln decided to press ahead and meet with them. Lincoln felt he had a moral obligation to see if peace without more casualties was possible.[9]

On the morning of February 3, Lincoln and Secretary Seward met with Alexander Stephens and the other peace commissioners for about four hours onboard the steam transport *River Queen*, which was anchored at Hampton Roads, Virginia. Several accounts of this meeting became part of the historical record, most of which agree on the larger points but differ on some of the details. All accounts agree that Lincoln, early in the meeting, completely ruled out an armistice or any other form of peace treaty that left the South to exist as a separate slave-holding nation. As one Confederate commissioner later recalled, Lincoln "distinctly affirmed that he would not treat except on the basis of reunion and the abolition of slavery."[10]

For those hoping to achieve some form of negotiated peace at Hampton Roads, Lincoln dashed that goal from the outset. Lincoln announced firmly that he would not negotiate anything less than surrender and reunification. Since the Confederate commissioners were not empowered to negotiate anything that led to such a result, that left very little of a substantive nature to discuss. Nevertheless, the parties decided to use the opportunity to share views on the issue of slavery, which all parties recognized to be the central issue that continued to divide them.

Secretary Seward's notes of the meeting recorded that "the anti-slavery policy of the United States was reviewed in all its bearings, and the President announced that he must not be expected to depart from the positions he had heretofore assumed in his proclamation of emancipation and other documents."[11] As Seward reported shortly after the meeting, the Confederate commissioners were notified of the recent passage of the Thirteenth Amendment and were told that "there is every

The *River Queen*, the steamer that hosted the Hampton Roads Peace Conference. Courtesy of the Steamship Historical Society Archives.

reason to expect that it will be soon accepted by three-fourths of the States, so as to become a part of the National organic law."[12]

The Confederate participants at the meeting recalled the discussion of the slavery issue somewhat differently. They acknowledged that Lincoln refused to even consider modifying any portion of his Emancipation Proclamation. They recorded, however, that Lincoln was much more open with the commissioners about his personal doubts and concerns. According to Stephens, Lincoln stated his doubts that the government possessed the power to end slavery except as a war measure; indeed, according to Stephens, Lincoln always favored gradual and not immediate emancipation, stating "Many evils attending [immediate emancipation] appeared to him."[13]

The South's best course of action, Lincoln counseled, was to give up fighting emancipation as a policy and attempt instead to mitigate the evil effects of immediate emancipation. "Slavery is doomed," Lincoln stated flatly.[14] According to Stephens, Lincoln suggested that the South's best strategy would be to slow adoption of the Thirteenth Amendment by maneuvering the state legislatures to provisionally adopt the amendment at some future date, perhaps five years in the future. Stephens also noted that Lincoln expressed interest in the possibility of having the government provide generous financial compensation to slaveholders impacted by emancipation, mentioning that one politician in his party suggested a figure of as much as four hundred million dollars for that purpose.[15]

At one point in the meeting, the subject of the impact of immediate emancipation arose. When pressed by the Confederate representatives, Lincoln admitted that the present result of emancipation might be devastating for the old and infirm, as well as women and children who were unable to support themselves. But Lincoln refused to accept any blame for this result. He instead chose to recite an anecdote that ended with an Illinois farmer being asked what his pigs would do for food in the winter. "Well," said the farmer, "let 'em root!"[16]

Lincoln's point in relating this unfortunate anecdote remains unclear. He may have told the story simply to lighten the tension in the room. He may have intended the story as an unsubtle effort to shift responsibility to the South for the very real hardships some of the emancipated slaves and their former masters would soon face. In any event, the meeting ended soon thereafter without any agreement on any issue. The Hampton Roads Peace Conference, as the episode became known, proved unremarkable, destined to be remembered only in the occasional memoirs of participants or the increasingly less frequent footnotes of Civil War historians.

If the Hampton Roads Peace Conference produced no tangible results, the reader might wonder why its story is related in this narrative. Why describe a negotiation where nothing was negotiated? The importance of the Hampton Roads Peace Conference lies not in what it accomplished; rather, its importance lies in what was not accomplished. The conference left unresolved a host of important issues that would cause tremendous difficulties at the end of the war and for decades thereafter, particularly the way in which slavery would end and freedom begin. The failure at Hampton Roads meant there would be no grand bargain between the North and the South in which the Confederacy agreed that slavery would end in a certain way or on a certain date. There would be no transition period, no compensation to slaveholders, no agreed system of wages, no requirement that former slaveholders continue to care for freed slaves who could not care for themselves. Issues like these would never be addressed by policymakers in a careful and methodical manner. The failure of the Hampton Roads Peace Conference meant that slavery would end not with a pen, but with the point of a bayonet.

Lincoln's assertion to the Confederate commissioners that the institution of slavery was "doomed" proved accurate. The way in which this doom transpired, however, would have meaningful consequences. After the failure of diplomacy at Hampton Roads, the end of the war revolved entirely around the maneuvers of the armies. When the Confederate armies ran out of military options, they surrendered. The documents of surrender addressed purely military considerations like the disposition of the captured Confederate artillery pieces and horses. The status of Southern slaves remained unresolved in these surrender documents. Instead, no real or lasting solutions to the problems facing the freed slaves were put forth. Ironically, even with the issue of slavery as its central cause, the Civil War produced no comprehensive program or planned transition to manage the end of that institution.

*Chapter 13*

## THE END IS IN SIGHT

At the outset of the Civil War, newspaper editors throughout the rapidly dividing country rushed to make bold predictions that their armies would quickly defeat the enemy, resulting in victory for their respective causes within a short period of time. Horace Greeley's newspaper, the *New-York Tribune*, followed Lincoln's call for volunteers in April 1861 with a demand that the Union army press "On to Richmond!" No time should be lost, the headlines thundered, urging the president to act so swiftly that the Confederate capital was in Union hands before the rebel legislature even had an opportunity to meet. This, the *New-York Tribune* declared, was the "Nation's War Cry."[1]

It turned out that the "Nation's War Cry" fell on deaf ears for a long time. Union armies captured Richmond, Virginia, almost four years after the *New-York Tribune*'s call for action. In the spring of 1865, the end of the Confederacy loomed and many wondered how much longer the war would last. The progress and events of the war had proven notoriously difficult to predict. It was still possible to imagine sequences of events in which the war might drag on in some form or fashion for an indefinite period.

One of the more plausible outcomes in which the Confederacy might survive involved a potential escape by Confederate President Jefferson Davis and his officials from Richmond to a different and more secure place in the South. At this new seat of government, possibly in Texas, Davis would continue to direct the war effort. Another possibility, one that particularly worried General-in-Chief Ulysses S. Grant, involved Confederate forces fleeing to Mexico, where they might receive aid from France and continue the war from a base across the Rio Grande. Both of these scenarios depended upon the escape of Jefferson Davis and Robert E. Lee's army from Virginia. Grant, determined to prevent such escapes if possible, scrambled to put together the resources needed to thwart that prospect. His task would not be easy.

On the afternoon of April 2, 1865, General Lee notified Confederate President Jefferson Davis that he saw no alternative but to evacuate his lines and leave Richmond unprotected. Lee's letter to Davis also stated that he was finally ready to appoint officers to attempt to recruit black troops to fight for the Southern cause. Such an action seemed to portend that the Southern cause was on its last legs.[2]

Faced with Lee's warning, Davis made immediate plans to flee, leaving Richmond on the night of April 2. Confederate supply officers in Richmond spent the night burning all the military supplies not easily moved. They then joined the exodus of Southern forces crossing the James River heading west toward Danville, Virginia. Shortly before dawn on April 3, Confederate engineers burned the last bridge over the James River and completed the Army of Northern Virginia's abandonment of the Confederate capital. The last uniformed Confederate to leave Richmond was Walter Husted Stevens, a New York-born soldier who graduated from West Point in the Class of 1848. Before the war, Stevens supervised the construction of Galveston's United States Custom House, completed just as the war got underway in 1861. Ironically, that building eventually served as one of the major Union office buildings when Texas was occupied in June 1865, and later served as one of the frequent locations for Juneteenth commemoration events.[3]

General Grant anxiously waited for Lee's Confederate army to complete its evacuation of Richmond and make its inevitable attempt to escape. The general viewed the potential of such a breakout with mixed feelings. Grant knew that Lee could not hold out much longer, and he did not need Northern newspapers to remind him that the loss of the Confederate capital would demoralize the entire South. Grant also knew that if Lee and Davis somehow managed to slip away, they could continue to stir up resistance in other parts of the Confederacy. "I was

Maj. Gen. Philip H. Sheridan. Photograph by Mathew Brady.
National Archives and Records Administration, NWDNS-111-B-2520.

afraid every morning," wrote Grant in his memoirs, "that I would awake from my sleep to hear that Lee had gone, and that nothing was left but a picket line."[4] If Lee managed to escape, as he had done so many times in the past, "he would leave me behind so that we would have the same army to fight again farther south—and the war might be prolonged another year."[5]

Commanders on both sides realized that Lee's best, and probably only, option was to maneuver his army around Grant's force and then proceed to North Carolina, where Lee could join his army with Gen. Joseph E. Johnston's and create a larger and more formidable Confederate force. To prevent such a combination, Grant needed to move ahead of Lee and prevent the Confederate army from reaching needed supplies. Such an operation required highly mobile cavalry and infantry, and to direct that force, Grant turned once again to Gen. Philip Henry Sheridan, a commander in whom he had the utmost confidence.

To look at him, there was not much impressive about Phil Sheridan. Called "Little Phil" at West Point because of his short stature, Sheridan was swarthy and ill-tempered. In 1864, Grant requested that Sheridan be named commander of the Army of Potomac's cavalry, despite his lack of experience as a cavalry commander. Grant later gave Sheridan command of the Army of Shenandoah, where he conducted a brilliant campaign that ended the region's position as a base of supplies for the Confederate war effort. Grant saw an aggressiveness in Sheridan that was a good fit with his own natural instincts. He later told Prince Otto von Bismarck that he believed Sheridan to be "one of the great soldiers of the world," saying that in his opinion, "No better general ever lived than Sheridan."[6]

Grant first encountered Sheridan in 1861 when Sheridan served as quartermaster on Gen. Henry Halleck's staff. Grant also served as a quartermaster at one time, and knew that successfully serving in such a demanding administrative position required the ability to make the most out of the available resources, even those outside the military. During a cavalry raid to threaten Richmond in March 1865, Sheridan accumulated a force of escaped slaves that numbered approximately two thousand. Sheridan tasked these freedpeople with destroying railroads and canals, some of which they may have originally helped build. Ultimately, when bad weather conditions turned Sheridan's raid into a "mud march," the freedpeople helped Sheridan's tired horses and heavily loaded captured wagons through the quagmire to the safety of Union lines.[7]

Sheridan found the freedpeople who aided his movements in enemy territory to be extremely useful. He also shared with General Grant the valuable intelligence that many of these people brought to him about enemy movements and defenses. Even as Sheridan witnessed the benefits of employing former slaves, the language of his communications to superiors displayed his racial prejudice. In a note to Orville Babcock on March 16, Sheridan wrote of his intention to cross the Mattapony River and "get rid of my 2,000 negroes and other debris at West Point."[8]

Sheridan may have viewed the freedpeople as "debris," as he put it, in the military context of 1865, but he remembered the useful service that these men and women provided him and his cause. Sheridan used the publication of his memoirs after the war as a long overdue opportunity to publicly complain about the policies of President Andrew Johnson and his unreconstructed rebel followers, noting that under these policies the black men who aided the Union cause should "have no political status at all, and consequently be at the mercy of a people who, recently their masters, now seemed to look upon them as the authors of all the misfortunes that had come upon the land."[9] Sheridan viewed President Johnson's policies as "inhuman," and used his post-war military influence to defend freedpeople whenever and wherever he could. As Sheridan saw the government's responsibility to the freed slaves, "freedom had been given them, and it was the plain duty of those in authority to make it secure, and screen them from the bitter resentment that beset them, and to see that they had a fair chance in the battle of life."[10]

## Chapter 14

## THE "NEW ORDER OF THINGS"

The collapse of the Confederate military apparatus, when it finally materialized, came at a rapid and accelerating pace. Robert E. Lee's surrender of the Army of Northern Virginia at Appomattox on April 9, 1865, was soon followed on April 26 by the surrender of Confederate Gen. Joseph E. Johnston's army to Union Gen. William T. Sherman near Durham's Station, North Carolina. Generals Sherman and Johnston attempted to broaden the terms of this second surrender to extend to all Confederate armies, and had signed a more comprehensive surrender document on April 18, just four days after President Lincoln's assassination, but officials in Washington viewed the terms as too liberal and disapproved them.[1]

Sherman always believed that Lincoln would have approved the broader surrender terms that he negotiated. The failure to accept the more comprehensive surrender Sherman attempted to negotiate in North Carolina meant that Johnston's surrender was eventually limited to the Confederate army he personally commanded in the field. The terms of Johnston's surrender remained limited to the purely military terms Grant extended to Lee. In disallowing Sherman's effort to broaden the surrender terms, Washington ensured that each Confederate force must sign a separate surrender. It also raised the possibility that some of those armies might choose not to surrender. Instead, Sherman worried, "the rebel armies will disperse; and instead of dealing with six or seven States, we will have to deal with numberless bands of desperadoes."[2]

There was indeed some sentiment in the Confederacy to continue fighting the war as a guerilla war, but after four long years of fighting, many, perhaps most, Southerners accepted that the South had lost the war and wanted to get on with their lives. Union soldiers eagerly awaited the war's end and the return to their families. But an unexpected obstacle appeared to delay that reunion. As Confederate armies surrendered, leaving the field clear for Union armies to take control, the issue of how to handle the multitude of liberated slaves that materialized throughout the conquered territory came sharply into focus. It was in many cases the number one issue confronting the victorious Union generals who became the chief civil authorities in the Confederate states their armies conquered. Dealing with freed slaves had not been part of the curriculum at West Point, and many Union officers found managing the relations between freed slaves and their bitter former masters completely distasteful.

One of the first Union commanders to complain about having to confront this issue was Gen. Henry Halleck, who had spent a good part of the war in Washington dodging and declining to give guidance on slavery-related issues. Halleck, who became commander of the Military Division of the James after Lee surrendered at Appomattox Court House, arrived in Richmond to find a large population of freed slaves clogging the streets. Halleck estimated their number to be between 30,000 and 40,000, making it approximately equal to the number of white inhabitants. The population of black refugees increased daily with the arrival of men and women who fled inactive or deserted plantations. To prevent starvation and avoid riots, Halleck authorized army quartermasters to issue emergency rations to the freedpeople.[3]

General Grant anticipated that Richmond needed urgent humanitarian assistance and appointed Lt. Col. Adam Badeau, a New York attorney, to assist Halleck by heading up a newly created Richmond Relief Commission. Badeau realized immediately that the key to dealing with the growing refugee population in Richmond was finding them sustainable employment, a task easier said than done. As Badeau reported: "The great difficulties existing in regard to furnishing employment in a captured and half-burnt city, the danger of fostering a spirit of idle vagabondism, the throngs of negroes recently freed, who have come from their homes in the country to add to the starving mouths in town, and the large

Maj. Gen. Henry W. Halleck. Library of Congress, LC-DIG-cwpb-06956.

number of disbanded soldiers, paroled prisoners of war, who also have flocked to Richmond, all have complicated the duties of this commission, and obstructed, in some degree, its operations."[4]

Halleck and Badeau both knew that the situation in Richmond was unsustainable and potentially dangerous. Once again, military leaders found themselves dealing with a social problem they were ill-equipped to handle. As Halleck reminded his former colleagues in Washington:

> As might naturally have been anticipated, the sudden emancipation by the termination of the war of a large part of the population, and their change of condition from bondage to freedom, produced no little excitement, both among the freedmen themselves and their former owners and masters. In the absence of all civil authority the regulation and direction of these excited and conflicting elements of society necessarily devolved upon the military. The task was ungrateful and disagreeable but could not be avoided.[5]

For Union military commanders, one of the most disagreeable aspects of handling issues involving emancipated slaves involved navigating the inherently complex and unstable relationship between former slaves and masters. To use a modern analogy, the situation put Union generals in a game as referees where the rules of the game had yet to be determined.

Halleck and other Union generals agreed on two issues concerning former slaves: first, all slaves were now free; and second, the best answer to food shortages in Union-occupied territory came from former slaves staying with their former masters and working for wages. As General Halleck put it, "[t]he idea that slavery has ceased must be everywhere impressed, but the freedmen must be made to understand that they are not to be fed by us. They must work for a living. They should not be permitted to leave the plantations and flock to the large cities, where they can get no labor."[6]

Other victorious Union generals joined Halleck with pleas to Washington for guidance on how to handle the thousands of freed slaves, often destitute, who migrated to Southern cities from rural areas. As Gen. John P. Hatch, in command at Charleston, South Carolina, complained, the "immense number of negroes flocking into the city threatens us with a pestilence and them with starvation."[7] He warned that "if something is not done, and that immediately, we will have starvation among the freedmen."[8]

Not all the problems involved feeding the former slaves. Union generals received numerous reports of criminal activities, many of which blamed "marauding negroes," "idle negroes," or "vagrant negroes." The number of these claims reflecting true crimes among the freedpeople remains lost to history, but as the Confederacy disintegrated, law enforcement suffered. Lawlessness from a wide variety of sources, including former Union and Confederate soldiers, expanded to fill the void. It seems likely, indeed almost inevitable, that one element of this lawlessness involved poor black men who banded together to provide for their families in the midst of a chaotic social setting. As one general complained, "The authority of the Government is weakened and brought into contempt by the impunity with which stragglers, deserters from either army, marauders, bummers, and strolling vagabonds, negroes and whites, commit outrages upon the inhabitants."[9]

Once again, Union military commanders looked to Washington leaders to issue general guidance on the way military authorities should handle freed slaves and their former masters. And once again, no such guidance proved forthcoming. President Lincoln signed legislation on March 3, 1865, creating the agency that became known as the Freedmen's Bureau. That agency was a long way from having any presence in the field, however, and in the short run, Lincoln's creation of the organization in March 1865 made Union military authorities even more reluctant to step in and act in ways that might eventually be questioned or reversed.[10]

President Lincoln's assassination on April 14, 1865, threw the entire policy-making apparatus in Washington even further into disorder. Left to their own devices, Union generals gradually began to use the language in Lincoln's Emancipation Proclamation as a template to create a new series of general orders intended to govern relations between freed slaves and their former masters. The wording of each of these orders differed slightly, but they all included common themes of reinforcing emancipation as policy while warning the freedpeople against vagrancy. As Halleck described their purpose, "the whites have been made fully sensible that they are no longer slaveholders, [and] their former slaves have been taught that their own well-being must depend upon their industry and good conduct."[11]

Examining a few of the general orders issued in the wake of the Confederate surrenders provides modern readers with a sense of their purpose and scope. One of the first such orders, issued at Petersburg, Virginia, by Gen. George L. Hartsuff on April 24, 1865, consisted almost entirely of a paternalistic lecture to the freedpeople about the nature of their newly acquired freedom:

> The delusion which many colored persons, formerly slaves, are laboring under concerning their rights and privileges having been in many instances productive of evil, and giving prospect of much trouble in the future, both to themselves and to their former masters, it is deemed necessary to correct it and explain what are the true relations their changed condition places them in toward the Government and their former masters, as well as what their own duties and responsibilities are. Their error consists mainly in the belief that with their liberty they acquire individual rights in the property of their former masters, and they are entitled to live with and be subsisted by them without being obliged to labor.... Their former master has the right to refuse them anything he might deny to a perfect stranger, and is no more bound to feed, clothe or protect them than if he had never been their master.... The fact must in time be learned by all negroes, and the sooner the better for themselves and all concerned, that they must work for their support now the same as

before they were free, in some instances perhaps even harder, the difference between then and now being that now they have the entire wages of their labor to themselves.[12]

Three days following Hartsuff's order in Virginia, Gen. John M. Schofield, commanding the Department of North Carolina, issued a much more balanced and succinct order that addressed both parties to the former master/slave relationship:

To remove a doubt which seems to exist in the minds of some of the people of North Carolina, it is hereby declared that by virtue of the proclamation of the President of the United States, dated January 1, 1863, all persons in this State heretofore held as slaves are now free; and that it is the duty of the army to maintain the freedom of such persons. It is recommended to the former owners of the freedmen to employ them as hired servants at reasonable wages, and it is recommended to the freedmen that when allowed to do so they remain with their former masters and labor faithfully so long as they shall be treated kindly and paid reasonable wages, or that they immediately seek employment elsewhere in the kind of work to which they are accustomed. It is not well for them to congregate about towns or military camps. They will not be supported in idleness.[13]

The language in General Schofield's order, designated General Orders No. 32, faithfully tracked the language in the Emancipation Proclamation and seemed to reach a good balance between warnings directed to the former masters and their former slaves. Schofield wrote later in his memoirs, "This order, which was the first public official declaration on the subject, was mentioned by one of the leading journals of New York at the time as having at least the merit of 'saving a world of discussion.'"[14]

Two facets of Schofield's General Orders No. 32 are important for the story behind Juneteenth. The language in Schofield's order is extremely similar—indeed parts are identical—to the language that ended up in the Juneteenth Order. Schofield issued his order in North Carolina exactly eighty-three days prior to the Juneteenth Order issued in Texas. Schofield was a friend and West Point classmate of Gen. Phil Sheridan. It is possible, even likely, that Sheridan possessed a copy of Schofield's order when he drafted a portion of what eventually became the Juneteenth Order's text.

Maj. Gen. John M. Schofield. Library of Congress, LC-B8172-1944.

The second feature of Schofield's order that is relevant involves the manner of its distribution. General Schofield hoped and expected (wrongly, as it turned out) that he might be appointed to serve as military governor of North Carolina. To that end, he started a policy of having his general orders published in newspapers throughout the state, even requiring the papers to publish all of them in sequence for several months following their issuance. This turned out to be an excellent distribution mechanism, and became precisely the same policy that General Granger eventually followed when he reached Texas on June 19, 1865.[15]

Schofield did not pretend to have all the answers regarding the best policies to follow with regard to freed slaves, but he knew that the problem had to be faced. North Carolina's freed slave population exceeded 300,000 individuals. Schofield understood that his order only touched the surface of the issues surrounding the freedpeople. Could black men vote, as Salmon Chase urged Schofield to declare?[16] Could they hold office? What rights and privileges did they enjoy under applicable state and federal laws? Many questions existed with unfortunately few answers.

Writing his friend William T. Sherman, Schofield candidly noted: "What is to be done with the freedmen is the question of all, and it is the all-important question. It requires prompt and wise action to prevent the negro from becoming a huge elephant on our hands."[17] Sherman responded that despite his personal conviction that every freed person in the State should be permitted "a way to make an honest livelihood, with his freedom secure," he did not see a way to help make that happen.[18] "It makes me sick to contemplate the fact," Sherman confessed, "but I am powerless for good, and must let events drift as best they may."[19]

Although willing to make public pronouncements about the equality of free slaves and masters, General Schofield, like General Sherman and many other Union military officials, entertained serious reservations about the true meaning of that equality. He shared his reservations with General Grant on May 10, offering his opinion that black men should not be allowed to vote because of the "absolute unfitness of the negroes, as a class, for any such responsibility."[20] Schofield pointed out that in his experience, the freedpeople "can neither read nor write; they have no knowledge whatever of law or government; they do not even know the meaning of the freedom that has been given them, and are much astonished when informed that it does not mean that they are to live in idleness and be fed by the Government."[21] There might come a time, admitted Schofield, when blacks were ready to vote. But he believed that "we certainly ought to teach them something before we give them an equal voice with ourselves in Government."[22]

Although Schofield's private reservations about the voting ability of former slaves sound paternalistic and racist to modern ears, the general at least attempted to deal with some of the very real complications that emancipation presented in states like North Carolina. On May 15, Schofield promulgated General Orders No. 46, which, among other things, prohibited the former masters of freedpeople from turning away the young or infirm, requiring the former slaveholders to provide their former slaves with food and shelter for the time being.[23] In defining the nature of the relationship between the former masters and their new "servants"— Schofield resisted calling the freedpeople "employees"—General Orders No. 46 provided only vague guidance:

> It will be left to the employer and servant to agree upon the wages to be paid; but freedmen are advised that for the present season they ought to expect only moderate wages, and where their employers cannot pay them money, they ought to be contented

with a fair share in the crops to be raised. They have gained their personal freedom. By industry and good conduct, they may rise to independence and even wealth.[24]

The order requested that all officers, soldiers, and non-combatants give publicity to the new rules and instruct the freedpeople as to their rights and obligations.[25]

Elsewhere in the conquered South, other Union generals followed Schofield's footsteps and issued public proclamations regarding the changed status of the relationship between masters and slaves. Many used Schofield's order as a template, making changes or emphasizing various portions of its language in accordance with their own individual circumstances and personal preferences. In Florida, for example, Gen. Israel Vogdes issued a general order declaring that "the freedom of the blacks" had been "fully declared by the President of the United States," but recommending that the freedpeople continue to labor for their former masters in return for compensation.[26] "In no case," the order warned the freedpeople, "will they be allowed to remain in idleness at the expense of the Government."[27]

More than just concern for order and the federal treasury pushed Union commanders to insert labor requirements in these orders. As spring turned into summer, the focus shifted increasingly to the coming harvest season. Union generals—who only months before devoted themselves to the disruption of Southern agricultural systems to bring about the end of the Confederacy—began to worry about reviving the system that would provide food for all those involved. Union military leaders speculated that if freedpeople fled to the cities or congregated around military installations, then a shortage of workers in the field would cause crops to go unharvested, a worry not only regarding food, but important commercial products like cotton and sugar as well. Many Union commanders agreed that they needed a way to persuade freedpeople to continue working at their previous agricultural pursuits until the crops could be harvested and normal order reestablished.

Generals responded to the demand for agricultural labor by issuing a series of orders designed to keep workers employed and to minimize disturbances. Typical of these orders was General Orders No. 24 issued by General Vogdes in Florida. Noting the "importance of the incoming crop as a means of support for the people of this district," the order directed "prompt and efficient measures" to ensure that the crops were properly cultivated and secured.[28] The edict instructed planters to enter into written contracts with their laborers providing either for stated wages or a fair division of the crops. One copy of each contract was to be furnished to the military, which was charged with the responsibility of strictly enforcing their terms.[29]

Orders directing freedpeople to continue working were usually worded in such a fashion that the military pledged to enforce the terms of the contracts against both parties, the planters as well as the laborers. From the wording of these orders, however, the laborers became the obvious target of these enforcement provisions. "Orderly and industrious habits are essential to the preservation of society," the Florida order recited, noting that "while all persons who show a disposition to submit to the authority of the United States and observe the orders in force will be protected in their rights and property, idleness, vagrancy, and all marauding, pilfering, or turbulence—the ills to which they lead—will be promptly and severely punished."[30]

Rapid and widespread distribution of these edicts became so essential that the military employed creative means to disperse the orders. In South Carolina, for example, Gen. Quincy Gilmore selected several reliable chaplains to go into the interior of the state to personally carry his message. "Call meetings among the planters and colored people," Gilmore directed, "for the purpose of instructing both classes in their duties to themselves, their country, and to each other under the new order of things."[31] The general advised the chaplains not to get too carried away on general subjects like religion, patriotism, or mutual respect, however. While tasked with meeting with former slaves and former slaveholders alike, the chaplains' main message was directed exclusively at the laborers. Gilmore told his messengers, "The colored people should be earnestly advised to remain with and work for their former masters, and they should not be led to expect pay in money the present year."[32] To many of the freedpeople who heard this message, their new freedom must have sounded remarkably like the bondage from which they had supposedly been liberated. What General Gilmore described as the "new order of things" for freedpeople sounded suspiciously and ominously familiar.[33]

## Chapter 15

## LOUISIANA

Although Louisiana started 1865, the last year of the war, as a state divided, it had been that way for some time. The Union army seized New Orleans and the area around the city in the spring of 1862 and an uncomfortable tension existed between the Union and Confederate-controlled regions ever since. Union Gen. Nathaniel P. Banks attempted a large campaign up the Red River in 1864, which would probably have given the North possession of virtually the entire state if that campaign had not ended in failure. By the spring of 1865, the territorial boundaries established between the two armies differed little from those that had existed for the last three years of the war, with the Confederates controlling most of the northern part of the state, while their Union adversaries controlled the southern portion.

Each army maintained a concentrated area of the state where it established civil and military power. New Orleans became the de facto capital of Union-controlled Louisiana, as well as the headquarters of the Union army and Department of the Gulf. At the northwestern end of the state, Shreveport became the provisional capital of Confederate Louisiana, as well as the headquarters for the Confederate Department of the Trans-Mississippi.

Commanders in both New Orleans and Shreveport followed developments in the eastern theater of the war with great interest, knowing that the spring campaigns of 1865 would most likely determine the outcome of the war. For Confederate Gen. Edmund Kirby Smith, in command of the Trans-Mississippi department at his headquarters in Shreveport, the news from the East was not good. As it became apparent that General Lee's army faced disaster, Kirby Smith issued a series of increasingly desperate patriotic messages and orders in an unsuccessful attempt to encourage public support and keep up his army's morale.

When news of Lee's surrender in April reached Louisiana, Kirby Smith challenged his troops to "show that you are worthy of your position in history," and "[p]rove to the world that your hearts have not failed in the hour of disaster, and that at the last moment you will sustain the holy cause which has been so gloriously battled for by your brethren east of the Mississippi."[1] The general offered one last bit of hope, noting "You have hopes of succor from abroad—protract the struggle and you will surely receive the aid of nations who already deeply sympathize with you."[2] The troops greeted these invocations with well-deserved skepticism. As one Union spy reported: "The men instantly became dejected. Mutiny and wholesale desertion was openly talked of. . . . [T]he Army of the Trans-Mississippi was in spirit crushed."[3]

Lt. Gen. Edmund Kirby Smith (C.S.A.). Library of Congress, LC-DIG-cwpb-06081.

Kirby Smith's unfounded claim of "succor from abroad" rang particularly hollow in his soldiers' ears. The Confederate soldiers reasoned if England and other European powers had not intervened to help the Confederacy during the course of four long years of war, little reason existed for them to risk doing so with the North clearly on the verge of winning a military victory. Most of the skeptical Confederate troops did not realize, however, that their general sought aid from a much closer and potentially more interested foreign source.

In January 1865, Kirby Smith wrote to the Confederate representative in France, requesting him to urge French Emperor Napoleon III to intervene in the American Civil War on behalf of the Confederacy. The Southern general insisted the move was necessary to protect French interests in Mexico. When nothing came of Kirby Smith's request to Napoleon, on May 2 he wrote a letter directly to Maximillian, the ruler of Mexico (installed by the French less than a year earlier) renewing his plea that Mexico provide military assistance against their common adversary. None of these diplomatic moves produced any tangible result other than to make Washington diplomats (who became aware of these machinations) even more suspicious of French motives in Mexico.[4]

With the fall of Richmond to General Grant, Kirby Smith turned his hopes to the possibility that Confederate President Jefferson Davis and his government officials might somehow find a way to escape to Cuba and then be smuggled back to Texas, where the South would reorganize and resume the fight. Kirby Smith even sent a representative to Havana to provide transportation for Davis when and if he materialized. All of Kirby Smith's hopes died when a detachment of Union cavalry captured Jefferson Davis near Irwinville, Georgia, on May 10, 1865. Time was about up for the Confederacy, whether Kirby Smith chose to publicly admit it or not.[5]

Unlike Kirby Smith, Confederate Gen. Richard Taylor recognized reality and saw that the time for fighting had ended. Taylor, the son of former President Zachary Taylor, feuded with Kirby Smith to the point that Taylor refused to serve under him. General Taylor had then been given an independent command across the Mississippi River, consisting of the Department of Alabama, Mississippi, and East Louisiana. After the surrenders of Generals Lee and Johnston, Taylor's army of about 10,000 men became the only large, organized Confederate force east of the Mississippi. On May 4, 1865, at Citronelle, Alabama, Taylor signed a memorandum containing surrender terms that mirrored those previously agreed to by Lee and Johnston. As Taylor later wrote in his memoirs, "The military and civil authorities of the Confederacy had fallen, and I was called to administer on the ruins as residuary legatee. It seemed absurd for the few there present to continue the struggle against a million of men. We could only secure honorable interment for the remainder of our cause."[6]

Taylor's "honorable interment" left only Kirby Smith and the Confederate forces west of the Mississippi River to make the decision whether to surrender or continue the hopeless fight. Even with Kirby Smith's headquarters in Louisiana, the largest territory under what remained of his command was actually the State of Texas. General Grant, commanding the Union war effort from Washington at the time, believed that Kirby Smith, when forced to consider his options, "will see that with the vast armies at our control the State of Texas can and will be overrun and desolated if the war continues."[7] He directed Gen. John Pope to demand Kirby Smith's surrender on the same terms accepted by the other Confederate generals east of the Mississippi. If Kirby Smith failed to surrender, Grant said, he intended to send a large enough force to "overrun the whole country west of the Mississippi."[8] This was no idle threat.

On May 9, Kirby Smith firmly but delicately rejected General Pope's surrender demand, stating that the "propositions for the surrender of the troops under my command are not such that my sense of duty and honor will permit me to accept."[9] On the same day, Kirby Smith wrote a letter to the Confederate governors in the Trans-Mississippi (which, in addition to Texas, included portions of Louisiana, Arkansas, and Missouri) in which he declared that "it is my purpose to defend your soil and the civil and political rights of our people to the utmost extent of our resources."[10] Noting that the government in Richmond could no longer direct his efforts, Kirby Smith invited the governors to assemble at Marshall, Texas, and create a coordinated statement of policy to support some continuation of the fight.[11]

On May 13, the Confederate governors and their representatives gathered in Marshall and received a candid report from Kirby Smith about the military situation and the increasingly dwindling options for holding out against the federal armies arrayed against them. The representatives at this "Marshall conference" found little reason for optimism. By this point, all present understood that defeat was inevitable, but they hoped for better terms of surrender if they held out and demanded concessions. Unsurprisingly, one of the revised terms that the men considered most necessary involved generous amnesty provisions for officers and officials like themselves.[12]

The attendees at the Marshall conference developed a five-point demand "in order that peace may be restored to the country."[13] The primary points in this demand included complete amnesty for all military and state officials, the recognition of the validity of the existing Confederate state governments, and the withdrawal of all Union occupation troops as of a future date. The governors hoped to send Gov. Henry W. Allen of Louisiana along with their proposal to Washington, D.C., to further negotiate the final details of the Marshall proposal.[14]

It seems unlikely that Kirby Smith believed the terms demanded by the governors would be accepted. The situation became even clearer when the group's spokesman, Governor Allen, was not even permitted to enter federal lines to discuss the demands with any Union military or political authorities. Instead, a Union officer carried the proposed "terms" back to General Pope with a curious personal "Memorandum" from Kirby Smith that attempted to provide some context for the group's various proposals and positions.[15]

Kirby Smith frankly conceded in his memorandum that he did not think his force in the Trans-Mississippi could "without assistance accomplish its independence against the whole power of the United States."[16] He wanted to "avoid the unnecessary effusion of blood and the attendant devastation of the country" that would inevitably result from further military resistance.[17] What troubled Kirby Smith, however, was his belief that he could not honorably surrender his army quite yet since his force was not closely threatened militarily.[18]

Kirby Smith's situation boiled down to a matter of appearances and timing. Unlike the circumstances that forced generals like Robert E. Lee to surrender, Union forces had not yet surrounded Kirby Smith's army. Instead, the Confederate general stated, "my force [is] menaced only from a distance."[19] He felt an officer could only honorably surrender his command when "he has resisted to the utmost of his power and no hopes rest upon his further efforts."[20] Kirby Smith encouraged the federal authorities either to threaten him more closely or to accede to the points demanded by the governors at the Marshall conference, noting hopefully that "the more generous the terms proposed by a victorious enemy the greater is the certainty of a speedy and lasting pacification."[21]

Although from Kirby Smith's perspective his army was not sufficiently threatened by the enemy to force a surrender, he knew all too well that his command was rapidly falling apart even without the Union's active assistance. Every day brought new reports of mass desertions, mutinies, and depredations by marauding bands of soldiers. On May 17, a Confederate officer in Alexandria, Louisiana, reported that "heavy desertions and plundering of Government property of every kind is the order of the day."[22] He summed up the situation very candidly, saying "in a word, colonel, the army is destroyed, and we must look the matter square in the face and shape our actions (personally and officially) accordingly."[23]

The Union commanders facing Kirby Smith's Confederate army understood the problems decimating the Confederates. The officers who worked so long and hard to destroy the Confederate armies began to worry about the logistical problems they would inherit when they moved inland. Many of their concerns centered on how to maintain order, how to supply the destitute civilian population, and how to feed the former slaves leaving plantations by the hundreds. To emphasize the last problem, Union Gen. Joseph Reynolds sent out a detachment of black troops on a routine patrol in Arkansas in late May, and it returned with two hundred starving former slaves. Writing to General Pope, Reynolds observed that "The thing is going to pieces so fast that one cannot count the fragments."[24]

In Shreveport, General Kirby Smith decided not to wait around and count the fragments of his disintegrating command. On May 18, his staff issued a terse announcement transferring the headquarters of the Trans-Mississippi Department to Houston. The logic behind this decision remains unclear, but Houston's proximity to Mexico was most likely not a coincidence since many Confederate officers (including Kirby Smith) eventually fled to that country.[25]

Gen. Simon Bolivar Buckner stayed in Shreveport with instructions to gather up what Confederate forces lingered in the area and head to Houston, but by the time the general was in a position to do so, only a few units had not either disbanded or deserted. When Kirby Smith reached Houston, essentially nothing remained of the Confederate army in Shreveport other than a few men from Missouri and North Arkansas with nowhere else to go. The situation in Shreveport became chaotic soon afterwards, and Buckner found it impossible to keep the public safe from the lawlessness accompanying the breakup of the army. General Buckner realized that to gain control of the situation required a Confederate surrender so that federal troops could step in and restore order. With Kirby Smith travelling to Houston and out of communication, Buckner started direct surrender discussions with federal forces.[26]

As with everything else associated with the end of the Confederate Army of the Trans-Mississippi, its surrender was a hopelessly complicated mess. At least three separate representatives or groups of representatives independently approached Union lines for the stated purpose of negotiating surrender terms, all claiming to speak for General Kirby Smith. Ironically, Kirby Smith himself was not a part of any of these discussions, largely because he was occupied dodging Confederate deserters and brigands on the roads between Shreveport and Houston. He arrived in Houston on May 27 to find that his army had disbanded and effectively surrendered in his absence. His only remaining role in the conflict was to sign his name on the final surrender paperwork.[27]

Lt. Gen. Simon Bolivar Buckner (C.S.A.).
Library of Congress, LC-DIG-ppmsca-41841.

On May 26, 1865, General Buckner signed a "Military Convention" with Union Gen. Edward R. S. Canby at New Orleans. The convention contained essentially the same surrender terms that Kirby Smith had rejected just a few weeks earlier. Canby became concerned by the absence of Kirby Smith from the surrender process and insisted on the Confederate general's signature on the convention to formally ratify its terms. On June 2, Kirby Smith boarded the Union steamer *Fort Jackson*, anchored near Galveston, and signed a document approving the terms of the convention. The Confederate Army of the Trans-Mississippi officially no longer existed.[28]

One of the first Union officers to realize that the last major Confederate surrender was imminent was Gen. Francis Jay Herron, who entertained two of the three Confederate surrender negotiation parties at his headquarters in Baton Rouge before sending them on to negotiate with General Canby in New Orleans. General Herron played a central role in the story behind the Juneteenth Order.[29] Born in Pittsburg, Pennsylvania, in 1837, Herron was a junior banker in a family-owned Iowa bank before the war. Sporting a set of huge, bushy sideburns to make himself look slightly older, Herron offered his militia company (the "Governor's Grays") for federal service in January 1861, making the unit one of the first to volunteer for service in the coming war.[30]

Because of his youth and lack of formal training as a soldier, Herron started the war as a captain in the First Iowa regiment. From that humble beginning, Herron steadily and swiftly rose in rank, reaching the status of brigadier general of volunteers in July 1862 after a particularly heroic performance at the Battle of Pea Ridge. Herron's actions at that battle, where he repeatedly rallied his men to acts of daring until Herron was himself wounded and captured, later won him the Medal of Honor.[31]

Herron's reputation for leadership and personal heroism strengthened after hard-fought battles like Prairie Grove, and he eventually became the youngest major general (on either the Confederate or Union side) in March 1863. Herron provided valuable service with General Grant's army at Vicksburg, in the process becoming one of Grant's favorite officers. Since Herron never attended West Point or any other military school, this feat was particularly impressive. Few officers had earned a more productive record of combat service. An Iowa biographer in 1867

Maj. Gen. Francis J. Herron. Library of Congress, LC-DIG-cwpb-05313.

accurately stated that Herron had "a military career of remarkable activity and full of heroic incident, developing a character of great force, a decision prompt, a military skill that found no equal among the veteran rebel leaders pitted against him, and an energy and determined will that never surrendered to obstacles, however formidable, in the path of his military enterprises."[32]

As the war wound down in the spring of 1865, General Herron found himself in command of the Northern Division of Louisiana. His immediate superior, Gen. Nathaniel Banks, had long recognized Herron's merits as a combat commander. Herron's new job in Louisiana called for a different set of skills, however. Perhaps because of his experience before the war as a banker, Herron turned out to be an able administrator. Banks told the secretary of war that not only had Herron's commands "always been efficient and prepared for service," but that his "administration in the districts he has commanded has been efficient and satisfactory."[33]

One feature of Herron's administration in Louisiana that particularly impressed his superiors centered on his focus on preserving law and order. As captured Confederate soldiers began to receive their paroles and return home, an increase in crimes associated with roving bands of outlaws arose throughout the area. General Herron, determined to stop this lawlessness, issued an order declaring that "in future any armed bands found prowling through the country for the purpose of plunder and robbery, will be held as outlaws and guerillas, and will be dealt with in the most summary manner. They are entitled to no mercy and need expect none."[34]

Herron's next assignment tested his reputation as a tough and efficient administrator. As soon as the military convention surrendering the Army of the Trans-Mississippi was signed in New Orleans, Herron received orders directing him to take 4,000 men and proceed to his new headquarters at Shreveport to gain control of West Louisiana and the area drained by the Red River. Herron knew from his conversations with surrendering Confederate officers that his command at Shreveport would be a challenging assignment. The more he learned about the situation at Shreveport, the worse the job sounded. Herron tried politely to decline the transfer but was told no other officer possessed the skills necessary to complete the task. Reluctantly, Herron began preparations to move his headquarters to Shreveport.[35]

General Herron's reluctance to take the position in Shreveport was understandable. The first concern Herron faced was the flooding of the Red River. A Union officer at Alexandria reported that the levees had broken, leaving the town and country beyond entirely flooded. His report stated: "owing to the high stage of water in Red River great numbers of the inhabitants, both white and black, have been thrown out of employment temporarily, and much destitution and suffering is likely to ensue."[36] Noting that the waters may not subside in time for the planters to bring in even a subsistence crop, the officer worried that "[i]t is hardly possible for many of these people to get along without some assistance from some source."[37] Herron worried that the only available source to help the beleaguered people was his army, but with Union supply lines already stretched to the breaking point, Herron possessed no spare resources to provide assistance to civilians.

The second issue concerning Herron was the roving gangs of disbanded Confederate soldiers in the area. As soon as General Buckner left Shreveport for New Orleans to surrender the army, the remaining Confederate forces fell into a state of complete disorganization, breaking into the army's stores of supplies and equipment and carrying away anything moveable. On his way to Shreveport, Herron arrived in the flooded City of Alexandria to find almost nothing in the way of supplies and no way to move anything that might be left. "All cavalry and artillery horses have been carried off to the country," he reported, while "everything with wheels has been sent to Texas."[38]

Herron's chief worry about his new Shreveport assignment centered on how to deal with the thousands of freed slaves in the region. He knew from previous experience that every time the Union army moved into an area previously unoccupied by Union forces, former slaves were quite naturally drawn to the army that they viewed as the source of their liberation. Earlier in May, a cavalry detachment arrived in Baton Rouge after a journey through enemy territory. "I was much annoyed," the general leading the force reported, "by negroes leaving their homes, taking animals with them, and attaching themselves to my command."[39] Once word got out that Herron and his men arrived in Shreveport, the general believed that a multitude of freed slaves would flock into the city, attaching themselves to his command and expecting rations and support. With no resources to share, Herron thought the situation perilous.[40]

All these concerns made Herron's movement up the Red River toward Shreveport cautious. He left Baton Rouge on May 31 and reached Alexandria on June 2, finding that city, as expected, flooded and devoid of provisions. As the level of the Red River started to decrease, Herron sent out an urgent call for more supplies. Before he continued up the river toward Shreveport, Herron decided to issue a few general orders that were sent ahead of him to prepare the way. Herron clearly intended to use his orders, published in the newspapers several days before he even arrived, as a way of preparing the inhabitants of Shreveport for the coming Union occupation.

Herron directed General Orders No. 20, the most important of his June 3 orders, at planters and others living within the limits of the general's new command. "There are no longer any slaves in the United States," the order stated, citing Lincoln's Emancipation Proclamation as the source of this action.[41] Noting that any attempt by the planters to evade this provision would be treated as a continuation of the rebellion and severely punished, Herron "recommended" that the freedpeople "be employed under specific contracts at reasonable wages and kindly treated."[42] Herron demanded the cooperation of the planters in negotiating fair labor contracts and said that such cooperation would assist the country to recover from "its present deplorable condition."[43]

As for the freedpeople themselves, Herron's order also set clear expectations:

> No encouragement will be given the [freedpeople] to leave their former masters, and they must learn that they cannot be supported in idleness or allowed to congregate at military posts. To be worthy of their freedom they must be industrious and honest. Their status will in no way be compromised by remaining at home and working for wages.[44]

On the day after he issued General Orders No. 20, Herron issued another order (General Orders No. 21) directed at his own soldiers. "The war is over," Herron noted, and in the future no foraging or lawless appropriation of private property would be permitted.[45] He continued, "In every way, therefore, the utmost care will be taken to teach the inhabitants that we are their friends and not their enemies, and that wherever the authority of the United States exists there is ample security for persons and property."[46]

Between potential misbehavior by his own troops, reports of roving bands of outlaws, and possible unrest among the hungry freedpeople, Herron realized his men were spread too thin. The general sent a frantic message to his superiors urgently requesting a force of cavalry. "They can do much good," he urged, "in preserving order among the negroes and putting down jayhawkers."[47]

Louisiana newspapers across the state published all of Herron's general orders. The orders were, at least publicly, well received by a population eager to put the war behind them and get on with their lives. A Shreveport newspaper observed that "the [free labor] system will operate harshly at first upon some individuals," but asserted that "when fairly tried it will be found to work well and to answer fully the purpose designed by those by whom it was established."[48]

Late on the evening of June 6, Herron finally reached Shreveport. As he had worried, the general found the city in a desperate situation. As the Confederate officers had warned, there remained little in the way of food and supplies. Herron reported to General Banks that "when it was known here that [peace] commissioners had gone to New Orleans to negotiate there was a general breaking up of the organizations, the troops scattering in every direction and carrying with them everything, public and private, they could lay hands upon."[49] Noting that the country was "badly off for supplies," Herron observed that it "would do much to restore good feeling" if supplies were expedited up the river to his new headquarters.[50]

To encourage the authorities in New Orleans to ship supplies to Shreveport, Herron offered a subtle bribe. He knew that military officials in New Orleans were under great pressure to expedite shipments of Louisiana cotton for eventual delivery to Northern textile mills. General Canby assured General Grant personally that Union commanders in the interior understood the urgency to bring in cotton for sale. Indeed, Canby issued an order on June 1 to all commanders in Texas and Louisiana stating that there must be "no military interference to [cotton's] coming out of the country."[51]

Herron reported to General Banks that an "immense amount" of cotton rested near Shreveport just "waiting to get down," and noted that good conditions for Union boats existed temporarily on the Red River because of its elevated water level.[52] In addition to cotton, Herron recounted the seizure of the official Louisiana state treasury from the site of the Confederate state offices and reported that he had in his possession one million dollars in bonds. Herron offered to send "all this property, which is exceedingly valuable" to Banks just as soon as the supply boats reached Shreveport.[53] Herron's tactics seemed to work, and shortly thereafter he received assurance that the requested supplies were on their way.[54]

As soon as Herron reached Shreveport, local planters besieged him with requests to meet and explain the new free labor system. Planters had a host of questions, and with harvest near, they wanted answers. What if the freedpeople refused to work or left the plantations and fled to the city? Was the general prepared to force them back to work? Many of the planters had been devastated financially by the war. How could they pay wages to the newly freed laborers?

Herron anticipated most of these questions. He met with the planters and assured them that he desired as much continuity in their labor supply as possible. Herron told the planters that he did not intend to get bogged down in the details of labor contracts and payment mechanisms. The Freedmen's Bureau, when the office became established, would monitor such issues. In the meantime, Herron's primary concern centered on ensuring order and making sure that crops were harvested in a timely manner. This message was exactly what the planters wanted to hear. As the local newspaper reported, "the planters left pleased with the purposes of the general to carry out a programme which will inure to the benefits of the agricultural interests of the country."[55]

Following his meeting with the planters, Herron issued General Orders No. 24 on June 11, which was in many ways an extraordinary document. Noting that "Great and sudden changes in the condition of any class of people are always productive of suffering, and the transition of the blacks from a state of slavery to freedom cannot fail to cause temporary suffering to all classes," Herron observed that this uncertain situation resulted in "the negroes leaving their homes and setting out *en masse* for the military posts, and with no definite purpose except to leave the scene of their former bondage."[56] Herron proclaimed this situation unacceptable because of two reasons: "the loss of the crops and the entire ruin of the agricultural interests in this part of the State," and the "untold suffering, starvation, and misery among the blacks themselves."[57]

Herron, like other Union military leaders, believed that the best course of action for the time being was for the former slaves to continue working quietly at the place of their former bondage. He ordered, therefore, that "all persons heretofore held as slaves remain for the present with their former masters and by their labor secure the crops of the present season."[58] The former slaves could not choose where to work but, instead, were expressly confined to the field "where they have been accustomed to work."[59] The edict stated that freedpeople could not travel by boat without a pass from their employer, and any caught wandering about the country or gathering at military posts would be arrested and punished.[60]

Herron's order also reinforced to the planters the temporary status of the arrangement and explained that to achieve a successful harvest the planters must be fair to their former slaves. The order stated: "But, while it is found necessary during the present unsettled state of the country to make these orders relative to the blacks, the planters are reminded that the matter depends largely on them, and that only by fair treatment of the hands can they hope to mature and harvest their crops and carry on their plantations."[61] If planters acted in good faith toward their former slaves, the order noted that they would be "assisted in all proper ways and will do much toward restoring quiet and confidence."[62]

General Herron demonstrated his enforcement of the policy soon thereafter. As a Shreveport newspaper reported:

> Our authorities have gone to work in real earnest in cleaning the city of its vast accumulation of filth. The work commenced on Thursday morning, by putting to work a number of idle negroes, who had left their homes in order to lounge in idleness around the city. But they found themselves greatly mistaken in their calculations, as General Herron is not the man to suffer idleness in either the whites or blacks about the place. The colored race had better learn at once that they are not to be supported in idleness: they must work, and work faithfully too, or they will be made to do it.[63]

General Herron's policy of making an example out of former slaves who left their place of enslavement apparently had its intended effect. Only a week later, the situation changed dramatically. Noting that the arrival of federal troops had resulted in the streets originally being clogged with a throng of black men "look[ing] after their rights," the local newspaper delightfully reported that after Herron's demonstration, "many of them have returned to their homes after an unsuccessful search for that commodity."[64]

General Herron knew that his solution to the labor situation in North Louisiana was temporary at best, but he hoped to keep things running well enough and long enough for the Freedmen's Bureau to arrive and take effective control of the situation. The question remained whether Herron's strategy would even last that long. William H. Clapp, Herron's adjutant, confessed to an officer in Alexandria that "The labor question is by far the most vexed one just now and will demand more patience than any other."[65] The chief objective was "to keep the negroes quiet and at work at present."[66] If they could just achieve that objective, Clapp thought, "Time will regulate the matter eventually and both employers and employed will come to know what they must do."[67]

On June 16, General Herron submitted a report to General Canby in New Orleans, explaining his actions concerning the planters and their former slaves:

> The greatest difficulty I have is with the negro population. This section of the country, not having been disturbed before, is filled with them, and within a few days after our arrival there was a combined movement of the blacks to the military posts. Prompt action was necessary, and I issued an order compelling them for the present to remain at home. This will prevent the scattering and demoralization of the hands and the ruin of the present crop. On the arrival of the agent of the Freedmen's Bureau the contracts for their wages can be fixed and other details settled. At the same time, I will look after the interests of the blacks until the agent arrives and see that they are not oppressed. Large crops of corn are in this season, and but little cotton. As a general thing the people are very poor, but I have given them to understand that they must support themselves.[68]

By this time, Gen. Philip Sheridan had arrived in New Orleans and, at General Grant's directive, had taken control of the Military Division of the Southwest. He closely monitored the situation in Shreveport and the actions that General Herron had taken to deal with the planters and their former slaves. He approved of Herron's steps in Shreveport and, even more importantly, thought that Grant would support Herron's scheme as a practical way to preserve order pending a more complete political and economic solution. Sheridan quickly concluded that Herron's approach represented a good temporary policy for other generals to follow in dealing with large populations of former slaves.[69]

As it turned out, the next Union general to face this situation would be Gordon Granger in Texas—the largest remaining Confederate territory which held the largest population of previously unliberated slaves. Neither Sheridan nor his subordinates clearly understood what Granger would face in Texas. But from all they gathered, conditions in Texas were bad and getting worse. No time could be lost in getting troops to Texas and gaining control of the chaos left by the failed rebellion.

*Chapter 16*

## PREPARING THE WAY

On November 10, 1896, John C. Walker delivered an address to the Texas Historical Society in Galveston. Much of his speech condemned the policies behind Reconstruction and is of limited historical interest today. But the opening line of that speech proved difficult to dispute. "If ever chaos reigned in any land," Walker began, "it did in Texas from May to August, 1865, following the news of Lee's surrender, which fell like a thunderbolt upon the army and the people."[1]

Unfortunately, Texas entered the last year of the Civil War under the direction of one of its least known, and probably least capable, governors. Pendleton Murrah, the last elected wartime governor of Texas, won election in 1863 after all his opponents, except three-time loser Thomas Jefferson Chambers, withdrew from the race. Murrah himself proved something of a mystery. He was an East Texas lawyer originally from the Deep South—accounts differed as to whether he was from South Carolina or Alabama—who quickly committed himself to opposing the Confederate military authorities and insisted on a very pure interpretation of the doctrine of States' Rights.[2]

Murrah wasted no time inserting himself into a series of increasingly heated power struggles with Confederate Gen. John B. Magruder involving issues such as conscription and the ability of the military to impress slaves to labor on military projects. All of these controversies weakened the Confederate war effort in Texas. They also seemed to weaken the governor's health. Murrah had long suffered from tuberculosis, and the stress of office and the complications of the disease weighed on the governor to the point that he was almost incapacitated by the beginning of 1865. Tired and ill, Murrah began privately sounding out influential Texans about the possibility of the state becoming a French protectorate if the Confederacy proved unsuccessful in achieving nationhood.[3]

Governor Murrah publicly endorsed the Confederacy and continued to deliver stirring speeches supporting the cause long after he knew that cause was lost. As late as April 27, 1865, as news of Lee's surrender circulated in Texas, Murrah encouraged Texans to "stand fast and firm in your colors and your country."[4] Urging Texans to "rise into the heroism," Murrah vowed that though the path to the war's conclusion would be "rugged and thorny," he intended to follow it with them fearlessly to the end—an end not long in coming.[5]

When General Kirby Smith convened the conference of Trans-Mississippi Confederate governors at Marshall in early May, illness prevented Murrah from attending. But Governor Murrah well understood the situation the Confederacy faced, and felt the conference would not accomplish much. For some time, Murrah had searched privately for a way to conclude the war without the end that every Texan dreaded: a devastatingly destructive invasion of Texas by massive Union armies. Murrah feared, with good reason, that Kirby Smith's pride might not allow him to surrender in time to avoid such an invasion. To prevent such an outcome, Murrah acted outside the Confederate military establishment and appointed his own peace commissioners. The governor carefully selected these representatives, men he believed were committed to a very difficult, perhaps impossible, mission.

Murrah met first with prominent Galveston attorney and Confederate Receiver William Pitt Ballinger to see how he might feel about accepting such a delicate assignment. On the morning of May 17, Murrah told Ballinger that while he publicly awaited the arrival of General Kirby Smith before deciding on his next move, he was inclined to send his own appointed commissioners to New Orleans to try and secure terms. Whether terms of peace or terms of surrender Murrah deliberately left vague, but Murrah asked Ballinger his thoughts about this course of action.[6]

Ballinger knew the governor's reference to "terms" was all window dressing and that nothing was really left to be negotiated. No Confederate army remained to oppose any federal invasion force whenever and wherever it chose to make an

William Pitt Ballinger. Courtesy of Galveston and Texas
History Center, Rosenberg Library, Galveston, Texas.

appearance on Texas shores. Ballinger said flatly that in his judgment, the Union
military would not treat with the governor nor anyone claiming political power
under the Confederate government. Ballinger felt the best course of action was for
representatives to informally assure the federals that there would be no opposition
to occupation and to seek a peaceful and orderly return to Union authority. Peace
commissioners, Ballinger said, could do nothing more than politely inquire
what "steps are necessary & facilitate reunion on acceptable terms."[7] In this way,
the Texans might soften the blow from the victorious Union military presence
in Texas. To Ballinger's surprise, Governor Murrah confirmed that privately he
agreed with this pessimistic analysis.[8]

It became clear to Ballinger that this proposed peace mission was not just a
theoretical exercise when Governor Murrah asked him to lead such a delegation.
Ballinger understood the heavy responsibility of this task and first tried to avoid
the assignment. The governor became insistent, asking Ballinger whether he
thought two representatives would be received better than one. Ballinger wrote
in his diary: "I told him I was frank in saying I did not wish to go—would much

prefer not to do so. If he should insist on it as a matter of public duty, I would then answer him—and mentioned that I thought two should go."[9]

Ballinger left his meeting with Governor Murrah with the strong impression that the governor meant to assign a very difficult, and almost impossibly delicate, mission to him and possibly other Texas leaders. Murrah spent a week choosing the commissioners to send on the peace mission to New Orleans. The governor knew that the men chosen for this task needed to satisfy two criteria: first, they needed to be experienced and credible representatives; and second, they needed to be readily available on short notice. The second qualification proved more difficult to satisfy. By summer 1865, few prominent Texas leaders resided close to the coast and were in a position to leave their homes, approach Union military forces, and travel to New Orleans to negotiate important matters.[10]

As soon as his initial meeting with Ballinger ended, Governor Murrah knew that he wanted the lawyer to serve as his primary representative. He recognized and understood Ballinger's reluctance to take the job but believed he would agree to do it as a matter of duty. Murrah settled on pioneer physician and statesman Ashbel Smith as his second representative. One of the most prominent men in Texas, Colonel Smith served as commander of what was left of the defenses of Galveston. The sixty-year-old Smith proved an obvious choice for such an assignment because he had previously served as secretary of state and diplomatic representative for Texas, in which capacity he had negotiated peace treaties with Comanches and settled difficult disputes with European powers. Smith's extensive diplomatic experience and personal credibility made him a natural choice for this assignment.[11]

On May 23, Smith received a telegram from Governor Murrah: "Will you consent to go as one of the Commissioners? Answer immediately."[12] Smith accepted the assignment despite his distrust of Murrah, whom he had once labeled a "hopeless trickster."[13] Smith left behind a rapidly deteriorating situation. On May 14, the troops in Galveston attempted a mass desertion, which was stopped at the last minute by a large force of armed and loyal Confederate troops with loaded artillery pieces positioned at the bridge leading to the mainland. Shortly thereafter, Smith commenced an orderly evacuation of the island, leaving just enough loyal troops to keep Galveston at least nominally under Confederate control.[14]

Col. Ashbel Smith (C.S.A.) by Boone Photo Co. Courtesy of Prints and Photographs Collection (di_01429), The Dolph Briscoe Center for American History, Austin, Texas.

If the situation looked bad in Galveston, the reports Smith received from Houston were even worse. On May 23, a group of soldiers broke into and sacked the stores for the ordnance, quartermaster, and medical departments. The soldiers then began stealing horses from the public stables. The commander in Houston reported to Smith that he wished "every one of our worthy soldiers was happily at home if they have a home."[15] The hopeless situation began to bring out the worst in the soldiers, leading the commander to despair. "The experience of the last few days," he wrote, "goes strongly to prove that man is not fit for self-government."[16]

After reconsidering the governor's offer, William Pitt Ballinger reluctantly agreed to Governor Murrah's request to serve as a peace commissioner. Like Ashbel Smith, Ballinger was horrified by the rapidly deteriorating situations in Houston and Galveston and knew that the war needed to be brought to a swift conclusion. Despite his protestations, Ballinger seemed the most logical choice to serve as the point man in the peace delegation. Articulate and well-connected, Ballinger had several relatives in high places. His uncle was a prominent Kentucky Unionist employed in the U.S. Department of the Treasury. His brother-in-law was Justice

Samuel F. Miller, a Lincoln appointee to the U.S. Supreme Court. Ballinger had a reputation for honesty and hard work. He also was experienced in mediation, a necessary skill during the coming negotiations.[17]

Not only did Ballinger have influential relatives and former clients in the North, he had also publicly opposed secession before the war, a fact that led one modern historian to brand him a "Reluctant Rebel." Governor Murrah probably hoped that Ballinger's reputation as a moderate might make him a more palatable choice to the Union representatives. Murrah understood the mission was a long shot, but he still held out hope that Ballinger might find some clever way to forge a peace treaty or surrender that would not further cripple the Texas economy. Like Ashbel Smith, Ballinger had encountered problems in dealing with Murrah in the past and had publicly opposed several of his policies as blatantly unlawful. Nevertheless, Ballinger came to believe that the mission was simply too important to turn down.[18]

With two men appointed to serve as peace commissioners, Murrah needed to define the role of each man. Governor Murrah chose Ballinger as his representative at the peace negotiations. His job entailed negotiating the civil and political questions that arose, and reporting to the governor on any settlement that might be possible regarding these issues. As a Confederate officer, Colonel Smith served as the military's representative at the talks. His primary responsibility involved analyzing and negotiating any issues relating to the army and its surrender. Smith would report back to General Magruder and Confederate military authorities in Texas on the outcome of the talks.[19]

With peace commissioners appointed and their roles defined, Murrah needed to get them in front of Union authorities as quickly as possible. On May 24, Murrah sent a message to the federal fleet requesting transportation to New Orleans for the peace commissioners. Capt. Benjamin Sands, commanding the Union fleet blockading Galveston, was only too eager to oblige. Smith and Ballinger boarded the USS *Antona* (a captured blockade runner converted into a Union dispatch boat), which promptly departed for New Orleans. In his enthusiasm at the prospect that an end to the war might be imminent, Captain Sands even agreed with General Magruder to an informal armistice along the Texas coast while awaiting the outcome of the peace mission.[20]

Ballinger may have been a "Reluctant Rebel" before the war, but once Texas entered the conflict, he gave his whole energy and professional talents to achieving a Confederate victory. Now that such a goal was impossible, Ballinger resolved to use his best efforts to secure the most favorable ending of the military conflict possible for Texas. Ballinger had handled difficult legal cases in the past, but none involved the high stakes that he believed faced him in New Orleans.

Col. Ashbel Smith and Ballinger had clashed in the past, and Smith would not have been Ballinger's first choice for a fellow peace commissioner. Despite these difficulties, both men endeavored to make the arrangement work. They discussed their strategy during the trip to Louisiana and found to their surprise that they quickly developed a good working relationship. Smith knew the governor had selected Ballinger as his primary representative and understood that his role was mainly to add authority and a military perspective. Despite his initial misgivings, Ballinger admitted in his diary that "I think Col. Smith and I will get along together very well. I shall defer to him as his experience & reputation render proper—He is quite as courteous & considerate toward me as I think proper."[21]

Neither Smith nor Ballinger held any illusions as to the chances of success for their stated mission. Governor Murrah and General Magruder told Texas newspapers that the commissioners were being sent to New Orleans to communicate a proposition from the state authorities that would result in a peace being "definitely concluded with the United States Government upon such terms as will insure it to be honorable and lasting."[22] Even as they conveyed confidence in the mission to the public, Murrah and Magruder knew that General Grant and the administration in Washington had clearly stated they would not negotiate any terms with Confederate officials. Grant and his superiors awaited only the surrenders of Confederate armies, and only on the same terms that Grant had extended to Lee in Virginia.[23]

In truth, the mission to New Orleans was not to negotiate terms—the two men never held any serious belief that any form of negotiated peace treaty could be signed. What Ballinger and Smith actually hoped to achieve in New Orleans was more limited, but in the end would prove equally problematic. In Ballinger's view, the goal was to convince Union authorities that Texas Confederates had given up and that the state and its inhabitants wanted to resume their peaceful status in the restored Union. "Our main and vital objects," Ballinger wrote in his diary, "are to prevent Federal troops being sent to Texas—prevent military Government—& get the peaceful solution of our condition."[24]

In between bouts of seasickness, Ballinger began rehearsing the arguments he would make in New Orleans in an attempt to keep a vast Union army from invading Texas and declaring martial law. On May 28, the steamer reached the entrance to the Mississippi River, where the ship's captain telegraphed ahead to let officials in New Orleans know that the commissioners from Texas were headed up the river. While doing this, the captain learned that Confederate Gen. Simon B. Buckner had arrived in New Orleans before them and signed terms of a Military Convention that surrendered the entire Army of the Trans-Mississippi.[25]

With the army surrendered, it became unclear what Ballinger and Smith could hope to accomplish. Their leverage to negotiate with the federal authorities no longer existed. Ballinger still thought there might be some utility in discussing the situation in Texas with Union authorities in New Orleans, as he deemed it

Maj. Gen. Edward R. S. Canby. Library of Congress, LC-B8172-6574.

important for the Union high command to realize that no military threat existed in Texas. "We must if possible prevent invasion—or sending troops there," Ballinger recorded.[26] He and Smith decided to press ahead.

Maj. Gen. Edward R. S. Canby led the federal military forces in New Orleans. Arriving in New Orleans on the morning of May 29, Ballinger sent a note to General Canby informing him of the commissioners' arrival and soliciting a meeting. Ballinger admitted that he had seen the terms of surrender printed in the newspapers but represented that he had fresh information on the situation in Texas and believed that a conference "would promote the pacification and settlement of affairs in Texas."[27]

While waiting for a reply from General Canby, the commissioners visited Confederate Gen. Simon B. Buckner at his hotel. It was Buckner, Kirby Smith's chief of staff, who had actually signed the Trans-Mississippi surrender document on May 26. Buckner explained to the Texans that he had essentially been forced into signing the document, asserting that without such a surrender, General Sheridan would have taken a force of 100,000 cavalry and "swept over Texas and desolated it."[28] The men knew this to be a serious threat, as Sheridan had done just that to the Shenandoah Valley.

The Texans did not quarrel with the decision to surrender, but Ballinger responded that the surrender document Buckner signed provided that all Confederate property must be turned over to the Union army. That was a physical impossibility in Texas, Ballinger and Smith noted, as the Confederate army had already disbanded and looted the public property. Canby needed to be told about this state of affairs as soon as possible, the commissioners argued, to avoid any potential claim that the Texans acted in bad faith or deliberately failed to fulfill the terms of the surrender. Buckner assured the commissioners that Canby understood the situation. Canby was a strict and rigid soldier, Buckner observed, but he was "a perfectly just & sincere man & his feelings were [as] kindly towards the South as was consistent with his duties."[29]

Canby soon responded with a note agreeing to see the Texas commissioners later that evening. The general made it clear, however, that his authority was limited purely to determining military questions. He wanted Ballinger and Smith to understand in advance that he possessed no authority to entertain any "questions of a civil or political character."[30] The cautious tone of Canby's note confirmed Buckner's assessment of Canby's careful and precise demeanor. Buckner continued to insist that Canby was a decent man, however, and even offered to accompany them to the meeting that evening to provide a formal introduction.[31]

While preparing for the meeting with Canby, Ballinger learned that Judge John Hancock, a prominent Texas Unionist, was staying in a nearby hotel. Ballinger knew Hancock well from Texas legal circles and decided to pay the judge a visit and test out the arguments he planned to use on Canby. Although Hancock received Ballinger very cordially, the judge was not very encouraging on Ballinger's main goals. He predicted that the commissioners could not prevent the military occupation of Texas. In fact, Hancock hoped for their failure on this point. In Hancock's opinion, "troops unavoidably will be sent to Texas, & ought to be sent."[32] The judge believed that a short period of military government was needed as the state transitioned from rebellion to restored statehood. "He doesn't think the troops should be kept there long," Ballinger recorded, "but that at first they will be essential."[33]

During his meeting with Hancock, Ballinger became even more convinced of the inevitability of a military occupation of Texas, but believed that a secondary objective for the meeting with Canby might provide more chance for success. If Union troops occupied Texas, Ballinger noted to Hancock, experience in other states suggested that the freed slaves would likely leave their fields, resulting in ruined crops and a devastated economy. Ballinger argued that the military needed to keep this from happening. Hancock seemed much more receptive to this argument and said he planned to meet with General Canby himself to seek an order keeping the freedpeople at work on the plantations until "their status and regulation should be defined & fully provided for."[34] On this point, the Texas peace commissioners and the Texas Unionist completely agreed.

Hancock seemed so supportive of controlling the freed slaves in Texas that Ballinger decided to bring the judge along to their meeting with General Canby that evening. When they arrived at Canby's residence, the Texans found the general to be just as Buckner described him: tall, quiet, and plain-spoken. Ballinger started out the meeting by saying how glad the Texans were to have Canby in charge of their future, and they firmly believed they could not be in

Judge John Hancock of Texas. Library of Congress, LC-DIG-cwpbh-00643.

more "honorable hands."[35] Ballinger went so far as to say that Texans admired Canby more than any other federal general. This praise proved embarrassing when Canby politely interrupted the lawyer to inform the group that they were flattering the wrong man. General Sheridan had recently been assigned the territory west of the Mississippi. If they waited a few more days, Canby suggested, they could speak to Sheridan and express their concerns directly.[36]

The embarrassing revelation that Canby was not in charge of their fate caused the commissioners to change the focus of the meeting. Since General Canby had signed the Convention by which the Confederate army in Texas had surrendered, the interpretation and effect of that document still seemed to be relevant and an appropriate subject for discussion. Ballinger described in detail the chaotic situation in Texas, noting that the Confederate army had effectively disbanded and headed for home, taking with them every ounce of public property that could be consumed, sold, or carried. Many of the Confederates believed that the stolen property was due to them in lieu of delinquent army pay. Ballinger noted that most Texans took their weapons home with them, guns being an essential resource in a frontier state like Texas. The commissioners knew that the surrender documents Canby signed called for the guns and public property to be turned over to the Union forces. This, Ballinger explained, was a practical impossibility.[37]

Canby assured the commissioners that he understood the situation they described perfectly well, and that he did not think there would be any difficulty with respect to the missing military property. They encountered similar difficulties in the western part of Louisiana, and the circumstances had not posed a problem there. As a practical matter, Canby told the commissioners, "they did not enquire carefully after public property and it would not give any trouble."[38] General Buckner noted that so many Confederate troops rushed to sign paroles in Louisiana that three times the expected number had been received. Buckner lightened the tone of the meeting with his observation that the list of Louisiana soldiers who received paroles included some men reported earlier to Confederate authorities as having been killed at the Battle of Shiloh.[39]

Ballinger made the argument, as he felt duty required, that there was no need to send federal troops to Texas. But General Canby quickly rejected that suggestion, noting his firm conviction that sending troops to Texas was "unavoidable."[40] Far from being a source of stress, Canby suggested that the presence of federal troops in Louisiana had been a necessary part of the process of restoring order. The troops became a calming influence, the general observed, and inhabitants requested garrisons in places where they had not originally been stationed. Troops were coming to Texas, and nothing the commissioners could say or do was going to change that fact.[41]

The commissioners then asked General Canby for any advice, but Canby, as expected, carefully and diplomatically declined to offer any such advice. He did suggest, however, that Ballinger might eventually want to travel to Washington to make his views known there. Toward the end of the meeting one last subject arose, the subject that all participants had carefully avoided discussing. The Texans wanted to know what the army proposed to do with the freed slaves.[42]

According to Ballinger's notes, in the discussions about freed slaves that followed the words "slave" and "master" were apparently never uttered by any of the parties. Similarly, the word "emancipation" and its variants were also absent. It seemed all parties knew the controversial nature of the issue and chose to discuss the situation in ways that would not reopen old wounds or spill into the realm of politics. Thus, the issue of freed slaves exercising their freedom to leave their place of enslavement became nothing more than a "labor problem," a situation that the army needed to address as part of its core mission of preserving order.[43]

In a strategic move, Ballinger let Judge Hancock take the lead in setting forth the basic problem as the Texans, including moderate Unionists like Hancock, saw it. If Union troops entered Texas in large numbers, as Canby projected and Hancock wanted, the Texans feared that their presence would act to "turn the negroes adrift."[44] A large force of Union soldiers would inevitably act to "withdraw the negroes from their homes, break up labor, abandon crops, & gather them as dependents on the skirts of the army."[45] The result of this labor shortage would be to devastate what remained of the Texas economy, possibly leading to ruin and starvation. Something needed to be done to avert this catastrophe, and the Union army was the only party in a position to offer any kind of solution.[46]

This discussion turned out to be one of the few subjects on which General Canby took a firm position. As Ballinger later recorded in his diary:

> [General Canby] said this would be prevented. There might be commotion a little while— but they would not be permitted to follow the army or be idle. & I understood him fully to favor the policy of keeping them on the plantations. He said that in Ala[bama] he had sent officers into the interior to keep the negroes from leaving their homes.[47]

Colonel Smith was equally confident about Canby's position on the issue of "the status of the negroes."[48] As Smith later reported back to General Magruder in Houston, Canby stated that "the negroes would be advised and required to remain at home on the plantations and to work until the subject should receive its final settlement."[49] Judge Hancock agreed, recording in his diary that the only thing General Canby made any sort of commitment about was keeping the former slaves at work until things could be sorted out. Hancock denigrated Colonel Smith's contribution to the meeting, writing that the colonel talked far too much for a former diplomat.[50]

At this point, the meeting at General Canby's residence reached a cordial end. Relatively little had been accomplished other than securing the general's agreement to find some way to keep the freed slaves at work on the plantations. Ballinger wrote Canby a lengthy letter the next day on behalf of the commissioners memorializing their discussions. He repeated his arguments about the lack of any necessity for a military government, but this was primarily to serve as evidence that he and Colonel Smith had at least raised the issue, thus faithfully carrying out the instructions they had received from Governor Murrah.[51]

Ballinger knew that a copy of his letter would be forwarded to authorities in Washington. He also assumed that the missive would be delivered to General Sheridan for review as soon as he arrived to formally take command of Texas and the area west of the Mississippi. Since his letter might help set the stage for whatever Union leaders planned for Texas, Ballinger decided to carefully spell out the nature of the "immense evils" that he felt certain would result if the labor disruption issue was not handled properly:

> More cotton is planted in Texas than in all other states. The crop is now far towards maturity. Its protection involves the interests of all who remain in the state, white or black, and also the manufacturing & general interests of the country. The loss of a few weeks [of] labor or a serious lack of labor during that period will be the irreversible loss of the crop.[52]

Ballinger's letter returned to General Canby's commitment to keep the freedpeople working at their plantations. It is "the greatest importance to all," Ballinger noted, that the "negro population" be required to "remain on the plantations & farms where they and their families now are."[53] Such a measure was not controversial, the letter concluded, it was simply one of the "proper precautions to secure & continue their labor & good order as at present until the whole subject receives its adjustment."[54] With their appointed task complete, Ballinger and Smith waited to see if the Union army would honor General Canby's commitment to maintain order and keep the freedpeople at work in the Texas fields.

While white men—Confederate and Union—disguised problems surrounding emancipation as "labor issues," the actual number of former slaves affected by these discussions remained estimates at best. Texas started the Civil War with slightly less than 200,000 slaves. As the Civil War proceeded, slaveholders from other states brought their slaves into Texas to escape the threat of losing them to the liberating effects of Union armies. In February 1865, a consul in Mexico reported to Union army officials in New Orleans that "I am abundantly satisfied that the State of Texas is filled to overflowing with negroes held as slaves, who have been sent thither from the States of Louisiana, Mississippi, Georgia, South Carolina, and even Virginia, in order to place them beyond the reach of the national arms."[55]

One early study estimated the number of slaves brought into Texas during the war at 32,000. Modern studies suggest the number was probably in excess of 50,000. Confederate General Magruder estimated that the number of imported or "refugeed' slaves was around 150,000, almost a doubling of the Texas slave population during the war. The validity of Magruder's estimate has been questioned by scholars, and is almost certainly an exaggeration. Whatever the increase, the slave population in Texas had grown substantially by the summer of 1865, making the state one of the largest remaining populations of people still held in a functioning form of slavery. For purposes of comparison, approximately 65,000 slaves remained in Kentucky and sixteen people remained "apprenticed for life" in New Jersey when the Thirteenth Amendment to the U.S. Constitution was finally ratified in 1866, ending slavery as a legal matter.[56] With a slave population in Texas that probably numbered more than 250,000 in June 1865, the end of that institution was going to have a major impact on the state. Emancipation would change the entire cultural, social, and economic landscape of the region in ways that no one at the time could predict or even begin to analyze.[57]

## Chapter 17

## TEXAS

As the Texas peace commissioners waited eagerly in New Orleans for General Sheridan's arrival, they were treated to a few days of comfort in a Southern city relatively far along in the recovery process. They also noticed something not present in Texas. On the way up the Mississippi River, they noted the presence of black troops in Fort Jackson's garrison, and many black sailors worked on the ship that carried them up to the city. Once they reached the City of New Orleans, they again encountered large numbers of black troops. Ballinger and Smith were all too aware that some of these troops might be coming to Texas if General Sheridan elected to send them.

Gen. Phil Sheridan had not expected to be anywhere near Texas or Louisiana in the summer of 1865. A "Grand Review" of all Union armies had been scheduled for May 23–24 in Washington, D.C., and Sheridan wanted to march in that greatest of all parades at the head of his victorious troops. But on May 17, General Grant ordered him to proceed as rapidly as possible to the Gulf of Mexico, where he would assume command of all Union forces west of the Mississippi. It was a tall and unexpected order.[1]

Sheridan immediately went to see Grant, hoping to delay his departure for the South until after the Grand Review, but Grant was adamant. Sheridan must leave immediately to get to his new command. At the time of Sheridan's meeting with Grant, Kirby Smith had not yet surrendered the Army of the Trans-Mississippi,

Maj. Gen. Philip H. Sheridan (left) and his staff (1865).
Library of Congress, LC-DIG-cwpbh-03133.

and Grant was deeply suspicious of the Confederate general's motives and actions. Grant believed that the Confederates might make one last desperate attempt to hold out against federal authority, using Texas as the base of their operations.

When Grant met with Sheridan, he told him of an even more significant motive behind his assignment to Texas, one carefully omitted from the general's formal written orders. Sheridan's true mission was no mere administrative assignment, Grant revealed, but more along the lines of a covert operation. Grant confided to Sheridan that he had received credible evidence of a growing threat along the Texas border that extended far beyond the dying Confederacy. It was this threat that Sheridan was being sent to evaluate and counter.[2]

During the course of the American Civil War, the French empire of Napoleon III skillfully used a debt position to maneuver its way into Mexican affairs, bringing Austrian Archduke Maximilian to the throne of Mexico as its purported "Emperor" in June 1864. Grant informed Sheridan that he viewed French interference in Mexican affairs "as a part of the rebellion itself, because of the encouragement that [French] invasion had received from the Confederacy, and that our success in putting down secession would never be complete till the French and Austrian invaders were compelled to quit the territory of our sister republic."[3] Secretary of State Seward opposed using U.S troops in any way that might provoke the French, which explained why Grant sent Sheridan to Texas with secret orders to get prepared to launch a possible invasion.[4]

Grant's suspicions about the Confederacy and Mexico proved valid, as Kirby Smith's secret correspondence with French and Mexican officials substantiated, but Grant's written orders to Sheridan could not mention these concerns. Instead, Grant instructed Sheridan that his duty was to "restore Texas and that part of the Louisiana held by the enemy to the Union in the shortest practicable time, in a way most effectual for securing permanent peace."[5] Grant could not tell Sheridan in writing to prepare to invade Mexico, but he did instruct him to place a strong force on the Rio Grande "in case of an active campaign (a hostile one)."[6] An outsider might view Sheridan's order as nothing more than routine preparation for a hostile campaign against Confederate forces in Texas. In reality, however, Grant wanted Sheridan to prepare to move against French forces across the border in Mexico if the situation warranted such an action.

By the time General Sheridan arrived in New Orleans on June 2, the Army of the Trans-Mississippi had surrendered and the threat from Kirby Smith's army had all but evaporated. But even without a Confederate army facing him, Sheridan still had two important tasks. The first task, his public assignment, involved distributing troops around Texas, installing federal authority, and preparing the state to resume its status as a peaceful member of the United States. The second task, the mission Grant privately assigned him, was to prepare for war with Mexico if that should prove necessary. Both tasks would be complicated and difficult, but Sheridan intended to do his best to satisfy both objectives.[7]

After receiving his orders from Grant, Sheridan took a steamer down the Mississippi River toward New Orleans. He arrived in Louisiana just as General Herron was heading up the Red River toward his new command in Shreveport. Sheridan met Herron's force at the mouth of the Red River and received a briefing on the situation in northwest Louisiana. Sheridan was alarmed; it seemed like everything that could go wrong in Herron's new command was in the process of doing so. Between Herron's reports about flooding, bandits, starvation, and large numbers of freedpeople flocking to the army seeking supplies, identifying the most pressing problem to address proved challenging.[8]

For the time being, Sheridan had to leave General Herron on his own to solve the problems on the Red River as best he could manage. Sheridan knew that his primary responsibility was to prepare for a Union occupation/invasion force in Texas. Indeed, Grant's orders explicitly stated that "no time should be lost" in getting a strong force to the Rio Grande.[9] Sheridan worried a great deal about what General Herron faced in northwest Louisiana, but his focus must be directed at Texas.

If the reports Herron sent from the Red River seemed alarming, the limited information Sheridan received from Texas over the past ten days appeared even worse. To begin with, quite a few Texans disagreed with the decision to surrender and openly talked about carrying on the fight in some form or fashion. Thomas North, an aptly named Northerner who found himself living in Texas at the time of the rebellion's end, observed that these people "did not accept the situation in good faith, have not yet, and never will so long as they can keep the waters muddy."[10] If not for the devastation that would have been inflicted on many innocent and well-meaning Texans, North said, "one could have desired Sherman's or Sheridan's armies to pass through the country [Texas] and give it a touch of devastation."[11]

The talk in Texas about continuing the fight was not confined solely to idle boasts and threats by civilians. During June 1865, several groups of Confederate officers, officials, and sympathizers took advantage of the chaos that surrounded the end of the war to roam across the state, moving generally toward the Mexican border with the stated intention of eventually renewing the fight. The most notable leader of these groups was Gen. Joseph Shelby, who commanded a division of Missouri Cavalry that became known as the "Iron Brigade" because of its tenacious fighting spirit.

Shelby refused to accept the surrender of the Confederate armies and, instead, delivered a series of increasingly incendiary speeches designed to keep his cavalrymen from relinquishing their arms. Inspired by Shelby, the men followed their bold commander on what became known as "Shelby's Expedition," a procession of more than five hundred men that visited various Texas towns, including San Antonio, to pick up supplies, arm themselves with a few light artillery pieces, and recruit like-minded men, before heading to the Mexican border.[12]

Near Eagle Pass, at a ford over the Rio Grande later referred to as the "Grave of the Confederacy," Shelby and his men symbolically sank their Confederate flag with stones in the muddy waters and crossed over to start a new life in Mexico. Other prominent Confederates joined Shelby south of the border, including high-ranking generals Kirby Smith, John B. Magruder, and Jubal Early. Several Confederate governors, including former Texas Gov. Edward Clark and Louisiana Gov. Henry Watkins Allen, also chose escape to Mexico instead of the uncertain fate that awaited them in the reunited United States.[13]

General Sheridan arrived in Louisiana with the intention of putting a strong federal presence on the Rio Grande, as Grant had directed, and to prepare to act against the French in Mexico. But when the general began receiving reports of multiple bands of former Confederates, like Shelby's Expedition, roving around Texas and threatening to continue the fight, he decided that a show of force at places other than the border was necessary. On June 4, Sheridan wrote to Grant's chief of staff, alerting him that nearly all of the Texas soldiers had disbanded before Kirby Smith's surrender, breaking into the magazines and supplying themselves with gunpowder. Although some Confederate soldiers returned home, others were either on their way to Mexico or considered violent, retaliatory action.[14]

Noting that "there is a very bad element in Texas," Sheridan advised Grant that a strong force be put ashore in Texas as soon as possible.[15] Sheridan told Grant that Gen. Frederick Steele, a West Point classmate of Grant's, was being sent to the Rio Grande and that a force in Mobile, Alabama, would head to Galveston as soon as transports could be arranged. "This may seem like the employment of a large force to you," Sheridan admitted, but experience taught him that when entering the heart of his enemy's country "it is always best to go strong-handed."[16]

When Sheridan pressed the quartermaster to find more shallow-draft steamers to transport occupation troops to Texas, he received a lecture about the nature of Texas maritime geography. Quartermaster Gen. Montgomery C. Meigs told

Sheridan: "There are few steamers fitted for the Texas coast in existence. Remember that ocean steamers are built on a different plan from the Western river steamers, and the Texas trade, never very large, had built up a few, and only a few, light-draft ocean steamers of special models, some of which have been destroyed during the war, and nearly all that remain have been taken into Government service."[17] No matter how bitterly Sheridan complained, the quartermaster simply could not locate additional suitable transports to charter.

Sheridan told Grant that the delay in obtaining transports for the forces he intended to send to Texas was "very bad," but admitted that the quartermaster was not entirely to blame for his failure to provide transportation for the thousands of men intended for the Texas expeditionary force.[18] The major ports along the Texas Gulf Coast, other than Galveston, were located on a series of large, relatively shallow bays. At these places, only shallow-draft vessels could make it into the ports to discharge their cargoes of men and supplies. Because of the war, and the Union blockade, very few shallow-draft steamers still operated on the Gulf Coast. There simply were not enough suitable vessels available to transport large armies and their associated supplies to Texas.[19]

As events later proved, even the relatively few ships available for troop transport were in an appalling state of disrepair. In fact, many of the chartered vessels were broken down even before their charters were approved. When Grant telegraphed complaining about the delay in getting troops to Texas, he learned from General Canby that just to transport the force he intended for the Rio Grande would absorb "everything that is seaworthy."[20] Although Grant and Sheridan were furious about the delays, they simply had to wait for the shipping situation to improve.

Union leaders hoped and expected that the surrender of the Confederate army west of the Mississippi put an end to French plans for Texas. A Union spy in Mexico, however, reported that the threat still existed. Writing from Matamoras on June 4, 1865, A. H. Cañedo warned that Mexican troops were fortifying the city and that a former rebel officer was raising a regiment of Texans for service with the French imperialists. French plans for Texas had received a "sudden shock" from the surrender, he admitted, but the plans were "by no means extinct."[21] Cañedo could not predict what would follow from current events, but from what he could see and hear "the feeling and spirit evinced by the Confederates generally and Texans in particular is most decidedly in favor of an uprising in Texas, at least assisting the Imperial [cause] against its enemies, particularly the United States."[22]

Union military leaders in New Orleans treated Cañedo's report as much more than idle gossip. General Canby furnished a copy of the report to the senior officers preparing to go to Texas, including Gordon Granger, noting that Canby hired the agent to procure information regarding "the place of landing rebels in Texas to establish in that State a definite republic under the protection of France."[23]

The reports from Mexico reinforced Grant's opinion that the real threat remaining in Texas came from across the Mexican border. While Sheridan waited for transports and further reports from the Rio Grande, he continued to receive disquieting reports about the situation at Galveston and other coastal ports far from the border. The most timely and direct reports came from the U.S. Navy, which was in direct communication with the townspeople and what remained of the Confederate military bureaucracy. Union Adm. Henry K. Thatcher notified army officials in New Orleans on June 1 that based on private information he had just received, "I infer that a mob has possession of Galveston and its defenses."[24]

Thatcher's report about Galveston was an exaggeration. While the situation remained very confused and unsettled in the city, the mayor and city officials went to great lengths to maintain order since the city's surrender. For the most part, their efforts proved successful. The end of the Galveston blockade provided a good example of their work. Capt. Benjamin Sands commanded the blockading Union fleet off Galveston when Kirby Smith signed the surrender terms on board his ship, the USS *Fort Jackson*, on June 2, 1865. Three days later, Sands personally witnessed the United States flag raised in a formal ceremony over the last major Confederate port.

As Captain Sands recorded in his memoirs, the flag raising at the Galveston Custom House on June 5 was a relatively orderly affair:

> Arriving at his office the Mayor made an address to the assembled citizens, informing them that I had come ashore to hoist the flag of the Union over the public property and expressing the hope that good order would be preserved and continued. I then spoke a

few words to them, expressing my hope and confidence that nothing would thenceforth
occur to disturb the harmonious feelings that should now prevail . . . We then proceeded
to the custom-house and there hoisted our flag, which now, at last, was flying over every
foot of our territory, this being the closing act of the great rebellion.[25]

Following the ceremony, Sands even strolled around the city without incident.

The order shown by Galveston's civilian population at the surrender ceremony may have impressed Captain Sands, but elsewhere in Texas the situation proved less orderly. When Kirby Smith signed the surrender documents on board the USS *Fort Jackson*, he frankly admitted to a Union observer that there was "complete disorganization" in his department, and that his troops had "mutinied simultaneously in all parts and plundered the Government stores, arms, ammunition, &c."[26]

Faced with reports like this, Sheridan was increasingly eager to get a large force in place on the upper coast of Texas. But the promised transport ships failed to arrive. "This delay is very annoying," Sheridan confessed to Washington officials, and issued an order to the chief quartermaster of the department directing him to "take immediate measures to secure, by seizure or otherwise, all steamers and other vessels that are suitable for the navigation of the Red River and the coast of Texas."[27]

Shortly after General Sheridan arrived in New Orleans, he and General Canby met with Ballinger and Smith, the Texas peace commissioners, who had patiently waited for such a meeting to again make their case against sending large numbers of troops to Texas. The contrast between the two Union generals could not have been greater. Canby was tall and reserved. Sheridan was short and possessed a fiery and impulsive temperament. President Lincoln once described Sheridan as "a brown chunky little chap, with a long body, short legs, not enough neck to hang him, and such long arms that if his ankles itch, he can scratch them without stooping."[28]

Ballinger noted the evident physical differences between the two Union commanders, but described Sheridan in his diary as "direct & no doubt a man of strong sense and decision."[29] He showed this last quality early in their meeting, saying that Washington had received multiple reports of "very great elements of disorder and violence in Texas," which required "the strong hand of the army for their control and rule."[30] Sheridan was not interested in hearing any talk about delaying the troops destined for Texas. If anything, he wanted to speed the deployment up. Even while the meeting progressed, a large Union force prepared to board ships headed for the Texas coast. The only thing the Texas peace commissioners accomplished in this meeting was to further convince Sheridan that the forces headed for Texas needed to be prepared to resolve the pressing labor issues that would accompany the liberation of so many slaves.[31]

On June 8, Sheridan reported to Grant that federal troops had landed at the Rio Grande and taken possession of Brownsville. As Union troops entered the city, the Confederate troops crossed the river into Mexico, where they quickly sold their artillery pieces to the French-supported imperial forces. Grant was incensed by this action and ordered Sheridan to demand the return of the artillery, which he promptly did. As far as Sheridan could determine, the situation on the border was still very much unsettled.[32]

Sheridan faced some difficult choices regarding troop deployments to Texas. He knew that Grant wanted a substantial, combat-ready force on the Rio Grande, both to keep forces of Confederates from crossing into Mexico and to prepare to battle the French if that should prove necessary. Sheridan sent a token force to occupy the area around Brownsville, but the general needed many more troops if an invasion of Mexico developed as Grant feared. In the meantime, Sheridan continued to forward troops down to the Rio Grande as fast as the transportation situation permitted.[33]

By the middle of June, Sheridan had shipped enough troops to the Rio Grande area to satisfy Grant. Sheridan turned his focus to occupying the major cities of Texas and reincorporating the state back into the Union—a tall order. The boundaries of Texas encompassed more than 260,000 square miles, with much of that land very sparsely inhabited. The general decided to send troops to the state's capital, Austin, as well as its chief commercial cities: San Antonio, Galveston, and Houston. He also employed a large force of cavalry to occupy some of the more important towns in the interior. Sheridan learned from previous experience in the war that cavalry movements through enemy country proved particularly effective at deterring resistance and exercising control of large pieces of territory.

Sheridan's preference for using cavalry in Texas seemed understandable given his previous experience as a cavalry commander. He also knew and trusted the men that he wanted to use for this operation. It was inherently difficult to move large bodies of cavalry very far by boat, however, and he already faced a shortage of transports. If Sheridan wanted the cavalry to play an important role in the Texas occupation force, many of the horsemen would have to ride from Louisiana, an enormous distance over some very bad roads, foraging as they went. To make matters worse, the lower part of Louisiana was very swampy, and the high-water situation meant the cavalry expeditions had to start farther up the Red River.[34]

Sheridan's plan for the occupation of the interior of Texas involved two forces of cavalry. One column, originally intended to include about four thousand men but ultimately expanded to more than five thousand, was to leave Shreveport, Louisiana, and travel through Marshall and Austin on their way to San Antonio. Gen. Wesley Merritt, newly appointed chief of cavalry for the Military Division of the Southwest, commanded this force. The second column, consisting of about four thousand men, was ordered to leave Alexandria, Louisiana, and head to Houston. The commander of this column was a brash, thirty-five-year-old officer, Gen. George Armstrong Custer.[35]

Sheridan later described Merritt's cavalry as the "finest which has marched during the war."[36] He also suggested that Custer's force was equally good. Both forces faced enormous challenges getting assembled at their starting places up the Red River and leaving for their objectives in Texas. Many of the cavalrymen arrived at their Red River camps dismounted, only to find no horses, nails, or horseshoes. A portion of Merritt's column started out on July 4. Custer's force was delayed four more days due to the absence of sufficient supplies in the recently flooded City of Alexandria, Louisiana.[37]

After a miserable journey through the summer heat, Merritt's column finally reached its objective at San Antonio. Even though its travel distance was shorter, Custer's column faced an even worse time, with many of the men complaining that their journey from Alexandria to Houston was the worst ordeal they suffered during the entire course of the war. Part of the reason revolved around Custer's autocratic leadership style, which manifested itself in punishments that his men considered arbitrary and excessive. Other men complained about the presence of Custer's wife Libby on the journey, as providing for Libby's support and comfort meant even more work for the hot and tired cavalrymen.

Finally, on August 25, Custer's column staggered into Hempstead, Texas, where they stopped to camp because infantry forces had already reached and occupied Houston. Many of Custer's men arrived barefooted and without supplies and rations. Some must have viewed their miserable journey as a waste of time. The last thing these troops wanted was to go on more long journeys through Texas spreading the news of emancipation. Because of the Juneteenth Order, however, they soon learned that another ordeal of long, dusty travel was one of their next assignments.[38]

## Chapter 18

# GORDON GRANGER

Gen. Gordon Granger, the general whose name is most associated in the public's mind with the subject of Juneteenth, had very little, if anything, to do with the Juneteenth Order. The order was written and promulgated by others, for reasons that had nothing to do with Granger and his command. Indeed, it seems likely that Granger's assignment in Texas resulted from an accident, which General Grant remedied by replacing Granger only a month following his famous arrival in Galveston.

That Granger's name became associated prominently with a political subject like emancipation would have surprised those who knew and worked with the general. It would have come as a particular shock to Generals Ulysses S. Grant and Philip Sheridan, each of whom knew Granger exceedingly well and were all too familiar with his limitations. Each of these officers also knew how events in wartime could be taken out of context and take on a life of their own, devoid of any connection to reality. Such proved the case with Gordon Granger and his association with the Juneteenth Order.

To understand the events of Juneteenth, and the delicate ballet that proceeded behind the scenes as Granger prepared to lead a Union occupation force to Texas, a look back to the conflicts and interactions between the key players becomes necessary. Three men, Granger, Grant, and Sheridan, each had much to do with the outcome of the war. They also shared many personal characteristics that alternately helped and hindered their interactions with each other. Indirectly, the relationship between these three men propelled the events that led to Juneteenth.

Gordon Granger was born in upstate New York near Lake Ontario in 1821, making him almost forty years old when the war broke out. Philip Sheridan, who was born not far away in Albany, New York, was ten years younger than Granger. Sheridan's family moved to Ohio when he was very young. Ulysses Grant, who was about six months younger than Granger, was born in Ohio.

All three men attended the military academy at West Point, where none achieved particularly impressive academic records. Grant graduated twenty-one out of thirty-nine in the class of 1843. Although older than Grant, Granger got a later start, graduating worst of the three future generals with a rank of thirty-five out of forty-one in the class of 1845. Sheridan, both because he was the youngest of the three and because he forfeited a year for assaulting a classmate, graduated in 1853, where he ranked thirty-fourth in a class of forty-nine. Granger's principal biographer speculated that Grant's dislike of Granger may have originated when they were both cadets at West Point. Interestingly, future Confederate Gen.

Maj. Gen. Gordon Granger. Library of Congress, LC-DIG-cwpb-05695.

Edmund Kirby Smith, who surrendered Texas to the Union in 1865, was also at West Point in the class of 1845, where he graduated ten places above Gordon Granger.[1]

Grant, Granger, and Sheridan all possessed strong and occasionally caustic personalities. It was not pleasant to be around any of these three generals when angered, but Granger and Sheridan were particularly subject to mood swings and volcanic displays of temper. The boldness and courage that made them effective as battlefield generals sometimes caused them problems in dealings with subordinates and, in Granger's case, even his superiors.

Although all three men had their eccentricities, Granger exhibited extremely unusual professional and personal behavior, even by the standards of army officers of his day. At a memorial for Granger, for example, Gen. David Stanley quoted an unnamed "brother officer" as saying that Granger was "of rather unshapely figure, and a little uncouth in his manner."[2] He went on to note that "while [Granger] was considered at times to be an 'Odd Dick,' he was of the stuff that real soldiers are made of."[3] If Granger's friends and fellow officers expressed this sentiment about him at his memorial, it must be wondered what his enemies would have said.

Even those who liked Granger, and there were some, admitted that he possessed no tact or subtlety at all. One observer noted that "Granger was almost gruff, not only in his criticisms, but in his language, and never disliked a man without showing it."[4] This frequently got him into trouble. On one occasion, he met a young woman whose uncle was Confederate Gen. Gideon Pillow. Granger told the young lady that he thought poorly of her uncle. When she castigated him for expressing this uncharitable opinion, Granger impolitely said that "I knew Gid Pillow in Mexico, and he was always an old fool."[5] With this example in mind, Granger's repeatedly unsuccessful attempts to secure a wife are unsurprising, though he did marry after the war at the relatively advanced age (for the time) of forty-seven.[6]

Granger's uncomfortable social interactions were not limited to members of the opposite sex. On one occasion, Granger watched over Gen. William S. Rosecrans' shoulder as he wrote an order to Gen. George H. Thomas. As the general wrote an elaborate order telling Thomas what to do and in what order, Granger interrupted his superior, telling him: "Oh that's all nonsense, general! Send Thomas an order to retire. He knows what he's about as well as you do."[7]

Granger had an unfortunate habit of telling his commander something he genuinely needed to hear, but in a deeply offensive manner. While Granger was usually right in these situations, his demeanor did not improve his relations with his peers. On one occasion, he told Gen. John Pope, who was one of his mentors and main supporters in the army, to watch closely as his troops drilled. When the general requested a reason for the requested observation, Granger replied: "You damned fool. You never saw a better-looking regiment nor a better drilled regiment in your life!"[8]

Even Pope, who both liked and admired Granger as a soldier, later said that "a coarser-grained man, both in looks and in manners, I never saw."[9] No matter how hard he tried, Granger's face seemed to always have an insolent and mocking expression on it. Soldiers who served with Granger came to respect him, but they seldom seemed to like him as a person. "The trouble with him," Pope wrote in his memoirs, was that Granger "could not help severely criticizing, indeed abusing, those to whom he professed friendship and to whom he really seemed attached. His tongue wagged at both ends and from both issued little except vitriol."[10]

For all his many personal idiosyncrasies, Granger became an extraordinary battlefield leader, cool under fire and possessing an indomitable courage. He proved his leadership qualities immediately after his graduation from West Point when America went to war with Mexico. Like Grant, Granger saw a great deal of action in the Mexican War, receiving two citations for gallantry and a promotion in rank.[11]

Unlike Grant and Granger, Sheridan graduated from West Point after the Mexican War; the first hostile forces he encountered were bands of Indians along the Rio Grande in Texas. Like Sheridan, Granger also spent the late 1850s scouting, tracking, and fighting Indians in Texas and New Mexico. One of his friends noted that the restless and high-strung Granger was well suited for this irregular mode of military service. "To follow, to intercept, and rout this wily foe, always cunning, and, when caught, always dangerous, was a most exciting life."[12] Something about the romance and adventure of activity on the frontier appealed to Granger, who later described this period as "the happiest period of his service."[13]

The coming of the Civil War brought an enormous change in fortune for Granger, but his new opportunity proved a challenging one. The firing on Fort

Sumter found Granger on sick leave in New York. Since many higher-ranking officers defected to the Confederacy, Granger finally received the promotion that eluded him in peacetime. In June 1861, Captain Granger left for Fort Leavenworth, Kansas, where he drilled raw troops and gained a reputation as a strict disciplinarian.

Granger was never very popular with the men who served under him. One officer in an Illinois regiment commented that "General Granger was unpopular in his own command, and an unwelcome visitor at headquarters. To his subordinates he was exacting and overbearing, while to his superiors he was discourteous."[14] Another soldier believed that Granger lacked focus on the job, noting that "if [Granger] had comfortable quarters, plenty of wine, and other enjoyments, he apparently cared very little for the comfort of the men in his command."[15]

On August 10, 1861, during the Battle of Wilson's Creek, Granger finally showed his merit as a combat officer. He began the battle, the second major battle of the war, occupying merely an administrative position as a staff officer. But the killing and wounding of several senior Union officers, and the desperate nature of the battle, pressed Granger into active combat service. He proved particularly adept at positioning artillery, an aspect of the service that always fascinated him. In his battle report, Maj. Samuel Sturgis said that Granger rendered "such excellent aid in various ways" that it was impossible to list them all.[16] One minute he was sighting a battery, the next he was reconnoitering the enemy or bringing up reinforcements. Of Granger's efforts during the battle, Sturgis stated, "To whatever part of the field I might direct my attention, there would I find Captain Granger, hard at work at some important service; his energy and industry seemed inexhaustible."[17]

Wilson's Creek proved to be the opportunity Granger needed to show his military skills. A month later, he was appointed colonel of the Second Michigan Cavalry, which was then being mustered into service. Granger lost no time in drilling that unit into a well-disciplined fighting force. Granger led his Michigan cavalry and several associated units through the successful campaign that resulted in the capture of New Madrid and Island No. 10, two key Confederate positions on the Mississippi River. After Granger's success, his command expanded to include a division and on March 26, 1862, Granger rose in rank to brigadier general of volunteers.[18]

Granger certainly did not spend the first year of the war demonstrating that he was a champion of black people or their liberties. In Missouri, he held runaway slaves in captivity until they could be reclaimed by their owners. In Kentucky, he issued orders forbidding runaways from entering his lines. Both of these situations resulted from official policies of the Union army at the time, and Granger was obliged to follow them. But Granger, like many other Union officers, showed no particular sympathy with the slaves or their cause.[19]

Granger's finest day as a commander in the Civil War undoubtedly came on September 20, 1863, when he commanded a group of inexperienced troops called the "Reserve Corps" at the Battle of Chickamauga. Granger's force was not even supposed to participate in the battle. As its name suggests, the Reserve Corps was stationed behind Union lines, supporting other troops in the line of battle.

In mid-September, the Union Army of the Cumberland, to which Granger's corps was attached, advanced out of Chattanooga into the northwest part of Georgia. Making his way through difficult countryside and trying to interpret a series of confusing orders directing him to conflicting locations frustrated Granger almost to the breaking point. The general eventually positioned his corps on the road leading to the Rossville Gap, a strategically important path through the mountainous Missionary Ridge. The trek was not easy. As one of his soldiers said, Granger had been "swearing his way through the woods and over the hills during the 19th, and on the morning of the 20th his temper was not angelic."[20] Part of the reason for Granger's frustration came from his desire to participate in the coming battle. His inexperienced corps, however, was stationed well behind the Union battle lines without even a clear view of the battlefield.[21]

On the morning of September 20, Confederate forces under Gen. James Longstreet exploited a hole in the Union defenses and launched a devastating charge through a gap that threatened to collapse the entire Union line. Only one force stood between the surging Confederates and the retreating Union army. Gen. George H. Thomas pulled together a small body of troops to make a desperate stand on a piece of elevated ground near Snodgrass Hill. Thomas was running short on ammunition and men and it looked like the Confederates were about to overrun his position.

From his location behind Union lines, Granger saw a great column of dust in the distance and told a staff officer: "They are concentrating over there. That is where we ought to be."[22] At about 11:00 a.m., Granger and his aide climbed to the top of a haystack to get a better view. After ten minutes watching through his glass, Granger jumped up and declared that he had seen enough; he could no longer stand by while the battle was being lost. He reportedly avowed, "I am going to Thomas, orders or no orders."[23] When the aide protested and pointed out the obvious risk in his decision, Granger contended firmly, "Don't you see [Confederate General] Bragg is piling his whole army on Thomas? I am going to his assistance."[24] Granger lost no time in moving his men toward the sound of the battle.

Granger arrived just in time to help save the day. Discussing the situation quickly with Thomas, Granger learned that a Confederate force needed to be driven from a commanding position on a nearby ridge. "Can you do it?" Thomas inquired. "Yes," Granger replied, "My men are fresh, and they are just the fellows for that work. They are raw troops and they don't know any better than to charge up there."[25] Twenty minutes later, Granger's men made their first charge and gained their objective. Again and again they repelled Confederate attacks, at one point fixing bayonets to make up for dwindling ammunition supplies. At the end of the day, Granger and his men helped Thomas save the army. Gen. David Stanley later wrote that the timely arrival of Granger "was splendid and probably saved our army from a terrible defeat."[26]

Thomas gained notoriety as the "Rock of Chickamauga" for his brave stand at Snodgrass Hill, but Granger also received credit for his part in the drama. In their official reports several Union generals serving with Thomas stressed the critical nature of the men and ammunition that Granger brought with him to the field. Gen. Thomas J. Wood was particularly complimentary of Granger's battlefield demeanor, noting that "the gallant bearing of General Granger during the whole of this most critical part of the contest was a strong reinforcement."[27]

After Granger's death in 1876, General Wood elaborated on his comments about Granger's inspiring leadership at Chickamauga:

It was worth a thousand men in its inspiring influence. On the field of hotly-contested battle, amid the roar of artillery and the sharp rattle of musketry, in the presence of imminent danger, and in the frenzied heat of assaulting columns and charging squadrons, Granger was a true hero. Never did he appear in grander proportions than then. . . . Had Granger never rendered any other service to the nation than he did on that illustrious occasion, he would have been justly entitled to its lasting gratitude.[28]

The disaster at Chickamauga resulted in a number of important changes in the command structure of the Army of the Cumberland. Granger found himself elevated to command of the Fourth Corps, with General Sheridan serving under him as a division commander. Sheridan remained unsure of Granger. He knew that Granger helped secure his promotion to division commander and thought that the general possessed a good heart and a generous nature. But, like every officer who ever served with Granger, Sheridan soon found that Granger tended to micro-manage his subordinates and got into disputes with everyone around him. What particularly annoyed Sheridan was "Granger's freaky and spasmodic efforts to correct personally some trifling fault that ought to have been left to a regimental or company commander to remedy."[29]

If Sheridan held mixed feelings about Granger, General Grant had made up his mind on the man. For unclear reasons, Grant loathed Granger and communicated his low opinion of the general to many around him. Grant undoubtedly heard all about Granger's sharp tongue and tendency to ignore orders, a reputation that caused Sheridan to believe that Grant "did not fancy" Granger as early as 1862.[30] But after the disaster at Chickamauga, Grant came to Chattanooga determined to restore honor to the Army of the Cumberland. This transfer gave Granger the opportunity to serve directly under Grant, and would be Granger's best chance to win the general's favor. Unfortunately for Granger, proximity to Grant made him even less popular with the general and only intensified Grant's low opinion of Granger.[31]

One of the main reasons that Grant disliked Granger so strongly stemmed from an unfortunate fascination that Granger developed with firing big guns. Granger became a "loose cannon" in perhaps the most accurate meaning of that modern expression. Granger liked, to the point of fixation and distraction, positioning and firing pieces of artillery. He focused on the artillery at the Battle of Wilson's Creek and at several subsequent engagements. Granger's enthrallment with artillery eventually became something of a standing joke in the army. Granger ignored his duties as commander of the infantry to play with cannon at a nearby artillery battery. Grant observed this odd behavior firsthand when Granger moved under his command, and it irritated him.

Grant's tolerance for Granger's odd behavior reached its breaking point at Chattanooga on the afternoon of November 25, 1863. Grant and his staff were on Orchard Knob at the center of the Union line facing the Confederate position on Missionary Ridge. Grant grew impatient and decided to order an attack on the Confederate rifle pits at the base of the ridge. But Granger, whose corps would necessarily be the first to charge that key position, was not present at the conference. He was eventually located at a nearby artillery position assisting an Illinois battery to aim its guns. John Rawlins, Grant's chief staff officer, was disgusted by Granger's conduct and complained bitterly to Grant. Eventually, Grant angrily ordered Granger to leave the battery to its captain and order the men under his command to move. The situation represented, as historian Peter Cozzens observed, an "idiotic act at so critical a moment."[32] Granger never regained Grant's trust. As Cozzens noted, "Granger's star, which had soared after Chickamauga, was fast falling in the estimation of Grant."[33]

Granger's conduct during and after the Battle of Missionary Ridge intensified Grant's unfavorable opinion of him. Granger's soldiers were ordered to seize the rifle pits at the base of the ridge, but in one of the most impressive and spontaneous soldier-led movements of the war they surged up the ridge and attacked the Confederate positions at the top. Grant was shocked to see the troops rapidly moving up the hill and asked Granger if he had ordered such a movement. "No," said Granger, "they started up without orders. When those fellows get started all hell can't stop them."[34] Angered by the insolent tone of Granger's answer, Grant responded that if the charge went poorly, somebody would suffer.[35]

The "somebody," presumably General Granger, got a reprieve when the charge up Missionary Ridge resulted in one of the most successful advances of the entire war, but Granger earned no credit with Grant for the action. Grant believed that Granger mishandled the orders directing the charge and then failed to follow up the fleeing rebels. Grant later told Gen. William T. Sherman that he no longer had any confidence in Granger. Word of Grant's bad opinion of him got back to Granger. When Granger protested bitterly about his harsh treatment by Grant in Sherman's presence, Sherman got a "bad impression" from Granger's "language and manner" and began looking for an opportunity to remove him as corps commander.[36]

The final straw for Grant's relationship with Granger took place on Christmas Day 1863, when Granger telegraphed Grant that he was prepared to hold Knoxville, Tennessee, "till hell freezes over." The message not only referenced the cold temperatures but also parodied a similarly worded telegram where General Thomas vowed to hold Chattanooga at all costs. The message from Granger's headquarters ended with the word "Tight," however.[37] Many believed that the word was inserted at the end of the message by a member of Granger's staff to alert the telegraph operator that the general was inebriated and that the message should not be sent. The operator failed to appreciate the meaning of this signal, however, and unfortunately went ahead and sent the entire message including the final, incriminating, word. Needless to say, General Grant was not amused.[38]

With some urging from General Grant, Sherman relieved Granger as commander of the Fourth Army Corps on April 5, 1864. Granger took the occasion to issue a congratulatory order that praised his troops and their accomplishments: "Soldiers, farewell! The memory of our common service in the past will ever remain fresh and green, cherished by me through all the vicissitudes of life."[39]

Granger knew that his chances of getting and keeping an active command would be better outside of Grant's purview. He eventually worked his way south to New Orleans and sought a position under Gen. Edward R. S. Canby, an old friend from the Mexican War. Granger's biographer suggests that the general secured his command under Canby due in part to the lobbying efforts of future Presidents Andrew Johnson and James Garfield. Canby offered Granger command of a relatively small body of troops who would coordinate with the U.S. Navy in a joint operation aimed at entering and securing the entrance to Mobile Bay.[40]

Commanding the land forces in a campaign directed at a high-profile objective like Mobile turned into an ideal assignment for Granger. In August 1864, he landed his troops on Dauphin Island and began a bombardment of Fort Gaines, one of the large forts at the entrance to the bay. Granger could not have asked for a better assignment, as he could legitimately satisfy his craving for positioning and firing heavy guns. By the end of August, after brief siege operations, both forts at the entrance to Mobile Bay fell to Union forces. While most of Granger's performance during the Mobile Campaign proved impressive, Granger received criticism from army inspectors for his use of black engineering troops for more than their share of hard labor and construction projects, a charge which Granger immediately, but not persuasively, denied. In any case, this episode does not sound like the actions of a commander who possessed strong feelings for the rights of black men.[41]

The campaign to capture the City of Mobile itself would not be launched until spring 1865. In preparation for that campaign, the Thirteenth Corps was reorganized with Granger as its commander—a controversial appointment. General Grant eventually learned of Granger's assignment and expressed the opinion that Canby had made a terrible mistake. "Tell Canby not to give Granger any large command," Grant warned General Halleck, "for if he does he is certain to fail."[42] When Grant learned that Canby had ignored his warning and appointed Granger to command the Thirteenth Corps, Grant was furious. He said, "I despair of any good service being done" and started looking for an opportunity to replace both Canby and Granger.[43]

After a vigorous campaign in which Granger played a significant role, the City of Mobile surrendered on April 12, 1865, three days following Lee's surrender at Appomattox. General Canby had previously been directed to prepare for an expedition to Texas but lacked the resources to fulfill that order. With Granger and his Thirteenth Corps free after the capture of Mobile, they became obvious candidates for such an expedition.

While awaiting his move to Texas, Granger interacted with the civilian population around Mobile. He became convinced that many of the inhabitants were ready to switch allegiance to the Union, and that the best way to promote that loyalty was to recognize the Alabama state legislature and allow them to rejoin the Union. This belief ran contrary to the course of action recommended by some prominent Alabama Unionists, who urged caution in dealing with existing institutions and citizens who claimed to have changed sides after the fall of Mobile. On May 29, 1865, Granger forwarded a petition by Mobile citizens of "standing and influence" directly to President Andrew Johnson with his personal approval.[44] Several in Washington viewed this action as evidence that Granger consorted with the Alabama slaveholders, a view that won him no friends among the more radical elements of the administration. It is unclear to what extent General Grant was aware of this correspondence, but Granger's direct communication with the president on a political matter would not have been viewed favorably by Grant.[45]

As discussed previously, General Grant's main concern with Texas was posting a strong Union presence on the Rio Grande to keep the French-led factions in Mexico from invading the Lone Star State. He also wanted to position American forces for a potential invasion of Mexico, should such a move prove necessary. Commanding Union troops on the border required a man with both good judgment and diplomatic skills. Above all, Grant needed someone on the Rio Grande he could trust—that man was certainly not Gordon Granger.

By this point, Grant lost trust in Canby's ability to appoint the right commanders for such a sensitive operation. He undoubtedly feared that, left without other orders, Canby might send Granger to the Rio Grande. Grant sent Canby orders directing him to send Frederick Steele (a West Point classmate and Grant's friend) to the Rio Grande with a force of 6,000 men. Grant pointedly made no reference to Granger's role in the coming Texas campaign, almost as if Granger no longer existed.[46]

General Sheridan arrived in New Orleans to find plans well under way to send General Granger and his Thirteenth Corps from Mobile to Texas as soon as suitable transportation could be arranged. This put Sheridan in an awkward position. He knew that Grant hated Granger and opposed giving him any important command. But Granger, as senior ranking general in the force to be sent, had been promised command in Texas by General Canby in May. It would not look good for Sheridan to remove Granger from command after the successful way he had handled his troops during the capture of Mobile. Sheridan also held a certain personal fondness for Granger and recalled that Granger had put in a good word for him earlier in the war. All in all, Sheridan decided that unless directly ordered by Grant not to do so, he would allow Granger to proceed to Texas in at least nominal command of the Union occupation force.

On June 2, 1865, the same day that Sheridan met with the Texas peace commissioners in New Orleans, he notified Grant's headquarters (but not Grant himself) that he intended to allow Granger to proceed to Galveston with 6,000 men as soon as transportation arrived. Sheridan assured Grant's chief of staff that the situation in Texas seemed to have quieted down a bit and that "the indications are that most of the Texas troops have disbanded and gone home."[47] Still worried about the situation on the Rio Grande, Sheridan advised Grant that a "strong force" was needed in Texas, but made it clear that the most important part of that force would be along the Mexican border under General Steele's direct command.[48]

By this point, Grant was intensely focused on the Rio Grande, where Sheridan himself was headed. On June 10, Grant sent a dispatch to Sheridan asking if the rebels had moved their artillery across the river to Matamoras after the surrender. If so, he wanted Sheridan to demand its immediate return. Granger was furnished copies of all the correspondence involving the Rio Grande for his information, but, as Grant had all but demanded, Granger was to play no direct role in the events in South Texas.[49]

As the day approached for Granger and his troops to head to Galveston, Sheridan kept Granger informed of the reports he had received about the situation on the island. Sheridan cautioned Granger again about the conditions he might face in Galveston. "There is not a very wholesome state of affairs in Texas," he observed, adding "The Governor, all the soldiers, and the people generally are disposed to be ugly, and the sooner Galveston can be occupied the better."[50] As it turned out, the Texas governor was not disposed to be "ugly" much longer. Two days after Sheridan wrote these words to Granger, a very sick Gov. Pendleton Murrah vacated his office and joined renegade Joseph Shelby on the journey to Mexico, where Murrah died less than two months later.[51]

On June 13, 1865, Sheridan submitted a report to General Grant advising him of the status of his forces on the way to Texas: General Merritt's force of 4,000 cavalry was riding from Shreveport to San Antonio; General Custer's force of 4,000 cavalry was riding from the area around Alexandria, Louisiana, to Houston; General Granger's division, expected eventually to number about 7,000 men (including those already on the Rio Grande), was heading for Texas within a few days; and the 16,000 men of Gen. Godfrey Weitzel's Twenty-Fifth Corps (largely black troops) were heading for Indianola, Corpus Christi, and Brownsville. Sheridan described this force as a "grand aggregate of 32,000 men" and advised against sending any more soldiers until the situation with Mexico and the French imperialist forces was clarified.[52]

Sheridan knew of Granger's imminent departure for Galveston in the next few days. He knew that the situation in Galveston was chaotic and feared that the unpredictable Granger might say or do something to embarrass him and bring down Grant's wrath on the whole Texas expedition. Sheridan was particularly concerned that Granger might be inundated with freed slaves as General Herron experienced at Shreveport. Indeed, the Texas peace commissioners had already warned him of such a possibility. Sheridan became convinced that Granger should be prepared for this eventuality and prompted Granger to draft a public announcement to be shared on his arrival. The proposed announcement was designed to reinforce the army's position on freedpeople seeking succor from Union forces. The language in this announcement was too important to leave to chance or the whims of General Granger. To ensure the proper statement would be issued on the subject, Sheridan referred to his copies of the orders issued by Generals Herron and Schofield and developed some specific language for Granger to use.

Accordingly, on June 13—the same date that he made his status report to General Grant—Sheridan sent Granger some very specific instructions:

> On your arrival at Galveston assume command of all troops in the State of Texas; carry out the conditions of the surrender of General Kirby Smith to Major-General Canby; *notify the people of Texas that in accordance with the existing proclamation from the Executive of the United States 'all slaves are free;'* advise all such freedmen that they must remain at home; that they will not be allowed to collect at military posts, and will not be supported in idleness. Notify the people of Texas that all acts of the Governor and Legislature of Texas since the ordinance of secession are illegitimate. Take such steps as in your judgment are most conducive to the restoration of law and order and the return of the State to her true allegiance to the United States Government. (emphasis added)[53]

The emphasized language about the end of slavery used by Sheridan appears almost verbatim in the Juneteenth Order that Granger's staff dutifully issued on the day the general arrived in Galveston six days later.

On June 16, 1865, the first transport carrying federal troops pulled up to the dock at Galveston. The people of Galveston made a serious effort to welcome their new guests. As the boat approached the wharf, a band played "Yankee Doodle," the first time in four years that song had been played in Galveston. Waiting on the dock to greet the boat stood a crowd of three to four hundred people, all of whom were quiet and respectful as the boat approached the shore. The news media knew how to flatter these new arrivals, saying in the next day's paper that they "appeared to be an orderly, intelligent set of men."[54] In fact, the reporter said, they were a better class of troops than the reporter had ever had the good fortune to encounter.[55]

One of the first Union regiments to reach Galveston was the Eighty-Third Ohio Volunteers (nicknamed the "Greyhound Regiment"). Their initial impression of Galveston was that the city was "a decidedly hot place."[56] The officers first directed the men to erect their tents close together in the middle of the courthouse square, but friendly local residents warned them that they would all get sick if they stayed crowded together in the square, as the tents could not receive the prevailing sea breeze. The officers soon relented, and quarters were arranged in the Island City House, a large hotel with wide porches facing the gulf. With "luxurious oleanders" still growing a wealth of blossoms and "one of the finest bathing beaches that is on any coast, anywhere," the soldiers from the Eighty-Third Ohio believed that "taking it on the whole, we were very well cared for in this tropical land."[57]

Three days after the soldiers of the Greyhound Regiment arrived, Gordon Granger finally arrived in Galveston, Texas, with his staff and portions of his Thirteenth Corps. Although no eyewitness reports of Granger's actual arrival seem to have survived, the scene that greeted him the morning of June 19, 1865, as he stepped off his vessel and entered the city must have been chaotic. Paroled Confederate prisoners (including members of Gen. John Bell Hood's Texas Brigade) had recently arrived and were preparing for the next steps of their journeys home. Galveston residents flocked back to the city, many to find their homes and businesses "pillaged and heavily devastated, and the evidence of grim war on every hand," as one history recorded.[58] With so many construction workers, unemployed workers, and former soldiers flooding the city, the crime rate soared and the same history records that "under the shadow of darkness many a damaging and damning deed was perpetrated."[59]

With the blockade ended, cotton from the state's interior flooded into Galveston by rail and boat and waited for departure through the rapidly expanding network of commercial outlets to textile mills desperate for raw materials. Not all cargo was outbound. As if by magic, Matamoros merchants appeared with merchandise that found eager Southern buyers long starved for luxury products. Activity was everywhere. The sounds of hammers and saws were heard from dawn to dusk as citizens and contractors worked to rebuild the city and its key buildings and residences. Even the Union soldiers eager to return to their homes in the North could tell that Galveston was a dynamic city in the process of resuming its place as one of the major commercial centers of the South.[60]

If all this activity were not enough, Gordon Granger got off the ship on June 19 to see many familiar Union soldiers, faces he had not expected to see. Various components of the Thirteenth and Twenty-Fifth Corps shipped out for Texas ahead of him, assigned to occupy places farther down the coast at ports like Indianola and Corpus Christi. A shortage of suitable ships and vessels that broke down *en route* resulted in all those troops being detained in Galveston until suitable replacement transportation could be arranged. In the meantime, the stranded troops added to the congestion and chaos in Galveston. Elements of the United States Colored Troops (USCT) also arrived in Galveston at the same time as General Granger, including one man in the Twenty-Ninth USCT regiment, William H. Costley, who some historians believe was the son of a slave whose freedom had been obtained by Abraham Lincoln in 1841 as part of his law practice.[61]

When General Granger disembarked, he proceeded to the first large building suitable for a headquarters and not already in use by other Union commands. That unused building turned out to be the Osterman building, which stood at the corner of 22nd and Strand. Unfortunately, the Osterman building no longer exists, having been destroyed by a storm in 1962. The site today is a parking lot, but also the location for the Texas Historical Commission's official Juneteenth historical marker. The location is also the proposed site of a large mural titled "Absolute Equality" that, when completed, will depict the dramatic events of Juneteenth.[62]

Rosanna Dyer Osterman, for whom Granger's headquarters building was named, came from a Texas pioneer family. Her brother, Leon Dyer, fought in the Texas Revolution. The Dyers were also one of the earliest Jewish families to take residence in Galveston. Born in Germany, Rosanna came to America through Baltimore at an early age. She probably arrived in Galveston in around 1839 along with her husband Joseph Osterman, an Amsterdam silversmith. Joseph bought the site of the Osterman building in 1849 and constructed a three-story building on it. By the time of the Civil War, Rosanna was a widow. She opened her house as a hospital during the Civil War, where she cared for Union and Confederate troops at various times. She felt such a sense of love for her town that she planned to leave her office building in trust to fund setting up a home for widows and orphans after her death. With the arrival of General Granger on June 19, 1865, her office building became one of the most important sites of military administration in Texas.[63]

For a famous establishment, it proved surprisingly difficult to find a high-quality photograph of the Osterman building. While the building was not unattractive, it was functional and did not have the elegant and more flamboyant

View of houses and businesses between 22nd and 23rd Streets, Galveston, Texas, c. 1865. Courtesy Galveston Photographic Subject Files: General City Views, Galveston and Texas History Center, Rosenberg Library, Galveston, Texas.

Victorian architecture that other buildings on the Strand possessed. Two vintage photographs of the building give the reader an impression of the structure and how it fit into the busy commercial environment near Galveston's wharfs and warehouses.

Granger probably chose the Osterman building for the site of his headquarters because of its proximity to the main wharf and its location on the Strand (Avenue B), Galveston's main commercial avenue. Up the Strand to the west lay Galveston's railroad station. Just down the Strand to the east stood the Hendley building, which served as the headquarters for Col. Frederick W. Moore of the Eighty-Third Ohio Regiment. Moore commanded the local troops. The Provost Marshal's office, under the command of Capt. Harry Beard of the Thirtieth Missouri Regiment, was located at the U.S. Custom House a few blocks away on Postoffice Street. The presses at the Custom House printed thousands of paroles, amnesty oaths, and oaths of allegiance.[64]

Granger had numerous documents printed and published soon after he arrived in Galveston. One of the first tasks a Civil War commander completed when setting up a new command was to issue a series of general orders establishing the details of his new command structure. Consistent with military precedent, General

Photograph taken in 1861 shows view looking west on the Strand from 20th Street, arrow depicts location of the Osterman building. Courtesy of Street Files Photograph Collection (Item FF2 #1), Galveston and Texas History Center, Rosenberg Library, Galveston, Texas.

Granger's staff released five general orders as soon as the general reached Galveston on the morning of June 19, 1865. The third of these orders was the Juneteenth Order.[65]

According to the most common manual for Union staff officers, "General orders announce whatever it may be important to make known to the whole command."[66] By contrast, a "special order" was usually directed at a single person or a smaller group of soldiers. General orders were numbered in the sequence in which they were issued, and a copy was kept as a permanent record in an indexed "General Order Book," as well as other related records and books. Staff officers commonly drafted such orders. The regulations provided that for a general order, the document "must be read and approved by the officer whose order it is, before it is issued by the staff officer."[67] With this background, the importance of having good staff officers who reliably handled most of the process of issuing orders and managing the paperwork becomes evident.[68]

Some confusion surrounds the first of Granger's orders, General Orders No. 1, since it was dated June 17, two days before Granger actually reached the city. Issuing general orders prior to reaching one's headquarters was not an unusual practice during the Civil War. General Herron did precisely the same thing before

Osterman Building (c. 1870s). Vintage Stereograph Slide, Author's Collection.

reaching Shreveport two weeks earlier. As was typical with the general orders of a commander entering a new command, Granger's first general order was little more than a statement of jurisdiction and authority, and was issued by the general himself. Citing a June 13 order issued by division headquarters in New Orleans, Granger announced formally in General Orders No. 1 that he "assumes command of all troops within the State of Texas."[69] From that point forward, all passes or permits relating to the Texas Coast required Granger's approval or that of his superiors. For all intents and purposes, Galveston had just become the administrative capital of Texas.

Each of the other four general orders issued by Granger's staff upon arrival in Galveston were dated as of the general's actual arrival date of June 19. General Orders No. 2 identified by name, function, and position each member of General Granger's staff. The order served as an office directory, designed to be posted and printed in the local newspaper. Granger's staff included officers from a wide variety of regiments, including men from Wisconsin, Michigan, New York, and Illinois. Granger's key administrative subordinate, identified first in accordance with military protocol, was Maj. Frederick W. Emery. Emery was Granger's assistant adjutant general, otherwise known as an "AAG." This title and position meant that Emery handled most of the formal paperwork, and he drafted and issued most routine orders and reports in the commanding general's name and authority. After General Orders No. 2, Emery issued the other three orders on June 19 with the designation "By order of Major-General Granger." This format aligned with generally recommended practices. It is highly likely that Major Emery composed all five of the Juneteenth orders and secured Granger's approval to issue them with little, if any, input from the general.[70]

The contents of the last two orders issued on Juneteenth set General Granger's mission and priorities. General Orders No. 4 was perhaps the most bellicose and actionable of the five orders issued on Juneteenth. It started with a proclamation that all actions of the governor and legislature of the State of Texas since the ordinance of secession were "illegitimate." General Sheridan instructed Granger to issue this proclamation, and the order used Sheridan's exact language in nullifying the rebel government's acts.

Apart from invalidating the actions of the existing Texas government, most of General Orders No. 4 demanded that Confederate officers and officials turn over all government property and apply for paroles at designated locations. This demand also originated with Sheridan, who considered it a high priority to get what remained of the official stores and supplies out of Confederate hands and into the possession and control of Union quartermasters. The Texas peace commissioners had warned Sheridan that little military property remained to be surrendered, but Sheridan insisted that whatever material was left should be gathered. Sheridan told Granger that General Grant was concerned about "extensive robberies taking place in Texas," and had urged the forces in Texas to be particularly vigilant "to prevent robbers and plunderers passing with their spoils from Texas into Mexico."[71] A good staff officer tried to protect the general he served against criticism for the orders issued in the general's name. Because Emery knew that "law and order" was important to Grant, he drafted General Orders No. 4 to document his general's compliance with this portion of Grant's instructions.[72]

Consistent with this "law and order" theme, the last paragraph of General Orders No. 4 contains language of a different tone than the language in the rest of the order. It reads as follows: "All lawless persons committing acts of violence, such as banditti, guerillas, jayhawkers, horse-thieve, &c., are hereby declared outlaws and enemies of the human race and will be dealt with accordingly."[73] Sheridan warned Granger that the people of Texas might be "ugly" and General Granger arrived in Galveston determined to get a firm grip on the situation and prevent the type of crime and civic unrest that had afflicted other Confederate cities at the end of the war. The language itself probably originated with General Herron in Louisiana, who issued a similar order in May stating that armed bands found robbing and plundering "will be held to be outlaws and guerillas, and will be dealt with in the most summary manner."[74]

General Orders No. 5, the last of the five orders issued on Juneteenth, was purely commercial in nature. The end of the war found Texas with a large quantity of cotton ready for market, but serious questions surrounded its legal ownership. Military and political authorities in Washington decided it was in the national interest to get all available cotton to market and sort out who was entitled to the proceeds later. General Grant instructed his subordinates to ship all available cotton north "as rapidly as possible."[75] For this reason, Granger's Order No. 5 directed that all available cotton be turned over to the quartermaster's department without delay so that it could be shipped to New Orleans or New York, there to be sold by U.S. purchasing agents. No cotton could be shipped from the "insurrectionary states" under other conditions.[76] Because of this policy, textile mills in the North gained preferential access to the cotton pouring out of Galveston and other former Confederate ports, with government purchasing agents able to keep a substantial portion of the proceeds for the United States Treasury. The language in General Orders No. 5 clearly tracked that of a similar order that General Herron issued in Baton Rouge in May, and demonstrated that staff officers and adjutants like Emery shared orders and other administrative resources to maintain continuity and uniformity in their official pronouncements.[77]

Before examining General Orders No. 3, the official Juneteenth Order, it is necessary to examine the background of one more, absolutely essential, player in the drama: Frederick W. Emery, the staff officer who issued the Juneteenth Order under General Granger's authority. Indeed, "F. W. Emery," as his name appears at the bottom of the order, deserves much of the credit for the language of the issued Juneteenth Order.

Emery was born in Portland, Maine, in 1836. With the passage of the Kansas-Nebraska Act in 1854, it became apparent that Kansas would eventually hold elections to determine its status as either a free or slave state. To influence that vote, a large number of New Englanders (including several families of Emerys) moved to Kansas in the 1850s, where they worked tirelessly for the cause of ending slavery. One such Emery family member was Frederick W. Emery, who moved to Palermo, Doniphan County, Kansas, and in 1858 (at the age of twenty-two) established a "Free-State" newspaper called the *Leader*. Emery was elected to the first state legislature of Kansas, where he served as chairman of the Committee on Printing because of his background as a newspaper editor.

When the Civil War broke out, Emery served with the Seventh Kansas Cavalry. Known as "Jennison's Jayhawkers," that regiment included Pvt. William F. "Buffalo Bill" Cody, a then unknown private. Company K, the company that

Carte de visite of Maj. Frederick W. Emery. Photographed by Armstead & White
in Corinth, Mississippi, during the Union occupation. Courtesy of Kansas State
Historical Society, Copy and Reuse Restrictions Apply.

Emery joined, had been established in in late 1861 by John Brown, Jr., son of the
famous martyr. As might be expected of such a company, the regimental history
states that Company K was "made up of abolitionists of the intense sort."[78] This
company famously held abolitionist meetings that closed with the invocation: "Do
you swear to avenge the death of John Brown?" followed by the chanted response
"We will, we will" and the singing of the John Brown hymn.[79]

The Seventh Kansas Cavalry regiment became a no-nonsense organization that
treated the war as an opportunity to settle old scores with their secessionist foes.
If Confederates attacked the wagons they guarded, the regiment wasted no time
in retaliating not only against the enemy forces but nearby civilian targets as well.
According to one history of this period, the Seventh Cavalry "stole livestock, freed
slaves, and generally wreaked havoc everywhere they went."[80] It may well have
been men from this unit that attacked a farm owned by President Harry Truman's

ancestor, so terrorizing the family that Truman's mother later refused to sleep in the Lincoln bedroom because it reminded her of the alleged Union atrocities.[81]

Emery proved himself to be a very capable officer with a talent for managing paperwork. He possessed an independent streak, however, that occasionally got him into trouble. As the regimental history noted, "Lieut. Fred Emery was a man of unusual ability and had a strong personality that would even override the regimental commander if his opinions went counter to the adjutant's idea of matters in question."[82] By the summer of 1863, Emery distinguished himself and was promoted to assistant adjutant general with the rank of captain.[83]

As might be expected of a newspaper editor, Emery proved adept at handling paperwork, an essential skill for an adjutant. Demonstrating these abilities, Emery moved steadily upward in rank to become the adjutant for the cavalry brigade of the Department of the Gulf. In this position he became known to Generals Phil Sheridan and Gordon Granger, each of whom for a time commanded the force of which Emery's brigade was a part. By the summer of 1865, the twenty-nine-year-old Emery had risen to the rank of major and became assistant adjutant general on the staff of Gen. Gordon Granger. This assignment proved a good fit for both men. Granger was not a capable writer and held little patience for administrative details. Emery, by contrast, handled details well and was a talented writer who knew how to work the system to the advantage of the commander he represented. Emery probably also served as a restraining influence on Granger, who possessed a well-deserved reputation as an unpredictable hothead.

In June 1865, Emery was extremely busy issuing all the orders necessary to coordinate the movement of Granger's command to Texas. In the middle of making these final preparations, Emery was handed the instructions from General Sheridan telling Granger to issue orders confirming the end of slavery as soon as he reached Texas. It was Emery's job as Granger's adjutant to take these instructions and create a general order covering the subject. Sheridan knew Emery and undoubtedly had more confidence in his ability to draft orders than he had in leaving the matter in Granger's hands. As General Sheridan probably hoped and anticipated, Major Emery served as the final draftsman of what became the Juneteenth Order. As a newspaper editor and crusader against slavery in Kansas, Emery was well versed on the subject of emancipation. He knew what General

Sheridan wanted to accomplish with such an order, and he intended to draft the order as carefully as he could to help appropriately define the nature of freedom and the army's commitment to ensure it.

The Juneteenth Order that Emery issued on Granger's behalf started out with a sentence notifying the people of Texas that in accordance with the president's Emancipation Proclamation, "all slaves are free." Although that phrase represents a fair summary of the president's action freeing slaves in some states, that language does not actually appear in Lincoln's final proclamation. To help his proclamation survive potential legal challenges, President Lincoln had been much more circumspect about the slaves he intended to free and those he intended to leave alone for the time being. The language "all slaves are free" appeared in General Sheridan's instructions to Granger, where it was misidentified as a quotation. Emery chose to copy and paste this portion of the order in accordance with General Sheridan's wishes, and the original Juneteenth Order included the language as a quotation. For unclear reasons, later published versions of the Juneteenth Order omitted the quotation marks around the "all slaves are free" language.

The next part of the Juneteenth Order presented a concise and, in some ways, elegant description of the changed relationship between master and slave brought about by emancipation: "This [freedom] involves an absolute equality of personal rights and rights of property between former masters and slaves, and the connection heretofore existing between them becomes that between employer and hired labor."[84] This phrasing did not appear in the language suggested by General Sheridan, nor did it appear in any of the other orders issued during the war by other army commanders dealing with the issues surrounding freedom. The language most likely did not originate with Gordon Granger. General Granger was not a lawyer, nor had his previous orders and correspondence shown any familiarity with philosophy or economics. Most likely, this language originated with Major Emery. In some ways, this phrasing turned out to be the most important and memorable language in the Juneteenth Order.

The final sentences in the Juneteenth Order, advising the freedpeople to "remain quietly at their present homes and work for wages" and warning them that they would not be "allowed to collect at military posts" or be "supported in idleness," came from General Sheridan's instructions to Granger. But even here, Emery exercised some editorial discretion. Sheridan's draft order said that the freedpeople should be advised simply that "they must remain at home." Emery chose to soften the language by advising them to "remain quietly at their present homes and work for wages." The portion regarding wages had not been in Sheridan's instructions to Granger, but Emery knew he could include this phrasing since it, unlike the "all slaves are free" language, had actually been present in President Lincoln's final Emancipation Proclamation.[85]

Because of Emery's changes, the Juneteenth Order as finally issued in Galveston contained a little something for everyone in the white audience. The abolitionists could point to the strong opening declaration that "all slaves are free." The former slaveholders could find comfort in the concluding portion advising the freedpeople to stay where they were and keep working. Even those seeking a middle ground could look to the language that sought to redefine the relationship between master and slave as evolving to become that "between employer and hired labor."

Since the order touched so many bases it had widespread circulation and relevance. Northern newspapers reprinted it, emphasizing the "all slaves are free" emancipation language. The *New York Times*, for example, printed the order in its entirety as part of its "interesting news from Texas" section.[86] Southern newspapers, including those in Texas, reprinted the order and noted that it showed Granger's intention to keep the former slaves working while the details of freedom and new labor relationships were sorted out. Granger's order, a Houston newspaper observed, resulted in the "changing of the negro into free labor and not free idleness."[87] Freedpeople "fleeing from the country to this city," the *Galveston News* reported with satisfaction, would not be allowed to live in idleness or become a burden to the people. Instead, it appeared that they will be "arrested as they arrived and forced to work on fortifications or be put to other labor."[88]

The wording of the Juneteenth Order proved so unobjectionable to slaveholders that they oftentimes read the piece to their former slaves. Many slaveholders used the order as a virtual emancipation script, emphasizing to the freed slaves that the army that freed them required that they remain where they were and continue to work. Thus, the Juneteenth Order became the critical "freedom paper" that many freed slaves remembered as the defining event that began their journey from slavery to freedom.

In March 2016, the author visited the National Archives and Records Administration in Washington for the purpose of locating the original hand-written version of the Juneteenth Order. The archives had been unable to locate the document after a standard research request, but the author was confident that it existed since the order was included in the published version of the *Official Records of the Union and Confederate Armies.* In fact, several copies of the order in various order books and record compilations existed. Since Granger's headquarters in Galveston functioned as the administrative center for the entire state, when his office issued a general order, the original remained preserved in the primary records (an order book or books) and copies were sent to all of the major command centers in the field. Copies were also sent to Washington and to General Sheridan, who commanded the Military Division of the Southwest (the department that

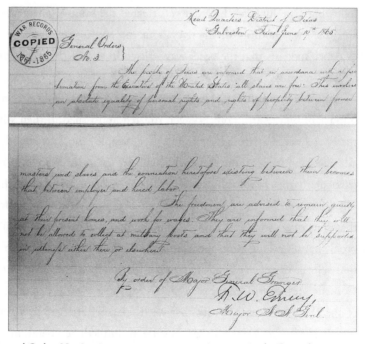

General Orders No. 3 as it appears on two successive pages in the General Orders Book, RG 393, Part II, Entry 5543, District of Texas, General Orders Issued. National Archives and Records Administration, National Archives Identifier: 182778372, HMS Entry Number(s): A1-2 5543.

included Texas). For this reason, the record collections in the National Archives contain multiple copies of the Juneteenth Order signed by Frederick Emery. General Granger signed the first two general orders himself, but, consistent with standard practice at other departments, Granger did not sign General Orders No. 3, the Juneteenth Order itself, nor the other orders that followed.

The record book at the National Archives titled "General Orders" contains a copy of the Juneteenth Order, clearly signed by Frederick W. Emery. As important as this order became, like other orders at the time, the Juneteenth Order did not get its own page in the order book, but simply followed the preceding order with just a small space in between and then continued to the next page when space ran out. Another record book, titled "General Orders and General Field Orders Issued," contained an identical version of the order, written in the same handwriting and signed with Emery's distinctive signature. In this version, the order was not located on two pages, but fell on a single page with portions of General Orders No. 4 following. The Juneteenth Order was treated the same as any other routine order and there was nothing distinctive about the way it was issued or preserved. No evidence suggests that the order was written in a form that facilitated a speech or a public reading.[89]

If the Juneteenth Order was not treated as particularly ground-breaking or important by the army officers who drafted and issued it, then why did it eventually resonate so strongly with the freedpeople who later heard it read? After all, the language of the Juneteenth Order contained no soaring rhetoric or particularly memorable phrases. The simple explanation is that it did not need to. The Juneteenth Order's message was one of action. The order basically reiterated that someone a long way away (President Lincoln in Washington) had issued a proclamation a long time ago (January 1, 1863) that provided in some manner that "all slaves are free." While none of that really mattered in 1863 because the Confederates controlled Texas, the freedpeople clearly heard in the language of the 1865 Juneteenth Order that we (the army) are here in Texas and you are free as of *right now*. It was that message of immediate liberation and the army's determination to enforce it that made all the difference. It was that message that made Juneteenth a day for the ages.

## *Chapter 19*

### "JUST LIKE THAT, WE WERE FREE."

Many people in Galveston received the news of General Granger's arrival with cautious optimism. They knew that his arrival meant the immediate control of all aspects of their lives by the Union military. They also knew that Granger's arrival in Mobile had probably kept that city from destruction and hoped that Union occupation of Galveston might lead to the resumption of law and order.[1]

With the arrival of General Granger's force and the issuance of the Juneteenth Order, Texas slaveholders faced a long-dreaded duty. It was time for slaves to receive notice of their actual and immediate liberation. Juneteenth celebrates the moment when enslaved people first received official notice of their actual freedom. For most of these men and women, that notice was not delivered in Galveston, Texas, nor was it received on June 19, 1865, the date of Granger's famous order. General Granger himself certainly did not deliver the news as he had relatively little to do with either the issuance or the distribution of the Juneteenth Order.

Texas slaves learned of their freedom in a wide variety of ways and from a wide variety of sources. Many heard of their freedom from their masters or overseers, who called the slaves together and made a special announcement. Other slaves learned of their freedom from Union soldiers or other officials sent by the government into the countryside for the express purpose of occupying the state and reestablishing federal authority. Some slaves never heard anything about freedom directly from masters or soldiers, but only heard the news indirectly from workers on other farms or passing travelers.

The end of slavery was an epochal event in American history and historians naturally have many questions about that event, particularly as it impacted millions of former slaves. How did slaves learn of their long-awaited freedom? How did masters or mistresses deliver the news to their slaves? How did slaveholders face the loss of what had at one time been viewed as their family's most valuable assets? How was the news of emancipation conveyed to the general public, and how did people react when they heard it? Given the length of time between 1865 and today, how did modern scholars learn about such events? After all, former masters probably had little interest in recording what might be called the "emancipation moment" for posterity, and most slaves did not write letters or keep diaries.

Most information about the coming of freedom to Texas slaves came from an extremely valuable, but also controversial, source. The "Slave Narratives," an archive consisting of thousands of interviews of former slaves, were compiled as part of a New Deal program called the Federal Writers' Project. From 1936–1938, more than 2,300 people were interviewed by writers and journalists. These interviews, in addition to some similar but smaller projects, represent the best remaining primary accounts of former slaves, and are the source to which researchers turn to learn how slaves heard and reacted to the news of emancipation.[2]

The problems surrounding the information contained in such interviews are numerous. A freed slave interviewed in the late 1930s was typically eighty years of age or older, and their experiences as children were presumably different than those of the adults. Researchers faced the challenge of determining how much a person could reasonably be expected to remember about events that happened so long ago. Even if the former slaves remembered such events, describing them fully and accurately to interviewers, people outside their friends, family, or community, seemed intimidating.

Other legitimate concerns surrounding the Slave Narratives interviews centered on the dynamic between interviewer and interviewee. Most of the interviewers were white, white-collar workers, some with little or no previous interaction with black people. Many researchers question the influence the interviewers had, both overt and inadvertent, on the former slaves. Some believed the former slaves felt pressured to tell the interviewer what the questioner wanted to hear, compromising the value of the interview. Others questioned the veracity of the transcription of the interviews since they typically came from the interviewer's handwritten notes. This procedure was the standard before the advent of modern recording equipment but was oftentimes an unreliable practice. Many of the people chosen to work for the project were not professional interviewers, but merely out-of-work writers and artisans; did they write and transcribe the interviews accurately? Scholars find this last area of particular importance since most of the interview transcripts clearly reflect an attempt by the interviewer to capture the subject's language and speaking mannerisms in what the interviewer believed was accurate "Negro dialect."

Given all the problems surrounding the Slave Narratives, historians still make extensive use of the interviews as valuable first-person accounts. When used carefully, these sources reveal much about the end of slavery. While significant questions remain about the value and accuracy of any individual slave narrative interview or any specific recollection by a particular former slave, historians understand that such limitations are true of any history based on the recollections of people who lived through important but traumatic events. Histories of emancipation simply must make careful use of the accounts in the Slave Narratives, taking them all together to form pieces of a larger picture.

For the purpose of a history of slave liberation, the nature of the event itself made the Slave Narratives particularly useful. Emancipation was a life-changing event for enslaved persons, and many interviews contain statements to the effect that the interviewee remembered the moment of freedom like it was yesterday. Just as people remember exactly where they were when they learned of some particularly important event (e.g., the bombing of Pearl Harbor, the first landing on the Moon, the terrorist attacks on 9/11), many historians believe that most of the freed slaves accurately remembered the general details of their emancipation.

The Slave Narratives create a picture of what it was like for Texas slaves to be told, both officially and unofficially, that their liberation was an accomplished fact. Many slaves knew, at least generally, about President Lincoln's emancipation efforts earlier in the war. In the spring of 1865, many slaves also knew that the South was losing the war. News of such matters travelled swiftly and effectively through informal channels. This word-of-mouth method of communication often functioned efficiently and effectively. In some parts of the Confederacy, the slaves knew about President Lincoln's emancipation proclamations well before their white slaveholders. For a slave to hear that somebody in a distant place had issued a decree freeing them was one thing; it was quite another to hear in 1865 that a large army had arrived in their midst and settled matters so that "all slaves are free." That was the central message they received from the Juneteenth Order.[3]

The process by which both black and white Texas learned of the freedom spelled out in the Juneteenth Order varied, though one persistent myth remains. Legend has long held that General Granger arrived in Galveston to take control of Texas and promptly delivered the Juneteenth Order in the form of a public speech, an assumption that gradually became an accepted part of the Juneteenth story. Sometimes this speech was claimed to have taken place from the balcony of the U.S. Custom House in Galveston; other sources suggested that the speech was delivered from a balcony at Ashton Villa (the location today of a Juneteenth Monument). An imaginative 1965 history of Texas even contained an illustration titled "Reading the Emancipation Proclamation," that depicted a Union general (surrounded by armed troops) reading a long paper from a balcony overlooking a crowd of black and white listeners. In the illustration, the Gulf of Mexico and a ship were seen only a few blocks away.[4]

The legends of a speech or reading by General Granger make for interesting historical imaginings, but seem to have no historical basis. No contemporary accounts of any such speech seem to exist. Such a pronouncement fell outside the military protocol for orders of this type, and General Granger was not given to writing or delivering public addresses. Making a speech even more unlikely, Granger knew that Grant and Sheridan watched his every movement and action, and he would not have made an effort to draw more of their attention by speaking out on a controversial subject like slavery. Instead, the Juneteenth Order was designed from its origination to be a written proclamation dispersed through an elaborate distribution network that included newspapers, messages sent by telegraph, and handbills carried by Union soldiers and cavalrymen. The Dallas Historical Society preserved one such handbill.

For the Juneteenth Order to have its intended effect, its message needed to be delivered to the freedpeople and their former owners. Relatively few slaves freed in the Trans-Mississippi region were physically present in the City of Galveston

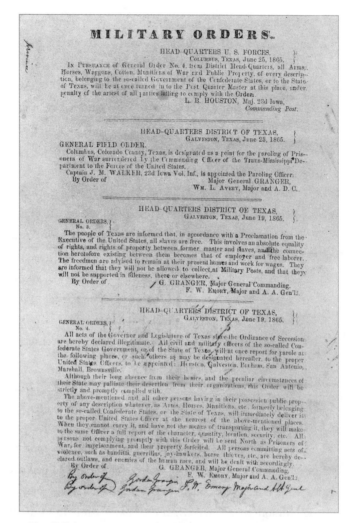

Handbill depicting Juneteenth Order and three other orders.
Courtesy Dallas Historical Society, Used by Permission.

when the Juneteenth Order was issued. In 1864, for example, only 957 slaves were reflected in the tax records for the entirety of Galveston County, less than .3% of the estimated statewide population of more than 250,000.[5] As this data confirms, announcing freedom to the slaves physically located in the City of Galveston would have made very little difference to the larger population of enslaved people spread across the state. Most of the slaves in Texas lived and worked on farms and small plantations. It took time, in some cases a lengthy period, for word of the Juneteenth Order and its liberation message to filter out from Galveston to the former masters and former slaves impacted by its issuance.

Due to the vast distances involved, slaves formally heard the news of their actual freedom in many different ways and places. The news proved electrifying, even if the hearers remained unsure of its exact meaning. As Felix Haywood, a former slave from San Antonio, recalled:

> Everybody went wild. We all felt like heroes, and nobody had made us that way but ourselves. We were free. Just like that, we were free. . . . Nobody took our homes, but right off colored folks started on the move. They seemed to want to get closer to freedom, so they knew what it was—like it was a place or city. We knew freedom was on us, but we didn't know what was to come with it. We thought we were going to get rich with the white folks. We thought we were going to be richer than the white folks, because we were stronger and knew how to work, and the whites didn't, and we didn't have to work for them anymore. But it didn't turn out that way. We soon found out that freedom could make folks proud, but it didn't make them rich.[6]

As Haywood's story emphasized, freed men and women reacted to the coming of freedom in a variety of ways. Susan Ross remembered that upon receiving news of freedom, her older brother gave a whoop, kissed his mother good-bye and told her he never expected to see her again. He ran off, jumped over a high fence, and that was the last she ever heard of him.[7] Not all of the reactions were this ecstatic. Mattie Gilmore noted that when the "paper came to make us free," nobody was quite certain how to react.[8] She continued, "Some of the slaves were laughing and some crying, and it was a funny place to be."[9]

In 1865 a Pennsylvania artist named Edmund Birckhead Bensell created an imaginative depiction of emancipation that he titled "The Day of Jubelo." In this popular image, freed slaves expressed their jubilation by dancing and drinking in their former master's plantation house while their children slid down the bannister of the main stairs.[10] This image may have reflected the way Northern abolitionists hoped Southern slaveholders suffered, and how they imagined freed

Felix Haywood, age 92, San Antonio, Texas. Federal Writer's Project, United States
Work Projects Administration Collection, Library of Congress, LC-USZ62-125235.

slaves celebrated at their former owner's expense. No evidence has been discovered, however, that anything like this depiction took place in Texas.

Many wonder why the news of emancipation was not received with the kind of joyous surprise so dramatically depicted in the "Day of Jubelo" image. While slaves undoubtedly received the news of their emancipation with joy, the news was not typically a surprise and did not generally lead to such an immediate and dramatic celebration. John Mason Brewer, a scholar famous for his research on the folklore of African Americans in Texas, believed that "as a general rule the Negro slave in Texas received the news of his freedom without very much outward demonstration."[11] Writing in 1935, Brewer expressed his belief that the news of emancipation spread quickly and widely through the informal network of the slave

The front of "The Day of Jubelo" by E. B. Bensell (1865).
Library of Congress, LC-DIG-ppmsca-10978.

community and, for this reason, the slaves were typically "not surprised when their freedom was proclaimed."[12]

Many former masters used the occasion of announcing freedom as an opportunity to try and persuade the slaves to stay on and work as employees. Sometimes such attempts proved successful, and other times they were a complete failure. James Brown recalled that his former master cried as he read the freedom "paper" and allowed his tears to fall all over the paper. Then, the tearful master offered $5.00 per month for those who would stay and bring in the crops. Many of the former slaves stayed for a while, but gradually drifted on to other, more lucrative, opportunities.[13] Isaac Martin's master said he wanted all his slaves to stay, and offered them wages of $8.00 per month. Most stayed on for at least the time it took to harvest the next crop.[14]

The number of freed slaves who stayed with their former masters and the number of others who left their former homes remains unknown. Complicating the understanding of this situation, early histories of this period tended to gloss over the evils of slavery and pretended that the relationship between master and slave had been almost consensual. Typical of this approach was John C. Walker, who told the Texas Historical Society in 1896:

> In the rural districts remote from military posts the behavior of the slaves upon acquiring their newfound liberty was better than what might have been expected. The crops for that year were growing and, in most instances, they remained with their former masters upon wages until after the harvest. Many refused to be emancipated, or, rather to leave their masters whom they regarded as their best friends. It is true that those whose idea of freedom was merely freedom from labor quit work and congregated about the small towns and villages, luxuriating in the enjoyment of undisturbed idleness, but as a rule the country negro in 1865 was industrious and peaceful.[15]

The relationship between former masters and former slaves was complicated and sometimes emotional. Walter Rimm recalled that his master cried as he read the freedom paper, saying "You is free as I is. What you gwine do?"[16] At first, Rimm's mother declared they would stay, but by the next day, she had changed her mind and the family moved away about sixty miles. Adding to this multifaceted story, eventually the family did move back to their former home and, for a period, lived rent free on the land they had formerly worked as slaves.[17]

Scholars find it difficult to generalize about the emancipation experience since every freed slave's memory of that most memorable event was unique. After analysis, however, historians concluded that the reactions of former slaves to their emancipation fell into certain broad patterns. Although some freedpeople stayed at their former master's home for many years, many left fairly soon after their emancipation. In general, older freedpeople tended to stay on at the place of their former captivity while younger people elected to leave and take their chances at

Walter Rimm, age 80, Fort Worth, Texas. Federal Writer's Project, United States
Work Projects Administration Collection, Library of Congress, LC-USZ62-125336.

starting a new life elsewhere. Understandably, former slaves tended to leave masters
regarded as cruel and threatening and to stay on and work with planters regarded
as more benevolent. For every freed slave, however, the coming of emancipation
meant change and uncertainty. One study of this experience accurately described
the season as "a time of jubilation and terror."[18]

Freedom proved traumatic for many former masters as well. At the end of the
war, most Southern planters found themselves "land poor," meaning they owned
their land, but possessed little reliable revenue or liquid assets. Compounding
their poverty, Confederate currency was worthless. All of this had a depressing
impact on the former slaveholders. John Bates said his master never called the
slaves together to tell them about freedom as others did. They finally heard the
news from people passing by and went up to the big house to ask the master about
it. Bates remembered, "He came out on the front gallery and said we were free and
turned around and went in the house without another word."[19] As the freed slaves

began to leave the farm, their former master's condition deteriorated. Ten or fifteen days later, he died. As Bates interpreted the event, "I think he just grieved himself to death, all his trouble coming on him at once."[20]

Despite the Juneteenth Order's admonition to the freedpeople to stay at their current location and continue to work for wages, many freed slaves promptly left their places of captivity to seek other opportunities. Molly Harrell, for example, recalled that most of the freed slaves around her wasted no time in getting on the road to the nearby town of Palestine. "We all walked down the road," she said, "singing and shouting to beat the band."[21]

Some former slaves found freedom confusing, as they were unfamiliar with any other way of life. Elsie Reece recalled the complete shock that accompanied her master's explanation that it was against the law for him to keep his workers on as slaves. "You should seed dem cullud folks," she explained, "dey just [in] plain shock. Dere faces long as dere arm and so pester dey don't know what to say or do."[22] Reece remembered that they fretted the whole night and approached their

Elsie Reece, age 90, Fort Worth, Texas. Federal Writer's Project, United States Work Projects Administration Collection, Library of Congress, LC-USZ62-125335.

former master the next day to ask, "When does we have to go?"[23] The master laughed and said that they could continue to stay and be paid wages or work as sharecroppers for half the crop.[24]

Elsie Reese described her master as reading the news of freedom to his slaves from the "long paper." By "long paper" Reese probably meant a newspaper. This reference to a "paper" or "long paper" was not unusual. Indeed, one of the most common descriptions of emancipation in the Slave Narratives involved a gathering of the slaves where the master, mistress, or an overseer delivered the news of liberation to the assembled people by reading it from some paper or papers. A lady in Houston named Laura Cornish, for example, described her master as reading the "freedom papers" to the assembled slaves.[25]

By the summer of 1865, the paper read to slaves was almost certainly not any version of President Lincoln's Emancipation Proclamations from 1862 or 1863. The paper that would have been in general circulation in Texas in June 1865 was General Granger's Juneteenth Order, which was widely distributed through newspapers and handbills throughout the state. As one planter described his course of action to a Houston newspaper shortly after the publication of the Juneteenth Order: "I received the orders yesterday in your paper and at noon called all my negroes up and read them [the Juneteenth Order], as well as General Herron's [order in Shreveport], and indeed all the orders on that subject, and explained, as far as I was able, the working of it."[26] Noting that he possessed no cash to pay them above the provisions he furnished them as slaves, the planter implored the newly freed people to stay and finish harvesting the crop. The planter reported that the strategy of reading and interpreting the order seemed successful, noting that all his hands elected to stay on with the exception of one "headstrong and foolishly smart" boy, who he predicted would ramble from town to town, doing nothing but "playing cards, stealing, and cutting up generally."[27]

Other newspapers soon joined in the call urging planters to read the Juneteenth Order and the associated orders to their freed slaves. As "Masters of servants," former slaveholders "have a duty to perform," one newspaper implored—a duty to read the Juneteenth Order to their former slaves and make them understand their responsibilities to remain usefully employed.[28] The orders should "be read to them by every person at all interested in their welfare."[29] By reading the orders and emphasizing the portions that advised the freedpeople to stay working at their present homes, the newspaper advised, "it is quite certain that [the freed slaves] will be kept out of mischief."[30]

The *Galveston Daily News* later claimed that "nearly every planter in the country," upon the issuance of Granger's order extending the Emancipation Proclamation to Texas, "immediately called his negroes together, read the proclamation to them and informed them that they were free and at liberty to go where they pleased."[31] This account seems an exaggeration, as numerous slaves recalled not learning of their freedom until long after the issuance of the Juneteenth Order. Many planters eventually staged such a reading, however, if only to emphasize the portion of the order that encouraged the freedpeople to stay working at their current location.[32]

Contemporary accounts confirm that many former slaves were gathered together as a group to hear the master or his overseer formally deliver the news of emancipation. *Flake's Daily Bulletin*, a Galveston newspaper noted for its pro-Union sentiments, quoted an account from Washington County recording that in the month following Juneteenth, "The order issued by General Granger on his first landing in Galveston, was generally read to the negroes."[33] Compliance with these orders by "both planter and negro," the newspaper observed, will "result favorably to both parties."[34]

It is likely that these accounts are accurate and that the Juneteenth Order was the paper that many former slaves vividly recall being read and discussed by their former masters. But using the Juneteenth Order as a script for delivering the news of freedom produced one immediate problem. Almost none of the slaves in the intended audience were literate. Indeed, most had been deliberately kept from literacy as part of their status and condition. A master reading the order almost certainly would have felt the need to interpret the language of the order as it was read, especially the second sentence of the Juneteenth Order that described freedom as involving "an absolute equality of personal rights and rights of personal property between former masters and slaves."[35] The concept of personal rights was hard to explain to enslaved people. Faced with this difficulty, many former masters paraphrased this language to something along the lines of "You are as free as I am." Thus, when researchers hear these phrases or something similar in a slave

Andrew Goodman, age 97, Dallas, Texas. Federal Writer's Project, United States Work Projects Administration Collection, Library of Congress, LC-USZ62-125225.

narrative, there remains an echo of the language that Frederick Emery inserted in the Juneteenth Order as it was read to and understood by the slave audience.

The "You are as free as I am" language appeared repeatedly in the Texas Slave Narratives. Andrew Goodman remembered his master telling his slaves, "You are just as free as I am."[36] James Brown recalled his master reading a paper and saying, "You darkies are as free as I am."[37] John James described his master as reading from the long paper and saying, "You is slaves no more. You is free, jus' like I is."[38] All these accounts seem to confirm that the Juneteenth Order was used as a script or series of talking points to communicate the message of free-dom, while emphasizing the Union army's instructions that the freed slaves should continue to stay and work under some type of employment or share-cropping arrangement.

Not all masters used the Juneteenth Order as a means to keep their former slaves working. Eli Davison said that his master always believed the South would win the war and boasted that no slave would ever be free. When freedom became an accomplished reality, the master turned his slaves loose with nothing to eat and no clothes to wear, saying "if he got up next morning, and found a nigger on his place, he'd horsewhip him."[39]

William Matthews of Galveston recalled that during the war his master transferred all his slaves to Texas to keep them out of the liberating hands of the Yankees. According to Matthews, "He say in Texas dere never be no freedom."[40] When freedom did come to Texas, the slaveholder pretended that nothing had changed. Eventually, a soldier came by and brought the news in a way that could not be ignored: "It was way after freedom dat de freedom man [the name Matthews gave the Union soldier] come and read de paper and tell us not to work no more 'less us git pay for it."[41] After the soldier left, Matthews' former mistress (Mary Adams) came out and delivered a threat that Matthews remembered with amusement the rest of his life

> When he gone, old Mary Adams come out. I 'lect what she say as if I jes' hear her say it. She say, "Ten years from today I'll have you all back 'gain." Dat ten years been over a mighty long time and she ain't git us back yit and she dead and gone.[42]

Not all freed slaves viewed Union soldiers as heaven-sent angels of liberation. Many believed their master's warnings that, as instruments of evil, Union soldiers would treat them worse than their masters. Abe Livingston received the news of freedom from about eighty laughing Union soldiers who seemed very happy that the war was finished and the fighting over. Livingston thought the soldiers "were more for eating than anything else."[43] They not only took all the horses, but absconded with forty turkeys and all the hogs and cattle. "How them Yankees could eat," Livingston remembered. "I never saw anything like it."[44]

Andrew Goodman recalled that when Union soldiers first marched by, "We were scareder of them than we were of the debil."[45] This opinion seemed confirmed when the soldiers came back, searched the stable for horses and mules, and then took whatever they wanted. Eventually, however, the soldiers spoke to the freed slaves and discussed their options. As one soldier told Goodman, "If you got a good master and want to stay, well you can do that, but now you can go where you want to, cause there ain't nobody going to stop you."[46] Some of the men on the farm with Goodman mistrusted the soldiers and went up to the big house to get their usual passes to leave. The master and mistress told them that such passes were no longer needed, saying, "All you got to do is just take your foot in your hand and go."[47] As Goodman and the other former slaves soon learned, freedom proved a great deal more challenging than his former master suggested.

Most of the slave population in Texas in 1865 centered on the former cotton plantations and farms in the rural eastern parts of the state. If the freed slaves left those areas, relatively few options remained in the immediate area. Times were hard and travel proved difficult. The more the freedpeople moved away, the more likely they were to encounter angry and violent people who resented their emancipated status. As the news of liberation filtered out from Galveston, freedpeople became aware of their actual freedom, though the reality and practical nature of that freedom still seemed uncertain.[48]

## *Chapter 20*

## PROBLEMS SURROUNDING FIRST FREEDOM

While none of the white inhabitants of Texas should have been surprised by the Juneteenth Order or its contents, many were still caught off-guard by the order. Perhaps the slaveholders were in denial, or perhaps they believed the poisonous editorials in the Texas newspapers that predicted Union soldiers could not and would not carry out the Emancipation Proclamation. Whatever the cause, the Juneteenth Order came as a tremendous shock to many Texans. After years of saying that their economy could not function without slave labor, and being conditioned to accept that belief, slaveholders had to face the reality of the end of slavery. Many white Texans saw General Granger's Juneteenth Order as the worst thing that ever happened to them. As historian Carl Moneyhon described the situation, they regarded the order as nothing less than "a virtual death sentence for the state's economy."[1]

Texas planters started the war with an estimated $400 million investment in slaves. The wealthiest 7% of Texans owned 72% of the slaves. While Texas planters ended the war with their land holdings intact, they no longer directly controlled the labor needed to work the land. The old order had been destroyed, with little certainty about what system would take its place.[2]

In an article accompanying the publication of the Juneteenth Order, a Houston newspaper observed that the order would "cause a sensation of sorrow and humiliation not to be described" for white Texans.[3] The newspaper also proclaimed that the end of slavery would "bear harder on the feelings of slave-holders in Texas than those of any other State."[4] The inhabitants of other states, the newspaper reminded its readers, had long been prepared for emancipation by large Union armies marching through their states and liberating slaves as they proceeded. But Texas, by contrast, "has never been overrun by armies."[5] Thus, the Juneteenth Order's "fiat for a new order of things finds her [Texas] with the old order of things undisturbed and operating precisely as it did before the war."[6] With the publication of the Juneteenth Order, the "old order of things" had to give way to a new way of life.

The end of slavery meant not only a new system of labor, but also a dramatic change in a wide variety of legal, economic, and social institutions. Before work in those areas began, however, Texas slaveholders faced a disagreeable task. As a Houston newspaper declared, "To wake up some morning and find it their duty to tell all their servants that they are free, that they no longer have any legal claim upon their time and labor, and to begin to make bargains with them for their hire, will be a hard, unhappy trial to the tastes and feelings of the people of Texas."[7]

As the Houston newspaper's commentary suggests, editorials in Texas newspapers still strongly influenced the "taste and feelings of the people of Texas" in 1865, and no newspaper held more influence than the *Galveston News*. Published in daily, weekly, and even tri-weekly versions, the *Galveston News* became the pulpit for its fire-breathing editor, Willard Richardson. Even though Richardson was born in Massachusetts, he spent his formative years in Alabama and South Carolina and became a strong proponent of the institution of slavery. Nicknamed "the Napoleon of the Texas Press" for his aggressive style, Richardson was an ardent supporter of secession. After the war ended, he set out to convince his readers to try to resist and even circumvent emancipation.[8]

On June 18, the day before Granger's Juneteenth arrival in Galveston, Richardson's newspaper (then being printed in Houston) published an article titled "The Negro—His Future" that referred to black people in the most bla-tantly racist language, saying that "Sambo" could not be trusted and "does not like to work—will not work if he can help it."[9] Instead, Richardson opined, the black man would "rather steal, lie and loaf for a living."[10] If slavery ended, and white men did not force black men to work, Richardson argued that they would

Willard Richardson, Editor of the *Galveston News*. Courtesy of Galveston and Texas History Center, Rosenberg Library, Galveston, Texas.

simply starve. "The extinction of slavery," Richardson concluded, "is simply the extinction of the negro race."[11]

With the arrival of large numbers of Union soldiers obligated to a policy of emancipation, the tone of the Galveston newspaper's language moderated slightly, but Richardson, like editors of many Texas newspapers, would not leave the institution of slavery behind just yet. Richardson understood that the Juneteenth Order meant an end to slavery in its current form for at least some period of time. Aware that every issue of his newspaper was read by Union army officers, Richardson stated that although the Juneteenth Order confirmed that slavery was going away in name, there remained a chance that it might be perpetuated in some other form like debt servitude or peonage. "The Northern view in favor of emancipation will soon be tested," Richardson wrote, "and there is but little reason to doubt that, whether or not slavery is perpetuated in name, there will be a return to a character of compulsory labor which will make the negro useful to society and subordinate to the white race."[12]

Richardson knew that the process to ratify the Thirteenth Amendment to the U.S. Constitution had started, but he did not see its adoption as likely. Instead, he viewed its probable rejection as an opportunity. "The amendment to the Federal Constitution abolishing slavery has not been ratified by three-fourths of the States, nor is it likely to be in the ensuing ten years. When the State governments, therefore, are reorganized, it is more than probable that slavery will be perpetuated."[13] For a time, Richardson's skepticism about the amendment's enactment seemed justified, as the ratification process slowed and former Confederate state governments struggled through the reorganization process. Other Texans shared Richardson's skeptical view, and some even continued to draft wills that "left" former slaves to designated beneficiaries in the event that slavery ever came back into existence.[14]

Richardson continued to argue that the institution of slavery, or an institution like it, needed to be retained in the long run in order to keep black workers occupied. He noted that the social and economic recovery in Texas could only take place if the state resumed growing and exporting large quantities of cotton. Cotton had become the life blood of Texas. The picking of cotton began seasonally in August and all hands were needed to perform that labor. If emancipation disrupted that sequence, and labor became unavailable to pick the cotton and transport it to market, it could be catastrophic to the business hopes and prospects of the state.

Richardson claimed in the *Galveston News* that only a black man could safely perform the grueling agricultural labor required to complete the task. August and September, Richardson warned, were the months of "dew, vapor and miasmas."[15] Only "the very fewest number of the Caucasian race can stand these two months in the cotton field without going down into the grave."[16] The black man, on the other hand, "is indigenous to the tropics," Richardson argued, and was well suited by nature and genetics to doing this work.[17] Whether Northern politicians chose to admit it or not, Richardson observed, "the South can only be cultivated successfully by those whom God, in his providence, seems to have marked out by their color to cultivate tropical soils."[18]

By modern standards, Richardson's words sound unbelievably racist and abhorrent. Richardson's views on black inferiority, however, ran similar to those of Gen. William T. Sherman, one of the principal heroes of the Union armies. Indeed, in some ways, they were not too different from those of President Abraham

Lincoln, who, even after issuing the Emancipation Proclamation, continued to favor some form of delayed compensated emancipation and supported schemes involving relocation of freed slaves to tropical countries.[19]

As Richardson wrote his newspaper columns about the desirability of finding some mechanism to keep blacks available as a class of perpetual working serfs, a different drama played out on the streets of Galveston, Houston, and other large Texas cities. Following the lead from General Herron's order in Shreveport, the Juneteenth Order strongly advised freedpeople to stay working at their location at the time of their emancipation. But the temptation to use their new-found freedom to leave the place of their former captivity proved irresistible to those who had lived in bondage for so long. First in small groups and then in floods, they poured into Galveston and other large Texas cities.

One of the first groups of black visitors to Galveston unfortunately crossed paths with the first Union officer to have a significant command in Galveston—Lt. Col. Rankin G. Laughlin of the Ninety-Fourth Illinois Infantry. Laughlin, previously assigned as Acting Inspector General on the staff of the Thirteenth Corps, was one of the highest-ranking officers on General Granger's staff. Granger appointed him Provost Marshal General for Texas on June 19, probably because Laughlin was a no-nonsense officer who had been promoted to the rank of brigadier general for gallant and meritorious conduct at Mobile.[20]

Laughlin, a physician who received his medical training at New York University, did not share Frederick Emery's generous feelings toward freed slaves. Laughlin arrived in Galveston on June 18, the day before General Granger, and wasted no time in opening his office in the U.S. Custom House, the most imposing public building in Galveston. After choosing his office, Laughlin immediately sent for Mayor Charles Henry Leonard. Laughlin was a high-ranking Mason and Mayor Leonard was the grand master of the Texas Independent Order of Odd Fellows. The two men shared similar interests and hit it off immediately. Laughlin assured Mayor Leonard that when General Granger arrived, he intended to provide the fullest protection to the people of Galveston and their property. Laughlin guaranteed the mayor, and gave the newspaper permission to print his assurance, that he would find "ample and uninterrupted employment for all vagrant or runaway negroes who should be found on the streets or elsewhere."[21] He said that "negroes fleeing from the country to this city would not be allowed to live in idleness or become a burden to the people, that they would be arrested as they arrived, and forced to work on fortifications or be put to other labor."[22]

This was welcome news to many white Galvestonians. Laughlin told Mayor Leonard to expect the federal authorities "cordially cooperating with him in suppressing such a nuisance."[23] As Leonard headed down the steps of the new Union headquarters, he came across a Union official with three black men in custody. Leonard learned that the men had come to Galveston after being freed from plantations located along the Brazos River. The mayor quickly returned to Laughlin to ask what the officer wanted done with the three men that waited below. Leonard inquired if they should be sent home or turned over to federal authorities. Laughlin responded that he would make an example of them by putting the men to work. Laughlin sent them to his quartermaster, who had no immediate work for them. The newspaper delightedly reported that Laughlin had instead "sent them to jail for safe-keeping till he should want them."[24]

Galveston Custom House (1861). Courtesy of Galveston and Texas History Center, Rosenberg Library, Galveston, Texas.

The irony of this action was undoubtedly lost on most of the involved parties. Emancipation in Texas had evolved into a very strange beast. In May 1861, Gen. Benjamin Butler made national headlines by taking three escaped slaves (whom he may or may not have termed "contrabands") into his care and refusing to return them to their owners. Butler's actions came at a time when no doubt existed about the slaves' legal status; at the time, the three men were slaves and legally belonged to their owners as a matter of then existing state and federal law. More than four years later, after a Civil War fought in part to free the slaves, Union officers in Texas thought nothing about placing three supposedly freed black men in captivity for no crime other than coming to the City of Galveston. The episode became a disturbing vision of what the future might hold for freedpeople and their relations with governmental authorities and at least some members of the military.

Other freed slaves soon joined the three men in jail, with no reason or provocation other than their failure to remain at their former place of enslavement. As the local newspaper lamented, "the people of Galveston were astonished at the number of colored individuals of all shades congregated here."[25] Former slaves wanted to exercise their newly found freedom, a course of action that many white Galvestonians found threatening and disturbing. According to the newspaper, "The good time so long promised to the darkies had in their estimation evidently come."[26] The report continued, "It appears that many persons in the country had allowed their slaves to take the emancipation ball at the first hop and meet their deliverers on the threshold."[27]

Many white citizens of Galveston became angry at some freedpeople moving to the island because it seemed the former slaves lived in better conditions than they themselves experienced. Willard Richardson wrote a blistering editorial criticizing white people who rented houses to former slaves:

> It is mortifying to find that there are so many in this city owning small houses willing to rent them to negroes regardless of all our past experience of the evil effects. The fact of the negroes being set free does not change their character or qualify them for the important duties of free citizens. It is painful and humiliating to see these darkies occupying genteel houses while many poor and respectable white people are unable to pay the rent, and are, to all appearance, in a more humble position than the negroes.[28]

As more and more black men and women poured into Galveston, Willard Richardson became more and more irate. "Everything in this city seems to be in the utmost confusion as regards the negroes. Nobody knows what to do."[29] Only the military could force the new black residents to work and Richardson believed that they lacked the willingness and resources to follow through on their promises. If city officials held any authority over the freedpeople, "nobody dares to exercise it, for fear of having negro complaints lodged against them."[30]

Delegations of concerned white citizens held a series of meetings with General Granger and Provost Marshal Laughlin to seek their aid with what they called the "negro problem." Laughlin responded by having his guards scour the streets one morning, where they rounded up "every loose negro they could lay their hands on to go to the country and cut wood, man steamboats, or assist in such labor as was necessary for the army."[31] The results of this crackdown met with the endorsement of Willard Richardson, who wrote approvingly the next day, "Yesterday afternoon you could not find a negro in Galveston who did not have, or pretend to have, some regular home and employment."[32]

Richardson believed that Laughlin's raid had, for the time being, achieved its intended effect. As far as he could tell, "our colored population have sensibly sobered down."[33] But this situation could not last. While Union leaders wanted freedpeople to stay in the fields to work, freed black people found more opportunities in larger cities like Galveston. As the number of blacks in the city again increased, the mayor publicly expressed his regrets that citizens in the town rented houses to the newcomers. These houses were allegedly used as bases by gangs to commit a wide variety of crimes and nuisances. A delegation of prominent Galveston citizens visited General Granger once again to ask for help in addressing the situation.[34]

On June 28, Provost Marshal Laughlin responded to these complaints by issuing a new order that reemphasized the provisions of the Juneteenth Order directing the freed slaves to "remain with their former masters, under such contracts as may be made for the present time."[35] No person would be subsisted by the government in idleness and "thus hang as dead weights upon those who are disposed to bear their full share of the public burdens."[36] In order to prevent the problem from reoccurring, Laughlin decreed, "No persons [who were] formerly slaves will be permitted to travel on public thoroughfares without passes or permits from their employers, or to congregate in buildings or camps at or adjacent to any military post or town."[37] While some former masters of slaves in the country told their freed slaves they no longer needed passes to move about, the Union army in Galveston officially demanded that they possess passes to enter the city or travel on public roads.[38]

Laughlin's order had some effect on the problem he sought to address, but it proved only a temporary success. By July 3, Willard Richardson once again complained that "Our city is constantly filling up with negroes, most of whom come from Houston."[39] The worst offenders, Richardson noted, were children of twelve to eighteen years of age "who seem to be going about without any home or anyone to take charge of them or exercise any control over them."[40] Richardson believed that the federal authorities shared his concerns about "having so large a servile population of all ages thrown here upon our city," but wondered if the military would take action to combat the problem.[41] He mused, "[H]ow this can be done consistently with the freedom promised them [freed slaves], and with which promise their expectations have been raised to the highest pitch, is now the great problem to be solved."[42]

Richardson's desire to find a solution to this problem did not include a way for freedpeople to responsibly exercise their new freedom. On July 4, 1865, an ironic choice of date, Richardson published an editorial titled "Negro Peonage," which repeated his racist argument that "the lands of the South cannot be cultivated by white labor."[43] He argued that only black labor could provide the needed agricultural workforce, and that black labor could not function properly without some form of direction and compulsion. If Northern sentiments rejected the term slavery, Richardson suggested that perhaps the new system could be called "peonage," and function much as slavery had before the war. He stated, "No other system than that of compulsory Peonage will induce the negro to work to advantage."[44] If whipping was considered offensive, perhaps the new system could work much like Northern penitentiaries, where they punished noncompliance by using "a system of shower baths, [and] solitary confinement in dark dungeons on bread and water."[45] Fortunately, no one took Richardson's peonage proposal seriously.

As the month of July proceeded, problems continued to develop between the white and black residents of Galveston. Laughlin's attempt to regulate the idle black population in Galveston using passes had some effect, but not as much as he hoped. When planters complained about their field hands leaving the plantations, federal officials said they possessed no authority to actually compel the former slaves to remain against their will. Their authority extended to patrolling the cities and "tak[ing] them [former slaves] up when they are found idle and without passes."[46] But as the system came increasingly to rely on written passes, Willard Richardson conducted an examination of these "passes" and determined that many were fraudulent. Although army officials did not know the residents of Galveston well enough to recognize their names, Richardson (who presumed to know everyone) found the names on many passes fictitious. Richardson reported with disgust, "The negroes say they paid 25 cents each for these passes."[47]

As Provost Marshal Laughlin and his subordinates checked passes and created forced labor gangs in Galveston, similar experiments took place in Houston, which faced its own large influx of freed slaves due to its status as a commercial hub and the central point in the Texas railroad network. A Houston newspaper reported on June 30:

> A trip to Houston is quite a fashionable excursion with the freedmen of the Brazos and Trinity [Rivers]. They travel mostly on foot, bearing heavy burthens of clothing, blankets, etc. on their heads—a long and weary journey. They arrive tired footsore and hungry only to learn what they were told before they left, that they were better off at home and that they had better go back again.[48]

Unlike Willard Richardson's *Galveston News*, the *Houston Telegraph* took a more moderate and constructive tone on the evolving relationships between freedpeople and their new employers. Edward H. Cushing, the editor of the *Houston Telegraph*, wrote an editorial on June 29, 1865, that characterized the practice of going to the Union army to get help with black labor problems as "unnecessary and absurd."[49] Cushing correctly noted that the suggestions of people like his rival, Willard Richardson, that the military might be cajoled or pressured into adopting some compulsory system like peonage were delusional.[50]

Instead of trying to fight battles that they could not win, Cushing advised planters to negotiate fair contracts with their former slaves. He urged, "Make the contracts, and then carry them out strictly. Let there be perfect equity between the black laborer and his old master, now become his employer. There is no wisdom in being stiff and moribund about this matter of making contracts with our former servants."[51] Cushing felt it useless to blame the Union for the end of slavery. He offered one final piece of advice: "Above all things treat your negroes kindly; they are not to blame; they have long labored for you; they are not prepared to take care of themselves; they are to be pitied and helped."[52]

The advice offered by Cushing, though patronizing, at least made sense. Unfortunately, many Texans dismissed his guidance. Indeed, many found it hard to make any arrangements with their former slaves. Impoverished by the war, Texas farmers possessed no currency with which to pay wages. Even those few who had the funds wondered what a "fair" wage was for an agricultural worker in Texas. Unlike places elsewhere in the country, relatively few competitive markets existed in Texas that could establish the appropriate level of a fair wage. The Union army adopted some market wages in the sugar growing regions of Louisiana, but serious questions arose regarding the application of the Louisiana sugar wage scheme to the cotton plantations of Texas. James Sorley, a prominent Galveston cotton merchant, met personally with General Granger and Provost Marshal Laughlin and published a letter in the *Galveston News* assuring planters that the Louisiana regulations about wages "are not in force here, and will not be."[53] Sorley calmed his fellow planters by stating: "your negroes will not be allowed to wander as vagrants in the country; they are advised to stay with you and work for wages, if they do not they will be made to work for the Government without wages."[54]

Sorley's advice, while accurate, did not assuage many planters' worries. Former slaveholders in Washington County rigged the process by agreeing among themselves that they would not hire black laborers from any other plantation. If no competitive offers existed, they reasoned, a freed slave would have to stay and work at whatever wage the planter chose to offer. At a meeting, the planters formally resolved that "each man present would not hire the servants of his neighbor without their consent until the present crops are gathered."[55] Deprived of competitive opportunities in the farm areas where they had previously been enslaved, it is no wonder that many freedpeople chose to move to the cities and look for other places to work and live.

Washington County was not alone in its unjust treatment of freed slaves. The City of Austin passed a sweeping "Ordinance Concerning Vagrants" that called for unemployed persons to be subject to a variety of harsh punishments. For the first offense, a white person or free person of color paid a fine. A freedman, however, could also be "punished by whipping at the discretion of the jury or Mayor trying the case, and returned to his former master or employer."[56] A few vagrants were arrested under this law and the Austin newspaper happily reported that the freedpeople "have partially withdrawn their besieging forces."[57]

Galveston tried a similar tactic to intimidate the freedpeople, but this attempt proved an embarrassing failure. The Galveston newspaper published an article informing the public that a "Freedmen's Fancy Ball" was planned for Saturday night, July 1, 1865. The newspaper made some silly comments about Othello being there "in his flowing robes," joined by "many an Egypt's dusky queen."[58] The article closed with the salutation that "Galveston is a fast place, and its colored population a fast people. Joy go with them."[59] The ball actually took place, and may be the first public celebration of the Juneteenth Order, issued less than two weeks before.[60]

The newspaper seemed content to let this harmless piece of frivolity proceed without interference, but the city fathers were suspicious about the event's purpose and impact. On the day after the ball, Mayor Charles Leonard ordered the arrest of the black promoter of the event and hauled him before the city recorder, where he was charged with violating the city ordinance prohibiting the hosting of a public ball without permission from city officials. The freedman insisted that he had obtained permission to hold the ball and tried to show a paper signed by a Union officer as proof. The city officials rejected his defense, and the defendant was fined and then sent to jail when he proved unable to pay the fine.[61]

The following morning, when Mayor Leonard presided over a regular meeting of the city's governing body, a group of Union soldiers appeared and arrested the mayor and took him to the same jail where the freedman had been confined. The soldiers acted on the orders of Col. Frederick W. Moore of the Eighty-Third Ohio Infantry, the officer who had given the jailed freedman written permission to hold the ball. A lawyer by profession, Moore viewed the mayor's action as contemptuous and a threat to his authority. Like Provost Marshal Laughlin, Moore received the brevet rank of brigadier general for his service in the campaign to capture Mobile. Moore was in no mood to have his authority overturned by any official of a captured Confederate city, and chose to make an example of Mayor Leonard's conduct.[62]

After two and a half hours in the same jail cell where the freedman had been confined, the mayor was released, with instructions to see the Provost Marshal the next day. Upon meeting with Laughlin the next morning, the mayor was informed that Col. Moore had ordered his arrest for overstepping his authority. Laughlin made it clear to Leonard that military orders and regulations stood superior to anything and everything the city might think necessary or appropriate. Two days later, in a carefully orchestrated meeting of Galveston's governing body, the mayor delivered his resignation, whereupon the board of aldermen unanimously requested him to withdraw his resignation, which he then did. It was a public and largely pointless demonstration. From this point forward, the city authorities exercised their authority much more carefully. Two weeks later, a second ball was held by the black residents of Galveston at which black Union soldiers were featured participants. On this occasion, the newspaper reported stiffly that "none of our white citizens [were] taking any stock in the concern."[63]

In the U.S. Custom House, Assistant Provost Marshal Capt. Harry Beard enjoyed what he assumed were the last few weeks of his military service. After spending the first week processing a large number of paroles, things settled into a quiet and comfortable routine. Beard used one of the elegant rooms for an office and sat there at a fine desk every day from nine in the morning to noon, and from two to four in the afternoon, answering questions, as well as "fining, imprisoning and writing."[64] One of the people Beard fined a lot was Mayor Leonard, who found it hard to comply with military regulations affecting his business and personal activities. Beard reported that almost every day the mayor came to see him with an excuse or an apology. Both men grew so tired of this conflict that the mayor said he thought he would resign, and Beard encouraged him to do so.[65]

Although Beard's usual duties included things like issuing fines to merchants who refused to accept U.S. currency, called "greenbacks," an unpleasant amount of his activity centered around processing paperwork relating to freed slaves and their new employers. Beard wrote home that he looked forward to the arrival of the Freedmen's Bureau because "this Negro question is more work and trouble than anything else."[66] Sometimes Beard was reminded that this question involved more than paperwork. "Back in the state," Beard noted, "I hear they are killing [negroes] off fast, and have some reason to believe it to be so, for nine dead bodies came floating down the river the other day."[67]

While Texas newspapers urged further restrictions on black laborers and applauded the army's periodic efforts to keep them working in the fields, a newspaper in the North reached exactly the opposite conclusion. On July 9, 1865, the *New York Times* published an editorial titled "The Negro Question in Texas" that took Colonel Laughlin to task for his treatment of black vagrants. Quoting Laughlin's publicly reported commitment to Galveston officials that "idleness on the part of the colored population would not be tolerated," the *New York Times* author asked if Laughlin also meant that idleness on the part of the *white* population was forbidden.[68] If so, the editorial sarcastically observed, the policy was a good one, since "there has been for a long period of time a number of people at the South [planters] in whom idleness has been so powerful that they have insisted on eating their bread in the sweat of other men's brows instead of their own."[69] Quoting with approval the Juneteenth Order's first sentence that "all slaves are free," the *New York Times* reporter warned that "the people will not rest satisfied with any result which shall by any indirection or juggle fritter away the emancipation which Abraham Lincoln proclaimed."[70]

*Chapter 21*

## SPREADING THE WORD THROUGH TEXAS

ity officials and military authorities in Galveston spent the month following Juneteenth feuding periodically with each other. A dramatic influx of people (black and white) to the city exacerbated the conflicts. With more people, many of whom were desperately poor, the crime rate in Galveston spiked. One of the biggest problems involved arson. One history recorded that "Fires were of almost nightly occurrence and were attended by the most bold and wanton attempt at plunder."[1] One such fire destroyed the Tremont House Hotel, the largest hotel in Galveston, a blaze most likely caused by Union soldiers stationed in the area. Deliberate arson caused other fires. A pattern emerged: a fire would be set at one building and while citizens fought to extinguish that fire other buildings away from the scene of the fire would be robbed and plundered by organized gangs of men. Reports showed many of these gangs included former slaves, making the army come down even harder on unemployed black men in Galveston. Eventually, the city and the army combined to deploy large enough forces to cause the nightly level of violence and arson to subside.[2]

Other cities besides Galveston experienced crime waves as Texas transitioned from Confederate to Union control. The State Treasury in Austin was looted, and bands of robbers appeared on all the prominent roads in Texas, holding up trains and stages. An unfortunate passenger on one stagecoach journey reported that his party was robbed by a gang of fifty men about forty miles after starting from Rio

Grande City and was stopped and searched by similar gangs about thirty more times before reaching San Antonio. Given that the distance was only 225 miles, his trip appeared to average about one robbery attempt every seven miles. Things had certainly become wild in the west.[3]

A Philadelphia journalist visited Galveston the first week in July and was not impressed with what he saw of the town. "Galveston is a city of dogs and desolation," he wrote, wondering whether a stranger would be more impressed with "the multiplicity of the canines or the poverty and degradation of the human species."[4] One thing he reported with certainty was the continued disloyalty of the inhabitants. "True loyalty," he recorded, "is an exceedingly rare pearl in Galveston."[5]

While Galveston coped with the tensions associated with the end of the war and the return to some form of normalcy, other cities around the state gradually began to make the same transition. The Union occupation plan called for small units of troops to deploy to cities in the interior, starting with posts located at important railroad junctions. In keeping with his abolitionist sympathies, Frederick Emery attempted to station sympathetic officers where he thought they might be of the most assistance in protecting freed slaves and handling the inevitable problems with sudden emancipation.

Emery received a letter from Col. George W. Clark of the Thirty-Fourth Iowa that presented him with an opportunity to help freedpeople. Clark and his men were in Houston at the time, the first federal troops who marched through that city's streets. Clark told Emery that a Confederate colonel named Carter had suggested that it might be useful to have federal soldiers "visit parts of the state where the negroes are the most turbulent and explain to them their present status."[6] Emery agreed with Carter's point, and probably with the unfortunate example of Col. Laughlin in mind, thought it best to task a less threatening officer with such a duty. After giving the matter some study, Emery approved the request to send a representative but suggested that a chaplain be chosen for this assignment.[7]

As the troops moved into the countryside and established formal posts, the reports that Emery received back from each post described similar sets of problems. Where large numbers of freed slaves existed, many of them remained understandably uncertain about their new status. Union officers spent much of their time answering questions. Many freedpeople wondered if they had to stay at their old homes. Others wondered about the practical realities of being a paid employee versus a slave. Some wanted to know what recourse they could take if their former master refused to pay them, or said he would pay them with a share of the crop only after it was harvested. Still others wanted to know if their former masters could beat them or punish them by withholding supplies.

Not all questions came from the freedpeople. Many planters believed that their newly freed laborers did not understand the meaning of freedom and thought they no longer had to work. Because the Juneteenth Order stated that the freedpeople needed to stay where they were and continue working, planters wanted troops to step in and explain to their freed slaves the restrictions on that freedom.

Stepping into the middle of such a poorly defined relationship inevitably led to trouble. Col. John H. Kelly and elements of the 114th Ohio Volunteers were sent to set up a post at Millican, Texas, a relatively large and prosperous town at the terminus of the Houston and Texas Central Railway. Emery assigned Kelly to go to Millican and provided instructions about the freedpeople. Emery warned that these instructions were "necessarily of a general character."[8] The situation was too fluid and unpredictable to give specific guidance. "Your sound judgment," Emery cautioned, "will often be called into action."[9] He advised the officers commanding posts to remember that one of the army's central missions was to see that "the colored people of the State are secure in their personal freedom and their right to hold, transfer and use their lawfully acquired property, and that they do not abuse these newly acquired rights both to their own injury and the injury of the white people of the State."[10]

Emery complicated an already precarious situation by advising Kelly on a wide variety of, sometimes contradictory, things he could and could not do. Although the army desired the freedpeople to continue working where they were living presently, Emery explained that they could not be forced to do so in the absence of a proper contract. Emery also reminded Kelly that the army was unable to provide food and shelter to civilians. Only in very limited circumstances was the quartermaster authorized to issue emergency rations to those who had become destitute by emancipation.

Emery told Kelly that freedpeople must under no circumstances be allowed to congregate at military posts and could not be permitted to become vagrants. Although the military would force them to abide by their contracts, it would also endeavor to protect them against cruel treatment. People who considered themselves cruelly treated could apply to the military and those found guilty of mistreatment would be fined or imprisoned.[11]

Soon after reaching Millican, Lt. Col. J. A. Callicott of the Twenty-Ninth Illinois Regiment replaced Kelly. Callicott immediately faced complaints of a recent robbery said to have been committed by a band of black men. He responded by arresting three of the alleged robbers and forwarding them to Houston for trial. The commander then listened to citizens who traveled as much as a hundred miles to complain about "roving bands of negroes, committing many depredations on their property."[12] These citizens wanted to form a posse or some form of self-defense organization but the men worried that by doing so they might run afoul of Union army restrictions intended to prevent armed bands of former Confederate soldiers. With Callicott's limited authority, all he could do was forward the request back to headquarters in Houston. As a small garrison, Millican could not provide the law enforcement assistance these citizens demanded.[13]

Callicott learned quickly that his new command involved more than listening to complaints by white citizens about the crimes and misdemeanors allegedly committed by freed slaves. A steady stream of freedpeople came to see him, most complaining about mistreatment by their former owners. Some of the complaints proved serious, but many the colonel believed to be "of quite frivolous character."[14] When Callicott followed the Juneteenth Order's language and instructed the complaining freedpeople to return to their present homes, some refused, saying they would be killed if they returned to the homes of their former masters. Callicott deemed one complaint, which alleged that a master had murdered one of his former slaves, credible enough that he ordered a force mounted on mules to travel thirty miles away to investigate the charge.[15]

Callicott's strategy of responding to the most serious complaints while leaving less important matters to sort themselves out appeared relatively successful from the army's point of view. By July 17, Col. Callicott reported that the area around

Millican was "in a quiet condition, and the negroes, though some of them are running off, are being employed by their former owners, as a general thing, and seem disposed to remain at home."[16] Colonel Callicott often talked candidly with groups of former slaves. The colonel understood that these people did not trust their former masters, but every time he explained the situation and the importance of their staying at their present location, with the promise of compensation for their labor, the freedpeople returned home seemingly satisfied to work the year out.[17]

Not too far away at another railway terminus in Brenham, Texas, Maj. Elijah P. Curtis of the Twenty-Ninth Illinois Volunteers experienced more difficulty in sorting out the various complaints. Washington County, of which Brenham was the county seat, had been one of the locations where planters tried to game the system by colluding not to hire workers from the farms of other planters. Despite this unfair advantage, white planters came in regularly with grievances about "negro mobs." Curtis thought such mobs, if they existed at all, posed little potential danger except where the former masters continued to whip their new "employees." He also reported that the planters in the area who made contracts with their former slaves generally entered into fair contracts with them. In cases where the former masters refused to employ their former slaves, the major noted that the German citizens of the area stepped in and often "employ[ed] negroes on fair terms where their former masters discharge[d] them."[18]

Curtis struggled to sort through the various complaints by former slaves regarding mistreatment by their former masters. As he reported to headquarters:

> Much trouble and annoyance is caused by the failure of planters to enter into contracts with their former slaves. Negroes come in daily with complaints that their former masters refuse to make any contracts with them, except a mere offer to allow them to remain and do as they have formerly done. Many of the negroes place a high estimate on their services, which increases the trouble.[19]

The end result of all these charges and countercharges was that, at least in Washington County, "the labor question is in quite an unsettled condition yet."[20]

The problems at Millican and Brenham are illustrative of the problems experienced at posts all across Texas when it came time to actually implement the provisions of the Juneteenth Order. It put army officers, particularly those at remote posts in the interior of the state, in an uncomfortable, indeed impossible, position as they tried to referee disputes between former slaves and former masters. When the army officers in these posts applied for guidance from their superiors, officers like Major Emery in Galveston told them to use their best judgment, and reassured them that officials from the Freedmen's Bureau would eventually arrive and assume supervision of these issues. The Freedmen's Bureau did not make an appearance in Texas for many months. Gen. Edgar M. Gregory, the first official from the Freedmen's Bureau in Texas, did not issue his first official circular until October 12, 1865, almost four months after liberation. Gregory arrived in Texas only to find that some slaves had not even been informed of their emancipation.[21]

Given the difficulties that Major Curtis experienced in Brenham, it was perhaps surprising that one of the more remarkable and illuminating speeches by a Union officer following the end of the war took place in that city just one month after June 19. The orator on that occasion, Maj. Gen. Christopher Columbus Andrews, was the son of a rural New Hampshire farmer. Andrews studied law and spent time in Kansas and Washington, D.C., before moving to Minnesota. When the war broke out, Andrews volunteered for service in the Third Minnesota Volunteer Infantry Regiment, where he rose through the ranks until his appointment as a brigadier general of volunteers in January 1864. Andrews led the Second Division of the Thirteenth Corps and participated in the campaign that culminated in the capture of Mobile. Andrews came to Texas with General Granger, who appointed him commander of the Military District of Houston.[22]

On July 20, 1865, General Andrews arrived in Brenham, one of the more important cities in his district. He had been invited by city officials to address a large crowd of not only planters and influential white men but also freedpeople. Noting the diversity of his audience, Andrews started by saying that he wished to use the occasion to say "true things instead of pleasant things" and proceeded to discuss what he called "the labor question."[23]

Addressing the black members of his audience first, Andrews said that while he understood their desire to cease work, leave their place of bondage, and exercise

Maj. Gen. Christopher C. Andrews. Library of Congress, LC-DIG-cwpbh-03213.

their freedom to travel, he regretted that it was not possible for them to fully take advantage of that particular freedom at the present time because of the urgent need to harvest crops in the field:

> The holidays must be put off until the crops are gathered. If the blacks were permitted to crowd into villages and military posts it would do them no good, but on the contrary would cause sickness and misery. The military authority, therefore, insists that they remain on plantations with their former masters—who treat them as freedmen and who engage to pay them fair wages—and cultivate and gather the crops. Having entered into a contract, they will not be permitted to violate it and stray off to some other place. Those who are industrious and well behaved will have the warm sympathy and friendship

> of the government; but those who violate their contract and do wrong, will be liable for
> punishment. The more industrious, the more obedient, the more patient and well behaved
> the freedmen are, the better it will be for them now and hereafter in all respects.[24]

Andrews then warned the freedpeople against ignoring his advice and walking away from their present situations without good cause, saying "freedmen will not be allowed to stray off and live in idleness around other plantations. The idea some freedmen have that the government is going to give them farms and build them houses is a great mistake. The object of government is not to feed and support able-bodied people, but to protect people in supporting themselves."[25]

Andrews then addressed the white planters in his audience, warning them that "All persons must treat the freedmen with good faith and in an honorable and humane manner, and if they treat them in a contrary manner they will be punished for it. Duplicity and bad faith are mean and criminal under any circumstances, but much more mean and criminal when practiced upon the ignorant and weak."[26] Responding to reports that some planters conspired not to hire each other's freed slaves, Andrews said that "it is not necessary for me to say that any coercion, or any conspiring together to thwart the policy of the government in this matter will not be tolerated."[27]

Andrews knew that many white men in his audience hoped, like the editor of the Galveston newspaper, that slavery might yet find some way to spring back into existence, perhaps with a slightly different name to placate Northern abolitionists. He knew also that many black members of his audience feared exactly the same thing, and worried that the provisions in the Juneteenth Order advising them to stay and work on the plantations were merely a cruel precursor to the return of slavery. Andrews addressed this concern firmly and directly:

> Let me say to the freed people that they need have no doubts about their liberty. Al-
> though circumstances now require them to continue at their former homes at work, their
> interests will in time be adjusted. They may rest assured they will never again be held
> or sold as slaves. The long war we have had has settled the question of slavery in this
> country forever, and the sooner all parties come to a realization of this fact the better.[28]

Many of the white men in the audience had signed the Amnesty Oath, which expressly pledged their support for the provisions of the Emancipation Proclamation. Andrews reminded them of this provision in their oath and said that it was a binding promise:

> We expect to treat those men who take the oath as brothers, and to be so treated by them. And when a man swears that he will abide by the proclamation freeing the slaves, he binds himself before God to consider it a finality. I consider that he violates his oath if he attempts to set aside the proclamation. That is not abiding by it. A man's duty to his country begins, not ends, when he takes the amnesty oath, and he cannot merely remain passive.[29]

As General Andrews neared the end of his speech, he offered some heartfelt practical advice to the planters. Noting that the army always sent officers to accompany and lead their men when an important objective was involved, he observed that the chance of success of the venture decreased if the officers just stayed in their tents. Similarly, he said, a planter could not expect to work his land successfully if he spent most of his time talking politics in town or disparaging his workers. "If a man intends to be a planter, he should be a thorough planter, and give his chief attention to the business."[30] To Andrews, this meant being physically present in the field where the planter could personally instruct and encourage his workers.

Andrews said that contrary to some expressed opinions, the people of the North and the army he represented did not wish to have the people of the South "humiliated or dishonored."[31] General Grant did not treat General Lee that way at Appomattox, and that was not the spirit that Andrews believed operated in the Union army in Texas. Some things needed to change, however. Andrews mentioned as an example that too many men thought themselves above the law. In his opinion, there had been "too much sway of bowie knives and revolvers." But it was time to leave all that in the past. "Loyalty to the Union and a patriotism which embraces the whole country will restore you to our affections."[32] The Galveston newspaper later printed the entire talk and reported that the general's speech had been "listened to with marked attention by a large and respectful crowd of whites and blacks, numbering several thousand persons, and gave general satisfaction."[33]

Three days following the Andrews speech in Brenham, Provisional Gov. Andrew Jackson Hamilton arrived in Galveston and delivered quite a different kind of speech. That speech held a much less conciliatory tone and did not give "general satisfaction" according to the Galveston newspaper. Instead, it abounded "in remarks calculated to wound and aggravate, in a remarkable degree, [Hamilton's] late political opponents."[34] Instead of the olive branch of peace that General Andrews offered, Hamilton arrived with what former Confederates dramatically characterized as "the flaming sword of discord and vengeance."[35]

On July 25, two days following his "flaming sword" speech, Hamilton released his first official proclamation as governor. Like his speech, Hamilton's proclamation made no effort to win friends among former Confederates. Instead, it was primarily an insult aimed squarely at *Galveston News* editor Willard Richardson:

> I shall not waste time or labor in the attempt to soothe those whose hearts are sore because of the extinction of slavery. It died because it made war upon the Government to whose protection it owed its power and influence. . . . There are those, I am told, who profess to believe that it is not yet extinct, that it still lingers and by vigorous application of stimulants may be kept in existence for some years to come, that the proclamation of emancipation was but a military order, which has now spent its force since the war is over and never had any effect except where, by the presence of Union armies, there was physical power to enforce it. There could be no greater delusion that this, and the man or men who encourage such opinions, if such there are, could not do the citizens of Texas, at this time, a greater disservice. The negroes are not only free, but I beg to assure my fellow citizens that the Government will protect them in their freedom.[36]

Hamilton admitted that he could never convince some Texans that "slavery was never a good, and emancipation not an evil."[37] He acknowledged that there were still "a few men in the South" who "differ with the whole world on that subject and I suppose that most of that few will go down to their graves, sore and complaining, but in the meantime, those who realize that a new era has dawned upon us and who take advantage of the present will leave far in the background the mourners over the past glory of slavery."[38]

The witnesses to the dawn of the new era of freedom in Texas would not include Gen. Gordon Granger, whose command lasted only a month after his famous arrival in Galveston on June 19. On July 1, General Sheridan confirmed to General Grant that the situation in Texas had stabilized. Among the successes he reported to Grant was that "Orders have been issued declaring all slaves free."[39] Sheridan did not tell Grant that Granger issued that order, nor did he reveal that his own detailed instructions led to that order. In fact, Sheridan carefully omitted any reference to Granger by name in his dispatches to Grant. Grant was well aware of Granger's presence in Galveston, however, and was already contemplating ways to remove him. On July 6, Grant notified Sheridan that his authority extended to all the troops in Texas and reminded Sheridan that he had authority to remove any officer "whose services were not required."[40]

Although Sheridan must have known that Grant's order was a subtle hint that he remove Granger from the picture, Sheridan was clearly reluctant to do so. Sheridan may have had some lingering affection for Granger, or he may have simply wanted to avoid publicly embarrassing him. On July 6, the same day that Grant's order arrived, Sheridan sent the general a communication addressed to "My Dear Granger." Sheridan held off on doing anything about Granger, probably hoping that Grant's focus on events near the border with Mexico might distract him and relieve the pressure to sack Granger.[41]

Grant's hatred for Granger, however, was so intense that Grant could no longer ignore his continued presence in Galveston. On July 13, Grant sent Sheridan a direct instruction: "Do you not think it advisable to relieve Granger from command in Texas? If so, relieve him."[42] Even with this not so subtle hint, Sheridan proved reluctant. On July 15, Sheridan telegraphed Grant that although he thought it best to relieve Granger, he believed the order should come from Washington. An hour later, Grant telegraphed back and directed Sheridan to relieve Granger and instruct him to wait for further orders.[43]

Thus, on July 19, 1865, exactly one month to the day after Granger's arrival in Galveston, the general received a formal order relieving him from command.

Sheridan tried to soften the blow by making it clear that the order had come from Washington. He suggested to Granger that his dismissal was probably due to a reorganization of the Thirteenth Corps, which was being consolidated into a division. Granger knew that Grant was behind his loss of command. After winding up a few loose ends, Granger left Texas in August with little fanfare. With Granger's departure from Galveston, his role in emancipation, the transition from slavery to "first freedom" as some historians call it, ended and the era of Reconstruction in Texas began.[44]

## Chapter 22

# LEGACY OF JUNETEENTH

As the Civil War ended and Reconstruction began, many wondered if former slaves would celebrate the end of slavery in any formalized commemorative fashion. No immediate consensus emerged regarding how and when slavery ended. Across the country, some groups chose to celebrate emancipation on January 1 (sometimes called "Freedom Day"), which commemorated the date of Lincoln's final Emancipation Proclamation. Others chose to celebrate emancipation on September 22, the date of Lincoln's first Emancipation Proclamation. Still others chose to honor April 9 or "Surrender Day," the day Lee surrendered his army to Ulysses S. Grant. In Richmond, Virginia, many people initially observed "Emancipation Day," the day that Union soldiers entered the city. While people in different regions celebrated the end of slavery on various dates, it was hard to find one particular day that really fit the arrival date of actual freedom for even a majority of the former slaves. Gradually, out of all of these potential dates, Juneteenth emerged through popular consensus as the date most often chosen by black people to celebrate emancipation. While some still argue for and celebrate other dates, Juneteenth's popularity has grown through the years.[1]

It would be foolish to suggest that "first freedom" resulted in a substantial or immediate change in working or living conditions for the freedpeople who came to celebrate its anniversary. In some cases, conditions for black people were even worse than before the war. In the months and years following the end of the war, numerous reports of white violence against freed blacks emerged, including

Emancipation Day parade in Richmond, Virginia (1905).
Library of Congress, LC-D401-18421.

a large number of murders. Elizabeth Hayes Turner, one of the leading scholars on the history of Juneteenth and its aftermath, argued in her article "Juneteenth: Emancipation and Memory" that Texas may have witnessed more cases of violence by whites against newly freed slaves than any other state. "The war may not have brought a great deal of bloodshed to Texas," Turner wrote, "but the peace certainly did."[2]

Like some of the events surrounding the issuance of the Juneteenth Order in Galveston, documentation regarding the early celebrations of Juneteenth remain elusive. Informal ceremonies conducted by African-American communities became the first celebrations of the anniversary of Juneteenth. Newspapers failed to record many of these smaller celebrations. Larger celebrations proved more visible, however, and newspapers covered their occurrence, leaving a documented trail for historians to travel.

One of the first large celebrations of Juneteenth recorded in the newspapers took place in Houston on Tuesday, June 19, 1866. When word of the planned anniversary barbecue and commemoration became apparent, some feared a violent reaction to that event. The *Houston Telegraph* informed its readers, "We earnestly trust that nothing will be done by the inconsiderate or ill-disposed to interrupt or mar the merry-making of the freedmen."[3] The newspaper acknowledged the right of freedpeople to celebrate their emancipation, and urged its readers to "Let them enjoy its celebration unmolested."[4]

The *Houston Telegraph* had good reason to be concerned about the celebration. General Sheridan and his staff watched carefully from nearby Galveston, waiting to see if the army needed to step in and protect the freedpeople from white antagonists. A clash between whites and blacks would almost certainly lead to a strong military response. In the end, the concerns turned out to be groundless. The *New York Times* printed a report from Galveston confirming that General Sheridan swiftly departed for New Orleans, noting "The freedmen's celebration of emancipation, at Houston, passed off quietly."[5]

The enthusiastic sponsors of the Houston event planned well for the first anniversary of emancipation. The Houston newspaper's account of the parade stated:

> The negro celebration of the anniversary of their freedom yesterday, turned out to be, as everybody expected, a very big thing. The various processions must have numbered in all at least some thousands. They were passing Main street from quite an early hour of the morning until after ten o'clock. The marshals or directors of the procession rode on horse-back and wore sashes, some of red, some of white, and some of blue. A great number of United States banners from the size of a pocket handkerchief up to a bed quilt. supplied no doubt for the occasion by the military, floated above them and added not a little to the imposing appearance of the scene. The darkies were nearly all dressed pretty well, and the women particularly shone in all their finery. We never saw such a multitude of smiling and happy faces all at once.[6]

Although the Houston newspaper account labeled the celebration a big success, it incorrectly assumed that the event would be a one-time occasion. Admitting that the freedpeople behaved in a "most proper manner," the editors expressed their hope that the celebrants would "long remember with pleasure their Houston celebration and talk of it for years to come."[7] The success of the first Juneteenth anniversary celebration, however, ensured that the event became an annual occasion. Future events followed a similar format, including parades, speeches, and community gatherings with shared food.[8]

As in Houston, a large emancipation celebration took place in the City of San Antonio on the first anniversary of Juneteenth in 1866. Several hundred freed-people gathered at San Pedro Springs, one of the oldest parks in Texas. At what the newspaper called a "grand affair," attended by a number of army officers and soldiers, a "good deal of dancing was done by the freedmen, and a good deal of lager was drunk by the whole gathering."[9]

The participants in the earliest Juneteenth celebrations included black soldiers, a large part of the Union occupation force in Texas. By the end of the war, almost 180,000 black men had joined the Union army. One estimate recorded only forty-seven of these men from Texas. This small number did not reflect black Texans' unwillingness to fight for the cause; the lower enlistment numbers merely indicate that slaves in Texas had a much harder time reaching Union lines. At the conclusion of the war, Union military leaders sent large numbers of black troops

Photograph of June 19, 1900, Emancipation Day Celebration in Austin, Texas. Photo by Mrs. Charles (Grace Murray) Stephenson. Austin History Center, PICA 05476, General Collection Photographs, Austin Public Library, Austin, Texas.

to help occupy Texas. Because black regiments were organized later in the war, more time remained in these soldiers' service commitments. As time wore on, white regiments gradually mustered out of service, thus increasing the role of black soldiers as part of the Texas occupation force. By January 1866, black men composed a majority of the troops stationed in Texas. These troops performed well in their postings on the frontier, which probably factored into the decision to create the Ninth and Tenth cavalry regiments in 1866. These men later became famous under the popular name "Buffalo Soldiers."[10]

Although large cities such as Galveston, Houston, and San Antonio developed successful Juneteenth festivities that began in 1866, large gatherings also took place in small country towns. In 1879, for example, Dripping Springs and Burton each held emancipation anniversary celebrations that included up to two thousand attendees. The Burton celebration included a brass band and a "grand ball out on an open platform, erected for that purpose."[11]

In 1870, a newspaper correspondent from Austin proudly proclaimed that "it has been the custom of the colored people of this section of the State, since the year 1865, to celebrate the 19th of June, the anniversary of the order of Gen. Granger, declaring them a free people."[12] Five years later, in 1875, Texas Gov. Edmund J. Davis spoke at a Juneteenth gathering at Pressler's Garden, a German beer garden in Austin, where the crowd number "amount[ed] to at least 1500 men, women and children, who indulged in dancing, chatting and speaking."[13]

In 1870, one group in Austin wanted to celebrate the anniversary of emancipation on June 19 while another group proposed changing the celebration date to coincide with the nation's independence on the Fourth of July. To resolve the issue, community leaders held a large meeting to consider the competing proposals. A local newspaper reported the result:

> A mass meeting of the colored people was called at the Courthouse and by a large majority stuck to the 19th of June. They said that the fourth of July was a very good liberty day for the white man, but that it never brought their freedom. They knew that "Freedom come" on the 19th of June, through the order of [General] Granger, which date is indelibly fixed in the ward's mind as the 19th of June.[14]

As the years went by, towns competed to see which community could put on the largest and most impressive Juneteenth festivity. One of the strangest and most elaborate of these events took place in San Antonio in 1883. It started with a morning salute fired by thirty-eight guns, which summoned the parade-goers to the military plaza for the start of a grand parade. The parade included not only the usual rifle companies and bands, but also a chariot drawn by four horses carrying thirty-seven girls representing the states in the Union plus "Miss Queen Rebecca" portraying the Goddess of Liberty. Eight carriages followed containing orators and dignitaries. The festivities during the day included baseball games, croquet, and target-shooting contests. The evening included a grand ball with dancing that went on until three o'clock in the morning. The only incident that detracted from the event's lavish success was that a man at the picnic attempted suicide (fortunately stopped by his friends) due to "the attention received by his wife in the face of his opposition."[15]

The custom of celebrating June 19 as the anniversary of emancipation gained traction in the 1870s when celebrations became larger and "emancipation parks" were developed to host them at various locations around the state. One of the most important such parks took shape in 1872, when Baptist minister and former slave John Henry "Jack" Yates led a community effort in Houston to purchase a tract of land to be used by the black community in perpetuity to celebrate emancipation. That property, eventually donated to the City of Houston in 1916, is still known as "Emancipation Park."[16]

Although African Americans probably referred to the annual commemoration as "Juneteenth" much earlier, the first recorded references to June 19 as "Juneteenth" appeared in newspapers in the early 1890s. After the civil rights era changed the way Americans thought about race, a resurgence of interest in celebrating emancipation emerged, and Juneteenth gained in popularity again through the 1970s. The theories as to why Juneteenth became the most popular emancipation commemoration date vary greatly. One writer concluded that its popularity arose in part because its commemoration date is conveniently located in summer, making it the perfect time for a picnic and outside celebration.[17]

Annual celebrations of Juneteenth and its legacy of freedom continue to inspire people. Opal Lee, a ninety-year-old retired schoolteacher from Fort Worth, walked from her home in Texas to Washington, D.C., in an attempt to bring attention to Juneteenth and persuade federal lawmakers to make it a formal national holiday. "Slaves didn't free themselves," Lee said. "We need to honor all those people who were responsible. . . . As old as I am, as long as I have breath, I'm going to keep that flame burning."[18]

Jamelle Bouie, chief political correspondent for *Slate Magazine*, called Juneteenth "the Black American Holiday Everyone Should Celebrate but Doesn't."[19] The movement to make Juneteenth a national holiday seems to be gaining traction. The Texas legislature made Juneteenth an official Texas holiday in 1979, and movements in other states to make the day either an official holiday, a day of remembrance, or a day of observance, have been successful or are pending. *Texas Monthly Magazine* once called Juneteenth "the greatest Texas export of the late twentieth century."[20]

Photograph of June 19, 1900, Emancipation Day Celebration Band in Austin, Texas. Photo by Mrs. Charles (Grace Murray) Stephenson. Austin History Center, PICA 05481, General Collection Photographs, Austin Public Library, Austin, Texas.

In 1990, Texas Gov. Ann Richards signed into law a bill designating Dr. Martin Luther King, Jr.'s birthday (January 15, 1929) as an official state holiday. She chose to do so on June 19, 1990, believing that Juneteenth was the perfect time to "honor the memory of Dr. Martin Luther King, Jr. and his living legacy of hope."[21] The association of Dr. King's legacy with Juneteenth became more publicly recognized in Austin when "19th Street" was officially designated "Martin Luther King, Jr. Boulevard."[22]

The rise and popularity of Juneteenth celebrations should not detract from remembering and celebrating other events relating to emancipation. Although Juneteenth reflects the army's attempt to bring Abraham Lincoln's Emancipation Proclamation into effect throughout the South, the true path to finally ending slavery required passage of the Thirteenth Amendment to the United States Constitution. That amendment, which Lincoln himself called a "King's Cure" for slavery, ended the institution in short and effective language: "Neither slavery nor involuntary servitude, except as a punishment for crime whereof the party shall have been duly convicted, shall exist within the United States, or any place subject to their jurisdiction."[23]

While the simple language of the Thirteenth Amendment concisely abolished the institution of slavery, the enactment of the amendment proved both difficult and complicated. The Senate voted in favor of the amendment by a wide margin on April 8, 1864, but the House of Representatives failed to pass it by the required two-thirds vote on June 16, 1864. President Lincoln thereafter heavily lobbied the representatives, and on January 31, 1865, the House finally passed the amendment by a vote of 119 to fifty-six. His enthusiasm regarding its passage prompted President Lincoln to sign the measure, a move later criticized since presidential approval was not required for its adoption.[24]

Although the Thirteenth Amendment received its required federal approval, there remained the delicate task of obtaining the required three-fourths approval by the states. After the addition of West Virginia, the country consisted of thirty-six states, meaning twenty-seven states needed to ratify the amendment to make it law. Obtaining the required number of state ratifications proved a formidable challenge since many former Confederate states did not yet have federally approved and functioning legislatures. Eventually, in December 1865,

Joint Resolution submitting Thirteenth Amendment to the States for
Ratification signed by Congress and Abraham Lincoln. Library of Congress,
Digital ID: http://hdl.loc.gov/loc.mss/ms000001.mss30189a.4361100.

Georgia became the twenty-seventh state to ratify the amendment, and on December 18, 1865, Secretary of State William H. Seward formally certified the amendment's ratification and enactment.[25] On February 18, 1870, more than four years after Georgia ratified the amendment, Texas became the thirty-third state to ratify the Thirteenth Amendment. Mississippi became the last state to ratify the amendment in 1995, though a mistake in its filing delayed its federal acknowledgement until 2013.[26]

The passage and ratification of the Thirteenth Amendment conclusively eradicated slavery throughout the United States, though several difficult legal questions lingered for years afterward. These cases concerned the status of slavery during the two-year gap between January 1, 1863, the effective date of Lincoln's final Emancipation Proclamation, and December 18, 1865, when the Thirteenth Amendment was ratified. Because the institution of slavery continued to function in Texas until the end of the war, large numbers of transactions relating to slavery took place during the gap period, and many wondered whether these transactions were invalid or not. If a person bought a slave in 1864 or early 1865, for example, could the buyer void the transaction, and thereby discharge his debt or get a refund of the purchase price? Could a lender invalidate a loan made during this period where slaves served as collateral? Large amounts of money hung in the balance on the question of when slavery ended in Texas as a legal matter.

The cases surrounding these issues, collectively referred to as the "Emancipation Proclamation Cases," took time to wind their way through the court system to the Texas Supreme Court. At that court, the justices considered at least three different potential dates to officially mark the end of slavery: January 1, 1863 (Emancipation Proclamation effective date), June 19, 1865 (Juneteenth Order issued in Galveston), or December 18, 1865 (Thirteenth Amendment Ratified). Advantages and disadvantages accompanied each of these dates.

As a practical matter, slavery continued to exist in Texas long after the 1863 date of Lincoln's Emancipation Proclamation. If the court chose January 1, 1863, as the date when slavery legally ended, then a large number of transactions would become invalid, leaving the Texas courts clogged with litigation for years. If the court chose the ratification date of the Thirteenth Amendment as the legal end date for slavery, its ruling would be largely meaningless. Slavery ended and emancipation occurred as a practical matter long before the December 1865 date of the Thirteenth Amendment. That left Juneteenth as the most logical date to define the end of slavery in Texas, a decision the Texas Supreme Court finally confirmed in 1868. The majority opinion in the Emancipation Proclamation Cases held that Lincoln's Proclamation did not free slaves in Confederate states immediately, but instead contemplated an end to slavery only if and when Union armies eventually liberated each state. As to Texas, that liberation date was June 19, 1865, when General Granger's headquarters in Galveston issued the Juneteenth Order. As one of the concurring opinions put it, "By general understanding, that was the day of jubilee of the freedom of the slaves in Texas."[27]

In 1868, when the Texas Supreme Court decided the Emancipation Proclamation Cases, Andrew Jackson Hamilton, former provisional governor for Texas, was then a sitting justice on the Texas Supreme Court. Hamilton wrote a blistering dissenting opinion arguing that Lincoln's Emancipation Proclamation should have been legally effective in Texas when issued, and that slavery should have been legally invalid after January 1, 1863. The court did not adopt Hamilton's position, however, and Juneteenth became the symbolic and legal end of slavery in Texas.[28]

Although Texas was among the last Confederate states to effectively emancipate slaves, people in other states still legally possessed slaves for many months after June 19, 1865. Since Lincoln's Emancipation Proclamation applied only to states under Confederate control, border states like Delaware and Kentucky continued to have slaves until the ratification of the Thirteenth Amendment in December 1865. Slavery continued in Indian Territory until 1866 when treaties outlawed the practice.[29]

Although the Texas Supreme Court officially recognized the issuance of the Juneteenth Order as the end of slavery in Texas, many forgot about the place where the order originated. In 2006, Galvestonians erected a statue commemorating Juneteenth, but the location of that statue was at Ashton Villa, a site on Galveston's main street where modern commemorations have sometimes taken place. The site where the Juneteenth Order originated, the Osterman building on the Strand, possessed no historical marker of any kind for many years.[30]

Sam Collins with Juneteenth Historic Marker on the 150th anniversary
of Juneteenth. Courtesy of Sam Collins.

In 2012, Sam Collins, III, a friendly and charismatic Galveston financial
planner, attended a historic preservation workshop where he learned that no historical marker commemorated the site of General Granger's headquarters. This
struck a chord with Collins, whose passion for historic preservation prompted
a newspaper article lauding him for preserving the home and gardens of a
Confederate soldier even though he is African American. Collins has become
a widely respected leader who serves on many committees and advisory groups
associated with historic preservation.[31]

At the 2012 workshop in Galveston, Collins pledged to secure the funding
needed for the Juneteenth historical marker, which he proceeded to do in the
months afterward. Collins wanted the marker dedicated in 2014 so that it would
be available for the 150th anniversary of Juneteenth on June 19, 2015. With a lot of
hard work from Collins and a variety of historical groups, the Juneteenth marker
went from an application form to a reality. The addition of the historical marker

to the community may not be the end of the story, however. In 2020, a group of government officials and community leaders began organizing an effort to create an "Emancipation National Historic Trail" that would begin at Galveston's Juneteenth historical marker (site of the Osterman building) and extend all the way to Houston's Emancipation Park with stops at various historic sites located along the way.[32]

At the formal dedication ceremony for the Juneteenth historical marker on June 21, 2014, many prominent people spoke about Juneteenth and its place in history. Collins said it best, "I think people need to realize Juneteenth celebrates freedom, and freedom is something we all value. . . . Juneteenth is not just an African American holiday, but a day that celebrates the evolution of our country to a more perfect union. The events that happened on June 19, 1865, in Galveston made us a better country."[33] Collins went on to say, "We encourage people to celebrate Juneteenth all over the state and world."[34] Increasingly, as Sam Collins hoped and predicted, people are doing just that.

# Notes

PREFACE

[1] General Orders No. 3, Galveston, Texas, June 19, 1865, *The War of the Rebellion: A Compilation of the Official Records of the Union and Confederate Armies*, 128 vols. (Washington, D.C.: Government Printing Office, 1896), Series II, 48:929 (hereafter cited as *OR*).

[2] For a listing of some of the celebrations around the country and the increasing number of international celebrations see the National Registry of Juneteenth Supporters and Celebrations website at: *https://www.juneteenth.com/worldwide.htm*.

[3] General Orders No. 3, *OR*.

[4] At the conclusion of the Civil War, most Union sources, including the Juneteenth Order, referred to the freed slaves as "freedmen," although some continued to use less complimentary terms. Recognizing that the emancipated slaves included women as well as men, however, this book will refer to the freed slaves using the more modern term "freedpeople" except where the context or direct quotations justify use of a different designation.

[5] Martin Luther King, Jr., "'I Have a Dream,' Address Delivered at the March on Washington for Jobs and Freedom," Speech, Lincoln Memorial, Washington, D.C., August 28, 1963, found online at: *https://kinginstitute.stanford.edu/king-papers/documents/i-have-dream-address -delivered-march-washington-jobs-and-freedom*.

INTRODUCTION

[1] "Barnes Institute was one of the First," *Galveston Daily News*, January 9, 2013; "Parting Guests: How Gen. Grant and Party Spent the Day Yesterday," *Galveston Daily News*, March 26, 1880.

[2] Ibid.

[3] "Address at Gettysburg, Pennsylvania," Abraham Lincoln, November 19, 1863, *Abraham Lincoln: Speeches and Writings, 1859–1865* (New York: Literary Classics of the United States, Inc., 1989), 536.

4    Ibid.

5    "Juneteenth Worldwide Celebration," accessed June 19, 2018, *http://juneteenth.com.*

6    General Orders No. 3, Galveston, Texas, June 19, 1865, *The War of the Rebellion: A Compilation of the Official Records of the Union and Confederate Armies,* 128 vols. (Washington, D.C.: Government Printing Office, 1896), Series II, 48:929.

7    Charles W. Hayes, *History of the Island and the City of Galveston,* 2 vols. (Cincinnati, OH: 1879; rpt. Austin, TX: Jenkins Garrett Press, 1974), 2:644–45.

8    For a thorough discussion of the number of slaves in Texas, including those "refugeed" to Texas during the war, see W. Caleb McDaniel, "Involuntary Removals: 'Refugeed Slaves' in Confederate Texas," in *Lone Star Unionism, Dissent, and Resistance: Other Sides of Civil War Texas,* Jesús F. de la Teja, ed. (Norman, OK: University of Oklahoma Press, 2016), 60–83. The trivia question and answer are taken from "How the Emancipation Proclamation Worked," accessed January 19, 2020, *https://history.howstuffworks.com/historical-events/lincoln-emancipation -proclamation.htm.*

9    "Preliminary Emancipation Proclamation," Abraham Lincoln, September 22, 1862, *The Collected Works of Abraham Lincoln,* 9 vols. (New Brunswick, NJ: Rutgers University Press, 1953), 5:433; "Emancipation Proclamation," Abraham Lincoln, January 1, 1863, *The Collected Works of Abraham Lincoln,* 6:28–30.

10   Kenneth C. Davis, "Juneteenth, Our Other Independence Day," *Smithsonian Magazine Online* (June 12, 2020), accessed July 6, 2020, *https://www.smithsonianmag.com/history/juneteenth-our -other-independence-day-16340952/.*

11   Ibid.; Edward T. Cotham, Jr., *Battle on the Bay: The Civil War Struggle for Galveston* (Austin, TX: University of Texas Press, 1998), 179–83; McDaniel, "Involuntary Removals," 60–83.

12   William Dobak, *Freedom by the Sword: The U.S. Colored Troops, 1862–1867* (New York: Skyhorse Publishing, 2013), 498–502.

CHAPTER 1

1    Alwynn Barr, *Black Texans, A History of Negroes in Texas: 1528–1971* (Austin, TX: Jenkins Publishing Co., 1973), 17; Randolph B. Campbell, *An Empire for Slavery: The Peculiar Institution in Texas* (Baton Rouge, LA: Louisiana State University Press, 1989), 55, 253.

2    Campbell, *An Empire for Slavery,* 253, 258; Andrew J. Torget, *Seeds of Empire: Cotton, Slavery, and the Transformation of the Texas Borderlands, 1800–1850* (Chapel Hill, NC: University of North Carolina Press, 2015), 265–66.

3    James L. Huston, "Property Rights in Slavery and the Coming of the Civil War," *The Journal of Southern History* 65, no. 2 (May, 1999): 249–86.

4    Donald E. Reynolds, *Texas Terror* (Baton Rouge, LA: Louisiana State University Press, 2007), 3.

5    W. O. Blake, *The History of Slavery and the Slave Trade, Ancient and Modern* (Columbus, OH: H. Miller, 1860), 260.

6    Thomas Jefferson, et al., July 4, 1776, List of Grievances, Preamble to the Declaration of Independence, found online at: *https://www.loc.gov/item/mtjbib000159/;* Robert G. Parkinson, "Did a Fear of Slave Revolts Drive American Independence?," *New York Times,* July 4, 2016.

7   Stephen B. Oates, *The Fires of Jubilee: Nat Turner's Fierce Rebellion* (New York: Harper and Row, 1975), 1–4; Patrick H. Breen, *The Land Shall be Drenched in Blood* (New York: Oxford University Press, 2015), 98, 231.

8   Stephen B. Oates, *To Purge this Land with Blood: A Biography of John Brown* (Amherst, MA: University of Massachusetts Press, 1984), 35–51.

9   *The Weekly Telegraph* (Houston, TX), July 31, 1860; Reynolds, *Texas Terror*, 29–43.

10  Reynolds, *Texas Terror*, 43.

11  Ibid., 43, 170–76.

12  Ernest W. Winkler, ed., *Journal of the Secession Convention of Texas: 1861* (Austin, TX: Austin Printing Co., 1912), 62.

13  Sidney Blumenthal, *A Self-Made Man: The Political Life of Abraham Lincoln, 1809–1849* (New York: Simon and Schuster, 2016), 288.

14  David Williams, *I Freed Myself: African American Self-Emancipation in the Civil War Era* (New York: Cambridge University Press, 2014), 16.

15  Gary W. Gallagher, *The Union War* (Cambridge, MA: Harvard University Press, 2011), 149–50.

16  Ronald E. Goodwin and Bruce A. Glasrud, "On the Edge of First Freedoms: Black Texans and the Civil War," in *The Seventh Star of the Confederacy: Texas during the Civil War*, Kenneth W. Howell, ed. (Denton, TX: University of North Texas Press, 2009), 274.

## CHAPTER 2

1   Michael Burlingame, *Abraham Lincoln: A Life*, 2 vols. (Baltimore, MD: John Hopkins University Press, 2008), 2:32–37.

2   Carl Sandburg, *Abraham Lincoln*, 6 vols. (New York: Charles Scribner's Sons, 1942), 3:121–22.

3   Burlingame, *Abraham Lincoln*, 2:60; David S. Heidler and Jeanne T. Heidler, eds., *Encyclopedia of the American Civil War: A Political, Social, and Military History*, 5 vols. (Santa Barbara, CA: ABC-CLIO, 2000), 4:1,919–21.

4   "First Inaugural-Final Text," in Roy P. Basler, ed., *The Collected Works of Abraham Lincoln*, 9 vols. (New Brunswick, NJ: Rutgers University Press, 1953), 4:263, 265 (hereafter cited as *CW*).

5   Ibid.

6   Abraham Lincoln to Albert G. Hodges, Washington, D.C., April 4, 1864, *CW*, 7:281.

7   Ibid.

8   James L. Huston, "Property Rights in Slavery and the Coming of the Civil War," *The Journal of Southern History* 65, no. 2 (May, 1999): 254; Abraham Lincoln, Address at Cooper Institute, New York, February 27, 1860, *CW*, 3:550.

9   "Speech at Chicago, Illinois," July 10, 1858, *CW*, 2:492.

10  *Population of the United States in 1860; compiled from the Original Returns of the Eighth Census* (Washington, D.C.: Government Printing Office, 1864).

11  James Oakes, *Freedom National: The Destruction of Slavery in the United States, 1861–1865* (New York: W. W. Norton and Co., 2013), 270–71; "Remarks and Resolution Introduced in the United States House of Representative Concerning Abolition of Slavery in the District of Columbia," January 10, 1849, *CW*, 2:20.

[12]  Abraham Lincoln to Orville H. Browning, September 22, 1861, *CW*, 4:532.

[13]  Abraham Lincoln to Horace Greeley, August 22, 1862, *CW*, 5:388–89.

[14]  *The Liberator* (Boston, MA), May 17, 1861.

[15]  Oakes, *Freedom National*, 66–68, 84–85; *The Congressional Globe*, 36th Congress, 2nd Session, John C. Rives, ed., 46 vols. (Washington, D.C.: Congressional Globe Office, 1861), Part 1, 30:342.

[16]  William H. Russell, *My Diary North and South*, Fletcher Pratt, ed. (New York: Harper and Brothers, 1954), 121.

## CHAPTER 3

[1]  A. J. Slemmer to L. Thomas, Fort Pickens, Florida, March 18, 1861, *The War of the Rebellion: A Compilation of the Official Records of the Union and Confederate Armies*, 128 vols. (Washington, D.C.: Government Printing Office, 1896) 1:362 (hereafter cited as *OR*).

[2]  H. Brown to E. D. Townsend, Fort Pickens, Florida, June 22, 1861, *OR*, 1:433.

[3]  Chandra Manning, *Troubled Refuge: Struggling for Freedom in the Civil War* (New York: Alfred A. Knopf, 2016), 32; Adam Goodheart, "How Slavery Really Ended in America," *The New York Times Magazine* (April 1, 2011).

[4]  Ezra J. Warner, *Generals in Blue: Lives of the Union Commanders* (Baton Rouge, LA: Louisiana State University Press, 1964), 60–61; David S. Heidler and Jeanne T. Heidler, eds., *Encyclopedia of the American Civil War: A Political, Social, and Military History*, 5 vols. (Santa Barbara, CA: ABC-CLIO, 2000), 1:329–31.

[5]  Benjamin F. Butler, *Autobiography and Personal Reminiscences of Major-General Benjamin F. Butler: Butler's Book*, 2 vols. (Boston, MA: A. M. Thayer and Co., 1892), 1:256.

[6]  Ibid., 1:257.

[7]  Ibid.

[8]  Allen C. Guelzo, *Lincoln's Emancipation Proclamation: The End of Slavery in America* (New York: Simon and Schuster, 2004), 32.

[9]  B. F. Butler to W. Scott, Fort Monroe, Virginia, May 24, 1861, *OR*, Series 2, 1:752.

[10]  Ibid.

[11]  John B. Cary to Benjamin F. Butler, Richmond, Virginia, March 9, 1861, in Benjamin F. Butler, *Private and Official Correspondence of Gen. Benjamin F. Butler*, 5 vols. (Norwood, MA: The Plimpton Press, 1917), 1:102–103; M. Blair to Benjamin F. Butler, Washington, D.C., May 29, 1861, in Benjamin F. Butler, *Private and Official Correspondence of Gen. Benjamin F. Butler* (Norwood, MA: The Plimpton Press, 1917), 1:116–17.

[12]  Benjamin F. Butler to W. Scott, Fort Monroe, Virginia, May 27, 1861, *OR*, Series 2, 1:754.

[13]  S. Cameron to Benjamin Butler, Washington, D.C., May 30, 1861, *OR*, Series 2, 1:754–55.

[14]  Ibid.

[15]  George McClellan to "The Union Men of West Virginia," Cincinnati, Ohio, May 26, 1861, *OR*, Series 2, 1:753.

[16]  George McClellan to B. Kelley, Cincinnati, Ohio, May 26, 1861, *OR*, Series 2, 1:753.

[17]  Resolution adopted by the House of Representatives, Special Session, July 9, 1861, *OR*, Series 2, 1:759; General Orders No. 33, Washington, D.C., July 17, 1861, *OR*, Series 2, 1:760; S. Hamilton to I. McDowell, Washington, D.C., July 16, 1861, *OR*, Series 2, 1:760.

18   Ibid.

19   Heidler and Heidler, eds., *Encyclopedia of the American Civil War*, "Confiscation Acts," 1:477–79.

20   Ibid.

21   S. Cameron to Benjamin Butler, Washington, D.C., August 8, 1861, *OR*, Series 2, 1:761–62.

22   Proclamation by J. Fremont, Saint Louis, Missouri, August 30, 1861, *OR*, Series 2, 1:221–22.

23   Abraham Lincoln to J. Fremont, Washington, D.C., September 2, 1861, *OR*, Series 2, 1:766–67; J. Fremont to Abraham Lincoln, Saint Louis, Missouri, September 8, 1861, *OR*, Series 2, 1:767–68; Abraham Lincoln to J. Fremont, Washington, D.C., September 11, 1861, *OR*, Series 2, 1:768; J. Holt to Abraham Lincoln, Washington, D.C., September 12, 1861, *OR*, Series 2, 1:769.

24   Ibid.

25   J. Lane to S. Sturgis, Kansas City, Missouri, October 3, 1861, *OR*, Series 2, 1:771.

26   J. Wool to S. Cameron, Fort Monroe, Virginia, September 18, 1861, *OR*, Series 2, 1:770–71.

27   Ibid.; S. Cameron to J. Wool, Washington, D.C., September 20, 1861, *OR*, Series 2, 1:771; General Orders No. 34, Fort Monroe, Virginia, November 1, 1861, *OR*, Series 2, 1:774–75.

CHAPTER 4

1    "Thomas West Sherman," in David S. Heidler and Jeanne T. Heidler, eds., *Encyclopedia of the American Civil War: A Political, Social, and Military History*, 5 vols. (Santa Barbara, CA: ABC-CLIO, 2000), 4:1,763–64; Ezra J. Warner, *Generals in Blue: Lives of the Union Commanders* (Baton Rouge, LA: Louisiana State University Press, 1964), 440–41.

2    Ibid.; S. Cameron to Thomas W. Sherman, War Department, October 14, 1861, *The War of the Rebellion: A Compilation of the Official Records of the Union and Confederate Armies*, 128 vols. (Washington, D.C.: Government Printing Office, 1896), Series 2, 1:773 (hereafter cited as *OR*).

3    Robert M. Browning, Jr., *Success is All that was Expected: The South Atlantic Blockading Squadron in the Civil War* (Washington, D.C.: Brassey's Inc., 2002), 40–41; R. Saxton to M. Meigs, Port Royal, South Carolina, November 9, 1861, *OR*, Series 2, 1:777.

4    *The Diary of Elias A. Bryant*, quoted in Robert Carse, *Department of the South: Hilton Head Island in the Civil War* (Hilton Head Island, SC: Heritage Library Foundation, 2002), 29–30.

5    Extract from Report of Secretary of War Simon Cameron, December 6, 1861, *OR*, Series 2, 1:783; Simon Cameron to Thomas W. Sherman, War Department, October 14, 1861, *OR*, Series 2, 1:773.

6    Thomas W. Sherman to L. Thomas, Port Royal, South Carolina, December 14, 1861, *OR*, Series 2, 1:785.

7    Ibid.; Thomas W. Sherman to L. Thomas, Port Royal, South Carolina, December 15, 1861, *OR*, Series 2, 1:785–86.

8    Ibid.

9    Ibid.

10   Thomas W. Sherman to L. Thomas, Port Royal, South Carolina, December 15, 1861, *OR*, Series 2, 1:785–86.

[11] Ibid.

[12] General Orders No. 9, Hilton Head, South Carolina, February 6, 1862, *OR*, Series 2, 1:805–806.

[13] Ibid.

[14] Thomas W. Sherman to Adjutant General, U.S. Army, Port Royal, South Carolina, February 9, 1862, *OR*, Series 2, 1:806–807.

[15] Ibid.

[16] Ibid.; Willie Lee Rose, *Rehearsal for Reconstruction: The Port Royal Experiment* (Athens, GA: University of Georgia Press, 1999), 20–21.

[17] "Saxton, Rufus," in Heidler and Heidler, eds., *Encyclopedia of the American Civil War*, 4:1,708–709.

[18] Extract from President Lincoln's Annual Message to Congress, Washington, D.C., December 3, 1861, *OR*, Series 2, 1:781–82.

[19] Ibid.

[20] General Orders No. 7, issued by C. Halpine for David Hunter, Fort Pulaski, Georgia, April 13, 1862, *OR*, Series 2, 1:815; "Hunter, David" in Heidler and Heidler, eds., *Encyclopedia of the American Civil War*, 2:1,019.

[21] General Orders No. 11, quoted in "Proclamation of A. Lincoln Revoking General Hunter's Order of Military Emancipation of May 9, 1862," May 19, 1862, Roy P. Basler, ed., *The Collected Works of Abraham Lincoln*, 9 vols. (New Brunswick, NJ: Rutgers University Press, 1953), 5:222 (hereafter cited as *CW*).

[22] Ibid.

[23] Ibid.; Resolution adopted by the House of Representatives, June 9, 1862, *OR*, Series 2, 1:820; Edwin Stanton to G. Grow, Washington, D.C., June 14, 1862, *OR*, Series 2, 1:820; P. Sturtevant to Abraham Lincoln, May 16, 1862, Abraham Lincoln Papers, Library of Congress.

[24] Proclamation of Abraham Lincoln, May 19, 1862, *CW*, 5:222–23.

[25] Ibid.

CHAPTER 5

[1] Proclamation of General Butler, New Orleans, Louisiana, May 1, 1862, in Benjamin F. Butler, *Private and Official Correspondence of Gen. Benjamin F. Butler*, 5 vols. (Norwood, MA: The Plimpton Press, 1917), 1:433–36.

[2] James Parton, *General Butler in New Orleans: History of the Administration of the Department of the Gulf in the Year 1862* (New York: Mason Brothers, 1864), 489.

[3] Benjamin F. Butler to Edwin M. Stanton, New Orleans, Louisiana, May 25, 1862, *The War of the Rebellion: A Compilation of the Official Records of the Union and Confederate Armies*, 128 vols. (Washington, D.C.: Government Printing Office, 1896) 15:440 (hereafter cited as *OR*).

[4] John W. Phelps to R. S. Davis, Camp Parapet, Louisiana, June 16, 1862, *OR*, 15:486.

[5] Ibid.

[6] William Howard Russell, *My Diary North and South* (London: Bradbury and Evans, 1863), 2:169.

7    Benjamin F. Butler, *Autobiography and Personal Reminiscences of Major-General Benjamin F. Butler: Butler's Book*, 2 vols. (Boston, MA: A. M. Thayer and Co., 1892), 1:488; John McClaughry, "John Wolcott Phelps: The Civil War General Who Became a Forgotten Presidential Candidate in 1880," *Vermont History* 38, no. 4 (Autumn 1970): 268–72.

8    E. Page, Jr., to Benjamin F. Butler, Kenner, Louisiana, May 27, 1862, *OR*, 15:446.

9    General Orders No. 32, New Orleans, Louisiana, May 27, 1862, *OR*, 15:445; Benjamin F. Butler to John W. Phelps, New Orleans, Louisiana, May 21, 1862, *OR*, 15:443; Benjamin F. Butler to John W. Phelps, New Orleans, Louisiana, May 23, 1862, *OR*, 15:443–44; Order to P. Haggerty, New Orleans, Louisiana, May 27, 1862, *OR*, 15:445.

10    John W. Phelps to R. S. Davis, Camp Parapet, Louisiana, June 16, 1862, *OR*, 15:486–90.

11    Benjamin F. Butler to Edwin M. Stanton, New Orleans, Louisiana, June 18, 1862, *OR*, 15:485–86.

12    Ibid.

13    John W. Phelps to R. S. Davis, Camp Parapet, Louisiana, July 31, 1862, *OR*, 15:535.

14    "From General Butler to Mrs. Butler," New Orleans, Louisiana, August 2, 1862, in Butler, *Private and Official Correspondence*, 2:148; Parton, *General Butler in New Orleans*, 505–506.

15    Ibid.

16    Parton, *General Butler in New Orleans*, 508–13.

17    Edwin M. Stanton to Benjamin F. Butler, Washington, D.C., August 7, 1862, *OR*, 15:543.

18    John M. Stanyan, *A History of the Eighth Regiment of New Hampshire Volunteers* (Concord, NH: Ira C. Evans, Printer, 1892), 107.

19    Entry on John W. Phelps, in Ezra J. Warner, *Generals in Blue: Lives of the Union Commanders* (Baton Rouge, LA: Louisiana State University Press, 1964), 368.

20    Benjamin F. Butler to Edwin F. Stanton, New Orleans, Louisiana, August 14, 1862, in Butler, *Private and Official Correspondence*, 2:191–92.

21    James G. Hollandsworth, Jr., *The Louisiana Native Guards: The Black Military Experience During the Civil War* (Baton Rouge, LA: Louisiana State University Press, 1998), 15–18; Order No. 426, in Butler, *Private and Official Correspondence*, 2:210–11; Donald E. Everett, "Ben Butler and the Louisiana Native Guards, 1861–1862," *The Journal of Southern History* 24, no. 2 (May 1958): 202–17.

22    Benjamin F. Butler to Edwin M. Stanton, New Orleans, Louisiana, September 1, 1862, *OR*, 15:559.

23    William A. Dobak, *Freedom by the Sword: The U.S. Colored Troops, 1862–1867* (New York: Skyhorse Publishing, 2013), 96; Everett, "Ben Butler and the Louisiana Native Guards, 1861–1862," 206–209.

24    Butler, *Butler's Book*, 1:493–94.

25    Frederick Douglass, "Fighting Rebels with Only One Hand," *Douglass' Monthly* 4, no. 4 (September 1861), 516.

CHAPTER 6

1    David S. Heidler and Jeanne T. Heidler, eds., *Encyclopedia of the American Civil War: A Political, Social, and Military History*, 5 vols. (Santa Barbara, CA: ABC-CLIO, 2000), 4:1,732–35.

2    Letter from George B. McClellan addressed "To Abraham Lincoln," July 7, 1862, Camp Near Harrison's Landing, *The War of the Rebellion: A Compilation of the Official Records of the Union and Confederate Armies*, 128 vols. (Washington, D.C.: Government Printing Office, 1896), Part 1, 11:73–74 (hereafter cited as *OR*).

3    Allen C. Guelzo, *Lincoln's Emancipation Proclamation: The End of Slavery in America* (New York: Simon and Schuster, 2004), 117–20.

4    Glenn David Brasher, *The Peninsula Campaign and the Necessity of Emancipation* (Chapel Hill, NC: University of North Carolina Press, 2012), 154, 161, 170, 187, 201, 213.

5    Michael Burlingame, *Abraham Lincoln: A Life*, 2 vols. (Baltimore, MD: John Hopkins University Press, 2008), 2:297–302.

6    Matthew Pinsker, *Lincoln's Sanctuary: Abraham Lincoln and the Soldier's Home* (New York: Oxford University Press, 2003), 5, 45–47; Elizabeth Smith Brownstein, *Lincoln's Other White House: The Untold Story of the Man and his Presidency* (Hoboken, NJ: John Wiley and Sons, 2005), 115–16.

7    Message to Congress, March 6, 1862, in Roy P. Basler, ed., *The Collected Works of Abraham Lincoln*, 9 vols. (New Brunswick, NJ: Rutgers University Press, 1953), 5:145 (hereafter cited as *CW*); Letter to Horace Greeley, March 24, 1862, *CW*, 5:169; Guelzo, *Lincoln's Emancipation Proclamation*, 27.

8    Pinsker, *Lincoln's Sanctuary*, 25, 27–28, 41; Charles E. Hamlin, *The Life and Times of Hannibal Hamlin* (Cambridge, MA: Riverside Press, 1899), 2:429.

9    Gideon Welles, *Diary of Gideon Welles: Secretary of the Navy Under Lincoln and Johnson*, 3 vols. (Boston, MA: Riverside Press, 1911), 1:70–71.

10    Ibid.

11    Ibid.

12    Ibid.

13    Message to Congress on the Second Confiscation Act, July 17,1862, *CW*, 5:328–31; Burlingame, *Abraham Lincoln*, 2:357–60.

14    Ibid.

15    Message to Congress on the Second Confiscation Act, July 17,1862, *CW*, 5:328–31; Daniel W. Crofts, *Lincoln and the Politics of Slavery: The Other Thirteenth Amendment and the Struggle to Save the Union* (Chapel Hill, NC: University of North Carolina Press, 2016), 234–37.

16    Burlingame, *Abraham Lincoln*, 2:151; Guelzo, *Lincoln's Emancipation Proclamation*, 215.

17    Letter to Orville H. Browning, September 22, 1861, *CW*, 4:531.

18    Ibid.

19    Francis Bicknell Carpenter, *Six Months at the White House with Abraham Lincoln: The Story of a Picture* (New York: Hurd and Houghton, 1866), 20–21.

20    Richard Hofstadter, "Abraham Lincoln and the Self-Made Myth," *The American Political Tradition and the Men Who Made It* (1948; rpt. New York: Knopf, 1973), 117–31.

21    Brian Dirck, *Lincoln the Lawyer* (Urbana, IL: University of Illinois Press, 2007), 167, 169, 171.

22    Salmon P. Chase, Diary entry for July 22, 1862, in John Niven, ed., *The Salmon P. Chase Papers*, 5 vols. (Kent, OH: Kent State University Press, 1993), 1:350–51.

23    Carpenter, *Six Months at the White House with Abraham Lincoln*, 21.

24    "Emancipation Proclamation—First Draft," July 22, 1862, *CW*, 5:336–37.

25    Ibid.

26  Carpenter, *Six Months at the White House with Abraham Lincoln*, 21–22.

27  Ibid., 22.

28  Abraham Lincoln, Letter addressed "To Horace Greeley," Washington, D.C., August 22, 1862, *CW*, 5:388–89; Horace Greeley, "The Prayer of Twenty Millions," *New York Tribune*, August 20, 1862.

29  Abraham Lincoln, "Address on Colonization to a Deputation of Negroes," August 14, 1862, *CW*, 5:370–75.

30  Abraham Lincoln, "Reply to Emancipation Memorial Presented by Chicago Christians of All Denominations," September 13, 1862, *CW*, 5:420.

31  Ibid.

32  Ibid., 421.

33  Niven, ed., Diary entry for September 22, 1862, *Chase Papers*, 1:394.

34  Ibid.

35  Burrus M. Carnahan, *Act of Justice: Lincoln's Emancipation Proclamation and the Law of War* (Lexington, KY: University Press of Kentucky, 2007), 108.

36  Preliminary Emancipation Proclamation dated September 22, 1862, *CW*, 5:433–36.

37  Ibid. The Preliminary Emancipation Proclamation, consisting of Abraham Lincoln's original draft and Secretary Seward's changes, is held in a double-chambered glass case filled with nitrogen at the New York State Library. An online exhibit of the document is found at: *nysl.nysed.gov/ep/*.

38  Preliminary Emancipation Proclamation dated September 22, 1862, *CW*, 5:433–36.

39  Ibid.; Niven, ed., *Chase Papers*, 1:394–95; Welles, *Diary of Gideon Welles*, 1:142–43;

40  "Reply to Emancipation Memorial Presented by Chicago Christians of All Denominations," September 13, 1862, *CW*, 5:420.

41  Preliminary Emancipation Proclamation dated September 22, 1862, *CW*, 5:433–36.

42  "Remarks to Union Kentuckians," November 21, 1862, *CW*, 5:503.

43  Emphasis added.

44  Guelzo, *Lincoln's Emancipation Proclamation*, 174.

45  Carpenter, *Six Months at the White House*, 23–24.

46  Welles, *Diary of Gideon Welles*, 1:143.

47  Ibid., 145.

48  General Orders No. 139, War Department, Washington, D.C., September 24, 1862, *OR*, Series 3, 2:584–85.

49  Letter to Hannibal Hamlin, September 28, 1862, *CW*, 5:444.

50  Ibid.

CHAPTER 7

1   John Russell Young, *Around the World with General Grant* (1879; rpt. Baltimore, MD: The Johns Hopkins University Press, 2002), 157–58.

2   Ibid.

3   Ibid.

4   Brooks D. Simpson, *Let Us Have Peace: Ulysses S. Grant and the Politics of War and Reconstruction* (Chapel Hill, NC: University of North Carolina Press, 1991), 5, 18; Ulysses S. Grant to Jesse

Root Grant, November 27, 1861, *The Papers of Ulysses S. Grant*, John Y. Simon, ed., 31 vols. (Carbondale, IL: Southern Illinois University Press, 1970), 3:227 (hereafter cited as *PUSG*).

5   Ibid.

6   Letter from Ulysses S. Grant to Jesse Root Grant, Camp Yates near Springfield, Illinois, May 6, 1861, *PUSG*, 2:20–22.

7   Ibid.

8   Ibid.

9   "The President's Proclamation," *New York Times*, September 28, 1862.

10   James Marten, "Slaves and Rebels: The Peculiar Institution in Texas, 1861–1865," *East Texas Historical Journal* 28, no. 1 (1990): 31.

11   John Eaton, *Grant, Lincoln and the Freedmen: Reminiscences of the Civil War* (London: Longman's, Green and Co., 1907), 3.

12   Ibid., 9–13.

13   Ibid.

14   Ibid., 2–3.

15   Ibid., 12.

16   Ulysses S. Grant, *Personal Memoirs of U. S. Grant*, 2 vols. (New York: Charles L. Webster and Co., 1885), 1:424–25.

17   William T. Sherman to John Sherman, September 3, 1862, in Brooks D. Simpson and Jean V. Berlin, eds., *Sherman's Civil War: Selected Correspondence of William T. Sherman, 1860–1865* (Chapel Hill, NC: University of North Carolina Press, 1999), 293.

18   Brooks and Berlin, eds., *Sherman's Civil War*, 293.

19   Eaton, *Grant, Lincoln and the Freedmen*, 12.

20   Ibid., 14.

21   Ibid., 14–15.

22   Ibid., 24; Grant, *Personal Memoirs*, 1:425.

23   Grant, *Personal Memoirs*, 1:424–26.

24   Special Order No. 441, issued at Headquarters, Department of the Gulf, New Orleans, Louisiana, October 1862, in Benjamin F. Butler, *Private and Official Correspondence of Gen. Benjamin F. Butler*, 5 vols. (Norwood, MA: The Plimpton Press, 1917), 2:397.

25   Benjamin F. Butler to G. Weitzel, New Orleans, Louisiana, November 2, 1862, *Private and Official Correspondence*, 2:439.

26   Ibid., 2:439–40; Murray M. Horowitz, "Ben Butler and the Negro: 'Miracles are Occurring,'" *Louisiana History: The Journal of the Louisiana Historical Association* 17, no. 2 (Spring 1976), 180.

27   Benjamin F. Butler to Abraham Lincoln, New Orleans, Louisiana, November 28, 1862, *Private and Official Correspondence*, 2:449–50.

28   Ibid.

29   Ibid.

30   Ibid.

31   Chandra Manning, *Troubled Refuge: Struggling for Freedom in the Civil War* (New York: Alfred A. Knopf, 2016), 32–35.

32   Ibid., 35.

CHAPTER 8

1   Michael E. Ruane, "D.C. Emancipation Tallied the Price of Freedom," *Washington Post*, April 11, 2012.

2   Preliminary Emancipation Proclamation, September 22, 1862, in Roy P. Basler, ed., *The Collected Works of Abraham Lincoln*, 9 vols. (New Brunswick, NJ: Rutgers University Press, 1953), 5:434 (hereafter cited as *CW*).

3   Ibid.; Harold Holzer, Edna G. Medford, and Frank J. Williams, *The Emancipation Proclamation: Three Views* (Baton Rouge, LA: Louisiana State University Press, 2006), 61–67.

4   Mary A. Livermore, *My Story of the War: A Woman's Narrative* (Hartford, CT: A. D. Worthington and Co., 1889), 556.

5   Holzer, et al., *The Emancipation Proclamation*, 61–67.

6   "Remarks to Union Kentuckians," November 21, 1862, *CW*, 5:503.

7   Michael Burlingame, *Abraham Lincoln: A Life*, 2 vols. (Baltimore, MD: John Hopkins University Press, 2008), 2:422.

8   "News from Washington," *New York Times*, December 20, 1862.

9   Diary entry for December 31, 1862, in Theodore C. Pease and James G. Randall, eds., *The Diary of Orville Hickman Browning*, 2 vols. (Springfield, IL: Illinois State Historical Library, 1925), 1:607.

10  Paul M. Angle, ed., *Created Equal? The Complete Lincoln-Douglas Debates of 1858* (Chicago, IL: The University of Chicago Press, 1958), 2.

11  Ibid.

12  Ibid.

13  Note 1 accompanying Abraham Lincoln to Henry J. Raymond, Washington, D.C., December 7, 1862, *CW*, 5:544–45

14  Emphasis in the original. Ibid.

15  Ibid.; "General News: The Finished Year," *New York Times*, December 31, 1862.

16  Annual Message to Congress, December 1, 1862, *CW*, 5:530.

17  Ibid., 5:537.

18  John M. Hay and John G. Nicolay, *Abraham Lincoln: A History*, 10 vols. (1917; rpt. New York: Cosimo Classics, 2009), 6:417; Memorandum from Salmon P. Chase to Abraham Lincoln, December 31, 1862, in John Niven, ed., *The Salmon P. Chase Papers*, 5 vols. (Kent, OH: Kent State University Press, 1993), 3:351.

19  Hay and Nicolay, *Abraham Lincoln*, 6:417–18, 421.

20  Ibid.

21  Preliminary Emancipation Proclamation, September 22, 1862, *CW*, 5:434.

22  Preliminary Draft of Final Emancipation Proclamation, December 30, 1862, *CW*, 6:24.

23  Emphasis added. Emancipation Proclamation, January 1, 1863, *CW*, 6:30.

24  Preliminary Emancipation Proclamation, September 22, 1862, *CW*, 5:434.

25  Emancipation Proclamation, January 1, 1863, *CW*, 6:30.

26  Preliminary Emancipation Proclamation, September 22, 1862, *CW*, 5:434.

27  Preliminary Draft of Final Emancipation Proclamation, December 30, 1862, *CW*, 6:24.

28 Emancipation Proclamation, January 1, 1863, *CW*, 6:29–30.

29 Burlingame, *Abraham Lincoln*, 2:469; Francis Bicknell Carpenter, *Six Months at the White House with Abraham Lincoln: The Story of a Picture* (New York: Hurd and Houghton, 1866), 87.


CHAPTER 9

1 Edward T. Cotham, Jr., *Battle on the Bay: The Civil War Struggle for Galveston* (Austin, TX: University of Texas Press, 1998), 124–35,143; Edward T. Cotham, Jr., *Sabine Pass: The Confederacy's Thermopylae* (Austin, TX: University of Texas Press, 2004), 52–56.

2 General Orders No. 12, New Orleans, Louisiana, January 29, 1863, *The War of the Rebellion: A Compilation of the Official Records of the Union and Confederate Armies*, 128 vols. (Washington, D.C.: Government Printing Office, 1896), Part 1, 15:666–67 (hereafter cited as *OR*).

3 Ibid.

4 Ibid.

5 "Negro Freedom and Vagrancy," *New York Times*, February 14, 1863.

6 General Orders No. 12, New Orleans, Louisiana, January 29, 1863, *OR*, 15:667.

7 Ibid.

8 Peyton McCrary, *Abraham Lincoln and Reconstruction: The Louisiana Experiment* (Princeton, NJ: Princeton University Press, 1978), 135

9 Ibid.; Letter from Ulysses S. Grant to Henry W. Halleck, Holly Springs, Mississippi, January 6, 1863, *The Papers of Ulysses S. Grant*, John Y. Simon, ed., 31 vols. (Carbondale, IL: Southern Illinois University Press, 1970), 7:186 (hereafter cited as *PUSG*).

10 Ibid.; Brooks D. Simpson, *Let Us Have Peace: Ulysses S. Grant and the Politics of War and Reconstruction* (Chapel Hill, NC: University of North Carolina Press, 1991), 36–38; David F. Bastian, *Grant's Canal: The Union's Attempt to Bypass Vicksburg* (Shippensburg, PA: The Bird Street Press, 1995), 17–35.

11 Ulysses S. Grant to Henry W. Halleck, Before Vicksburg, February 18, 1863, *OR*, Part 1, 48:18.

12 Simpson, *Let Us Have Peace*, 41–42.

13 General Orders No. 50, Vicksburg, Mississippi, August 1, 1863, *OR*, Part 3, 24:570.

14 General Orders No. 51, Vicksburg, Mississippi, August 10, 1863, *OR*, Part 3, 24:585.

15 Ibid.

16 Ibid.

17 Order No. 53 note, *PUSG*, 9:136.

18 John Eaton, *Grant, Lincoln and the Freedmen: Reminiscences of the Civil War* (London: Longman's, Green and Co., 1907), 65, 87–92; Note, *PUSG*, 8:343.

19 Ulysses S. Grant to E. B. Washburne, *PUSG*, 9:217–18.


CHAPTER 10

1 Ulysses S. Grant to Edwin M. Stanton, Headquarters in the Field, Virginia, May 11, 1864, *The Papers of Ulysses S. Grant*, John Y. Simon, ed., 31 vols. (Carbondale, IL: Southern Illinois University Press, 1970), 10:422 (hereafter cited as *PUSG*); Ulysses S. Grant to Henry W. Halleck, Near Spotsylvania Courthouse, Virginia, May 11, 1864, *PUSG*, 10:422.

2    J. William Jones, *Personal Reminiscences, Anecdotes, and Letters of Gen. Robert E. Lee* (New York: D. Appleton and Co., 1875), 40.

3    Ibid.

4    Ulysses S. Grant, *Personal Memoirs of U. S. Grant*, 2 vols. (New York: Charles L. Webster and Co., 1885), 2:292.

5    Thurlow Weed to William H. Seward, August 22, 1864, quoted in Note 1, in Roy P. Basler, ed., *The Collected Works of Abraham Lincoln*, 9 vols. (New Brunswick, NJ: Rutgers University Press, 1953), 7:514 (hereafter cited as *CW*).

6    Abraham Lincoln, Memorandum Concerning His Probable Failure of Re-election, Washington, D.C., August 23, 1864, *CW*, 7:514.

7    John C. Waugh, *Reelecting Lincoln: The Battle for the 1864 Presidency* (New York: Da Capo Press, 2001), 276–92.

8    William T. Sherman to Henry W. Halleck, Near Lovejoy's Station, September 3, 1864, *The War of the Rebellion: A Compilation of the Official Records of the Union and Confederate Armies*, 128 vols. (Washington, D.C.: Government Printing Office, 1896), Part 5, 38:777.

9    Grant, *Personal Memoirs*, 2:176.


CHAPTER 11

1    William T. Sherman to Ulysses S. Grant, Allatoona, Georgia, October 9, 1864, *The War of the Rebellion: A Compilation of the Official Records of the Union and Confederate Armies*, 128 vols. (Washington, D.C.: Government Printing Office, 1896), Part 3, 39:162 (hereafter cited as *OR*).

2    William T. Sherman, *Memoirs of W. T. Sherman* (1875; rpt. New York: Penguin Books, 2000), 541.

3    Ibid.

4    Ibid.

5    Ibid., 545.

6    Ibid.; Edmund L. Drago, "How Sherman's March Through Georgia Affected the Slaves," *Georgia Historical Quarterly* 57 no. 3 (Fall, 1973), 364–65.

7    Sherman, *Memoirs*, 545–46.

8    Ibid.

9    Ibid., 549–50.

10    Report of Maj. Gen. Henry W. Slocum, Savannah, Georgia, January 9, 1865, *OR*, 44:159.

11    James P. Jones, "General Jeff C. Davis and Sherman's Georgia Campaign," *Georgia Historical Quarterly* 47, no. 3 (September 1963): 242–44; Sherman, *Memoirs*, 604–605.

12    Sherman, *Memoirs*, 588–89, 592–93.

13    Ibid.

14    Ibid., 607.

15    Ibid.

16    Salmon P. Chase to William T. Sherman, Washington, D.C., January 2, 1865, in John Niven, ed., *The Salmon P. Chase Papers*, 5 vols. (Kent, OH: Kent State University Press, 1993), 5:3-4.

17    Sherman, *Memoirs*, 562–63;

18  Salmon P. Chase to William T. Sherman, Washington, D.C., January 2, 1865, *Salmon Chase Papers*, 5:3.

19  William T. Sherman to Salmon P. Chase, Savannah, Georgia, January 11, 1865, in Brooks D. Simpson and Jean V. Berlin, eds., *Sherman's Civil War: Selected Correspondence of William T. Sherman, 1860–1865* (Chapel Hill, NC: University of North Carolina Press, 1999), 795.

20  Ibid.

21  Ibid., 794

22  Ibid.

23  Ibid.

24  Sherman, *Memoirs*, 606–607.

25  Ibid.

26  Ibid., 607.

27  William T. Sherman to Andrew Johnson, Washington, D.C., February 2, 1866, in Paul H. Bergeron, ed., *The Papers of Andrew Johnson*, 16 vols. (Knoxville, TN: University of Tennessee Press, 1992), 10:20–21.

28  Ibid.

29  Special Field Orders No. 15, Savannah, Georgia, January 16, 1865, *OR*, Part 2, 47:60–62.

30  Ibid.

31  Sherman, *Memoirs*, 609.

32  Howard C. Westwood, "Sherman Marched and Proclaimed, 'Land for the Landless,'" *The South Carolina Historical Magazine* 85, no. 1 (January 1984): 43–48.

## CHAPTER 12

1  Jefferson Davis to Francis P. Blair, Richmond, Virginia, January 12, 1865, in Roy P. Basler, ed., *The Collected Works of Abraham Lincoln*, 9 vols. (New Brunswick, NJ: Rutgers University Press, 1953), 8:275 (hereafter cited as *CW*).

2  Ibid.; Abraham Lincoln to Francis P. Blair, Washington, D.C., January 18, 1865, *CW*, 8:275–76; William C. Harris, "The Hampton Roads Peace Conference: A Final Test of Lincoln's Presidential Leadership," *Journal of the Abraham Lincoln Association*, no. 1 (Winter, 2000): 32–35.

3  "The President's Message and Proclamation," *Brownson's Quarterly Review* 26, no. 1 (January 1864): 94.

4  Abraham Lincoln to James M. Ashley, Washington, D.C., January 31, 1865, and note 1, *CW*, 8:248.

5  Ibid.

6  "Resolution Submitting the Thirteenth Amendment to the States," February 1, 1865, and note 1, *CW*, 8:253–54.

7  "Response to a Serenade," February 1, 1865, *CW*, 8:254–55.

8  Ibid.

9  Harris, "The Hampton Roads Peace Conference," 45–46; Ulysses S. Grant, *Personal Memoirs of U. S. Grant*, 2 vols. (New York: Charles L. Webster and Co., 1885), 2:422–23.

10  Robert M. T. Hunter, "The Peace Commission of 1865," *Southern Historical Society Papers* 3, no. 4 (April 1877): 173.

11    William H. Seward to Charles F. Adams, Washington, D.C., February 7, 1865, *The War of the Rebellion: A Compilation of the Official Records of the Union and Confederate Armies*, 128 vols. (Washington, D.C.: Government Printing Office, 1896), Part 2, 46:473.

12    Ibid.

13    Alexander H. Stephens, *A Constitutional View of the Late War between the States; Its Causes, Character, Conduct and Results, Presented in a Series of Colloquies at Liberty Hall*, 2 vols. (Philadelphia, PA: National Publishing Co., 1870), 2:614.

14    Ibid.

15    Stephens, *A Constitutional View*, 2:614; Hunter, "The Peace Commission of 1865," 174; John A. Campbell, *Reminiscences and Documents Relating to the Civil War During the Year 1865* (Baltimore, MD: John Murphy and Co., 1887), 12–14.

16    Stephens, *A Constitutional View*, 2:615; John A. Campbell, "Memorandum of the Conversation at the Conference in Hampton Roads," *Reminiscences and Documents Relating to the Civil War During the Year 1865* (Baltimore, MD: John Murphy and Co., 1887), 14.

CHAPTER 13

1    James M. Lundberg, "On to Richmond! Or Not," *New York Times*, July 28, 2011.

2    Robert E. Lee to Jefferson Davis, Petersburg, Virginia, April 2, 1865, in *The Papers of Jefferson Davis*, Lynda L. Crist, ed., 14 vols. (Baton Rouge, LA: Louisiana State University Press, 2003), 11:496–97.; Robert E. Lee to Jefferson Davis, Petersburg, Virginia, April 2, 1865, *The War of the Rebellion: A Compilation of the Official Records of the Union and Confederate Armies*, 128 vols. (Washington, D.C.: Government Printing Office, 1896), Part 3, 46:1,378 (hereafter cited as *OR*).

3    Ezra J. Warner, *Generals in Gray: Lives of the Confederate Commanders* (Baton Rouge, LA: Louisiana State University Press, 1959), 292; Donald J. Lehman, *Lucky Landmark: A Study of a Design and its Survival* (Washington, D.C.: General Services Administration Public Buildings Service, 1973), 34, 60, 71.

4    Ulysses S. Grant, *Personal Memoirs of U. S. Grant*, 2 vols. (New York: Charles L. Webster and Co., 1885), 2:424–25.

5    Ibid.

6    Entry on "Sheridan, Philip Henry," in David S. Heidler and Jeanne T. Heidler, eds., *Encyclopedia of the American Civil War: A Political, Social, and Military History*, 5 vols. (Santa Barbara, CA: ABC-CLIO, 2000), 4:1,760–61; Grant, *Personal Memoirs*, 133; John Russell Young, *Around the World with General Grant* (1879; rpt. Baltimore, MD: The Johns Hopkins University Press, 2002), 156.

7    Report of Maj. Gen. Philip H. Sheridan, New Orleans, Louisiana, July 16, 1865, *OR*, Part 1, 46:478; Orville E. Babcock to John A. Rawlins, White House, Virginia, March 16, 1865, *OR*, Part 3, 46:14.

8    Philip H. Sheridan to Orville E. Babcock, Mangohick Church, Virginia, March 16, 1865, *OR*, Part 3, 46:15.

9    Philip H. Sheridan, *Personal Memoirs of P. H. Sheridan*, 2 vols. (New York: Charles L. Webster and Co., 1888), 2:262.

10    Ibid.

CHAPTER 14

1   William T. Sherman, *Memoirs of W. T. Sherman* (1875; rpt. New York: Penguin Books, 2000), 719.

2   Ibid., 717.

3   Report of Henry W. Halleck, Richmond, Virginia, June 26, 1865, *The War of the Rebellion: A Compilation of the Official Records of the Union and Confederate Armies*, 128 vols. (Washington, D.C.: Government Printing Office, 1896), Part 3, 46:1,296 (hereafter cited as *OR*).

4   Adam Badeau to E. W. Smith, Richmond, Virginia, April 21, 1865, *OR*, Part 3, 46:884.

5   Report of Henry W. Halleck, Richmond, Virginia, June 26, 1865, *OR*, Part 3, 46:1,296.

6   Henry W. Halleck to John M. Schofield, Richmond, Virginia, May 5, 1865, *OR*, Part 3, 47:404.

7   John P. Hatch to W. L. M. Burger, Charleston, South Carolina, April 19, 1865, *OR*, Part 3, 47:256.

8   Ibid.

9   J. R. Hawley to J. A. Campbell, Wilmington, North Carolina, April 3, 1865, *OR*, Part 3, 47:92; J. R. Hawley to J. A. Campbell, Wilmington, North Carolina, April 1, 1865, *OR*, Part 3, 47:79; E. L. Molineux to W. L. M. Burger, Augusta, Georgia, June 26, 1865, *OR*, Part 3, 47:666.

10  Patrick Rael, *Eighty-Eight Years: The Long Death of Slavery in the United States, 1777–1865* (Athens: University of Georgia Press, 2015), 301.

11  Report of Henry W. Halleck, Richmond, Virginia, June 26, 1865, *OR*, Part 3, 46:1,296.

12  General Orders No. 11, Petersburg, Virginia, April 24, 1865, *OR*, Part 3, 46:932–33.

13  General Orders No. 32, Raleigh, North Carolina, April 27, 1865, *OR*, Part 3, 47:331.

14  John M. Schofield, *Forty-Six Years in the Army* (New York: Century Company, 1897), 368.

15  An example of the publication in sequence of General Schofield's General Orders is found on page 4 of the *The Daily North Carolina Standard* (Raleigh, NC), June 20, 1865.

16  James L. McDonough, *Schofield: Union General in the Civil War and Reconstruction* (Tallahassee, FL: Florida State University Press, 1972), 160.

17  John M. Schofield to William T. Sherman, Raleigh, North Carolina, May 5, 1865, *OR*, Part 3, 47:405.

18  William T. Sherman to John M. Schofield, Morehead City, North Carolina, May 5, 1865, *OR*, Part 3, 47:405–406.

19  Ibid.

20  John M. Schofield to Ulysses S. Grant, Raleigh, North Carolina, May 10, 1865, *OR*, Part 3, 47:462.

21  Ibid.

22  Ibid.

23  General Orders No. 46, Raleigh, North Carolina, May 15, 1865, *OR*, Part 3, 47:503.

24  Ibid.

25  Ibid.

26  General Orders No. 22, Jacksonville, Florida, May 24, 1865, *OR*, Part 3, 47:623–24.

27  Ibid.

28  General Orders No. 24, Jacksonville, Florida, June 3, 1865, *OR*, Part 3, 47:624–25.

29  Ibid.

30  Ibid.

[31] Quincy A. Gilmore to J. P. Hatch, *OR*, Part 3, 47:628.

[32] Ibid.

[33] Ibid.

## CHAPTER 15

[1] Address to "Soldiers of the Trans-Mississippi Army," Shreveport, Louisiana, April 21, 1865, *The War of the Rebellion: A Compilation of the Official Records of the Union and Confederate Armies*, 128 vols. (Washington, D.C.: Government Printing Office, 1896), Part 2, 48:1,284 (hereafter cited as *OR*).

[2] Ibid.

[3] Ibid.; John K. Damico, "Confederate Soldiers Take Matters into Their Own Hands," *Louisiana History: The Journal of the Louisiana Historical Association* 39, no. 2 (Spring 1998): 191–92; Report of C. S. Bell, scout, no date or place, *OR*, Part 2, 48:400.

[4] Edmund Kirby Smith to J. Slidell, Paris, France, January 9, 1865, *OR*, Part 2, 48:1,319–20; Edmund Kirby Smith to R. Rose, Shreveport, Louisiana, May 2, 1865, *OR*, Part 2, 48:1,292–93; Damico, "Confederate Soldiers Take Matters into Their Own Hands," 197; Carland Elaine Crook, "Benjamin Theron and French Designs in Texas during the Civil War," *Southwestern Historical Quarterly* 68 (April 1965): 432–33.

[5] Damico, "Confederate Soldiers Take Matters into Their Own Hands," 196; John D. Winters, *The Civil War in Louisiana* (Baton Rouge, LA: Louisiana State University Press, 1991), 419.

[6] Richard Taylor, *Destruction and Reconstruction: Personal Experiences of the Late War* (1879; rpt. New York: Time-Life Books, 1981), 226.

[7] Ulysses S. Grant to John Pope, Washington, D.C., April 17, 1865, *OR*, Part 2, 48:110.

[8] Ulysses S. Grant to John Pope, Washington, D.C., May 1, 1865, *OR*, Part 2, 48:283.

[9] Edmund Kirby Smith to John Pope, Shreveport, Louisiana, May 9, 1865, *OR*, Part 1, 48:189.

[10] Edmund Kirby Smith to H. W. Allen, et al., Shreveport, Louisiana, May 9, 1865, *OR*, Part 1, 48:189–90.

[11] Ibid.

[12] William R. Geise, "Missouri's Confederate Capital in Marshall, Texas," *The Southwestern Historical Quarterly* 66, no. 2 (October 1962): 205–206.

[13] Unnamed document advising Gen. Edmund Kirby Smith from H. W. Allen, et al., Marshall, Texas, May 13, 1865, *OR*, Part 1, 48:190–91.

[14] Ibid.

[15] Memorandum for Col. John T. Sprague from Edmund Kirby Smith, undated, *OR*, Part 1, 48:192–93.

[16] Ibid.

[17] Ibid.

[18] Ibid.

[19] Ibid.

[20] Ibid.

[21] Ibid.

[22] D. F. Boyd to L. A. Bringier, Alexandria, Louisiana, May 17, 1865, *OR*, Part 2, 48:1,310.

[23] Ibid.

24 J. J. Reynolds to John Pope, Little Rock, Arkansas, May 31, 1865, *OR*, Part 2, 48:700.

25 General Orders No. 48, Shreveport, Louisiana, May 18, 1865, *OR*, Part 2, 48:1,312; Joseph H. Parks, *General Edmund Kirby Smith, C.S.A.* (Baton Rouge, LA: Louisiana State University Press, 1954), 472, 481; Damico, "Confederate Soldiers Take Matters into their Own Hands," 201.

26 Winters, *The Civil War in Louisiana*, 425; Damico, "Confederate Soldiers Take Matters into their Own Hands," 203.

27 Winters, *The Civil War in Louisiana*, 425–26; Parks, *General Edmund Kirby Smith*, 474.

28 Military Convention, New Orleans, Louisiana, May 26, 1865, *OR*, Part 2, 48:600–602; Andrew W. Hall, "Closing Act," *The Civil War Monitor* 5, no. 2 (Summer 2015): 40, 74–76.

29 Francis J. Herron to Edward R. S. Canby, Baton Rouge, Louisiana, May 23, 1865, *OR*, Part 2, 48:562.

30 "General Francis J. Herron Dead," *New York Times*, January 10, 1902; Ezra J. Warner, *Generals in Blue: Lives of the Union Commanders* (Baton Rouge, LA: Louisiana State University Press, 1964), 228–29.

31 Ibid.

32 Ibid.; Sanford W. Huff, "Major General F. J. Herron," *The Annals of Iowa* 167, no. 1 (1867): 807.

33 Nathaniel P. Banks to Edwin M. Stanton, New Orleans, Louisiana, May 10, 1865, *OR*, Part 2, 48:380.

34 General Orders No. 18, Baton Rouge, Louisiana, May 14, 1865, *OR*, Part 2, 48:437–38.

35 C. T. Christensen to Francis J. Herron, New Orleans, Louisiana, May 30, 1865, *OR*, Part 2, 48:681; Philip H. Sheridan to John A. Rawlins, New Orleans, Louisiana, June 2, 1865, *OR*, Part 2, 48:726.

36 O. McFadden to N. Burbank, Alexandria, Louisiana, June 1, 1865, *OR*, Part 2, 48:719–20.

37 Ibid.

38 Francis J. Herron to Nathaniel P. Banks, Alexandria, Louisiana, June 3, 1865, *OR*, Part 2, 48:747–48.

39 Report of J. Bailey, Baton Rouge, Louisiana, May 24, 1865, *OR*, Part 1, 48:262–64.

40 Ibid.

41 General Orders No. 20, Shreveport, Louisiana, June 3, 1865, *OR*, Part 2, 48:749.

42 Ibid.

43 Ibid.

44 Ibid.

45 General Orders No. 21, Shreveport, Louisiana, June 4, 1865, *OR*, Part 2, 48:769–70.

46 Ibid.

47 Francis J. Herron to A. De Blanc, Natchitoches, Louisiana, June 5, 1865, *OR*, Part 2, 48:778.

48 "New Labor System," *Shreveport Semi-Weekly News*, June 10, 1865.

49 Francis J. Herron to Nathaniel P. Banks, Shreveport, Louisiana, June 8, 1865, *OR*, Part 2, 48:816–17.

50 Ibid.

51 Edward R. S. Canby to Ulysses S. Grant, New Orleans, Louisiana, May 30, 1865, *OR*, Part 2, 48:673; Letter to O. S. Curtis, Purchasing Agent, New Orleans, Louisiana, from Secretary of the Treasury Hugh McCullock, Treasury Department, n.p., May 27, 1865, Francis J. Herron Papers, New York Historical Society; General Orders No. 3, New Orleans, Louisiana, June 1, 1865, *OR*, Part 2, 48:713–14.

52  Report of Francis J. Herron to Nathaniel P. Banks, Shreveport, Louisiana, June 8, 1865, *OR*, Part
    2, 48:816–17; Francis J. Herron to Nathaniel P. Banks, Shreveport, Louisiana, June 8, 1865, *OR*,
    Part 2, 48:816.

53  Ibid.

54  Ibid.; Philip H. Sheridan to Francis J. Herron, New Orleans, Louisiana, June 14, 1865, Francis J.
    Herron Papers, New York Historical Society.

55  Notes accompanying publication of General Orders No. 24, *The South-Western* (Shreveport,
    LA), June 14, 1865; Letter to Francis J. Herron from a Delegation of Planters, Thomas J.
    Land, Chairman, Shreveport, Louisiana, June 11, 1865, Francis J. Herron Papers, New York
    Historical Society.

56  General Orders No. 24, Shreveport, Louisiana, June 11, 1865, *OR*, Part 2, 48:854–55.

57  Ibid.

58  Ibid.

59  Ibid.

60  Ibid.

61  Ibid.

62  Ibid.

63  *Shreveport Semi-Weekly News*, June 10, 1865.

64  *The South-Western* (Shreveport, LA), June 14, 1865.

65  W. H. Clapp to J. H. Coates, Shreveport, Louisiana, June 13, 1865, *OR*, Part 2, 48:867–68.

66  Ibid.

67  Ibid.

68  Francis J. Herron to C. T. Christensen, Shreveport, Louisiana, June 16, 1865, *OR*, Part 2,
    48:903.

69  Indorsement by J. W. Forsyth by order of Philip H. Sheridan, on letter from Francis J. Herron
    to C. T. Christensen, New Orleans, Louisiana, June 16, 1865, *OR*, Part 2, 48:903.

CHAPTER 16

1  John C. Walker, "Reconstruction in Texas," *Galveston Daily News*, November 15, 1896.

2  Benny R. Deuson, "Pendleton Murrah," in *Ten Texans in Gray*, W. C. Nunn, ed. (Hillsboro,
   TX: Hill Junior College Press, 1968), 122–24; Ralph A. Wooster, "Texas," in *The Confederate
   Governors*, W. Buck Yearns, ed. (Athens, GA: University of Georgia Press, 1985), 208–209.

3  Wooster, "Texas," 210–15; John Anthony Moretta, *William Pitt Ballinger: Texas Lawyer, Southern
   Statesman, 1825–1888* (Austin, TX: Texas State Historical Association, 2000), 162.

4  Pendleton Murrah to "My Countrymen," Executive Department, Austin, Texas, April 27, 1865,
   Records of Pendleton Murrah, Texas Office of the Governor, Archives and Information Services
   Division, Texas State Library and Archives Commission.

5  Ibid.

6  William Pitt Ballinger Diary, entry for May 17, 1865, Typescript, Galveston and Texas History
   Center, Rosenberg Library, Galveston, Texas, 1865 volume, p. 58 (hereafter cited as TS).

7  Ibid.

8  Ibid.

9  Ibid., 59.

10  Moretta, *William Pitt Ballinger*, 170.

11  Elizabeth Silverthorne, *Ashbel Smith of Texas: Pioneer, Patriot, Statesman, 1805–1886* (College Station, TX: Texas A&M University Press, 1988), 168–69; Elizabeth Silverthorne, "Ashbel Smith" *The New Handbook of Texas*, Ron Tyler, ed., 6 vols. (Austin, TX: The Texas Historical Association, 1996), 5:1,090–91.

12  Pendleton Murrah to Ashbel Smith, May 23, 1865, Ashbel Smith Papers, Dolph Briscoe Center for American History, The University of Texas at Austin.

13  Silverthorne, *Ashbel Smith*, 165.

14  Silverthorne, *Ashbel Smith*, 167.

15  W. Cravens to Ashbel Smith, Houston, Texas, May 24, 1865, Ashbel Smith Papers, Dolph Briscoe Center for American History, The University of Texas at Austin.

16  Ibid.

17  Kenneth R. Stevens, "William Pitt Ballinger: Galveston's Reluctant Rebel," *East Texas Historical Journal* 40, no. 1 (2002): 41.

18  Moretta, *William Pitt Ballinger*, 170.

19  Silverthorne, *Ashbel Smith*, 168–69.

20  Benjamin F. Sands, *From Reefer to Rear-Admiral* (New York: Frederick A. Stokes Co., 1899), 272–75.

21  Ballinger Diary, entry for May 27, 1865, TS, p. 63.

22  John B. Magruder to "The People of Texas," Houston, Texas, May 26, 1865, *The War of the Rebellion: A Compilation of the Official Records of the Union and Confederate Armies*, 128 vols. (Washington, D.C.: Government Printing Office, 1896), Part 2, 48:1,319-20 (hereafter cited as *OR*).

23  Ibid.

24  Ballinger Diary, entry for May 27, 1865, TS, p. 63.

25  Ibid., entry for May 28, 1865, p. 64.

26  Ibid., entry for May 28, 1865, p. 65.

27  Ibid., entry for May 29, 1865, p. 66; Ashbel Smith and William P. Ballinger to Edward R. S. Canby, New Orleans, Louisiana, May 29, 1865, *OR*, Part 2, 48:648–49.

28  Ballinger Diary, undated entry, TS, p. 68–69.

29  Ibid.

30  Edward R. S. Canby to Ashbel Smith and William P. Ballinger, New Orleans, Louisiana, May 29, 1865, *OR*, Part 2, 48:649.

31  Ballinger Diary, undated entry, p. 71.

32  Ballinger Diary, entry for May 30, 1865, TS, p. 73–74.

33  Ibid.

34  Ibid., p. 74.

35  Ibid., p. 76.

36  Ibid.

37  Ibid., p. 76–77.

38  Ibid.

39  Ibid., p. 77.

40  Ibid.

41  Ibid.

42 Ibid., p. 78.

43 Ibid.

44 Ibid., p. 78–79.

45 Ibid.

46 Ibid., p. 78–79; William P. Ballinger to Pendleton Murrah, New Orleans, Louisiana, June 1, 1865, William Pitt Ballinger papers, Dolph Briscoe Center for American History, The University of Texas at Austin.

47 Ballinger Diary, undated entry, TS, p. 79.

48 Ashbel Smith to E. P. Turner, New Orleans, Louisiana, June 1, 1865, Ashbel Smith Papers, Dolph Briscoe Center for American History, The University of Texas at Austin.

49 Ibid.

50 John Hancock Diary, p. 143, Archives and Information Services Division, Texas State Library and Archives Commission.

51 Letter from William P. Ballinger and Col. Ashbel Smith to Edward R. S. Canby, New Orleans, Louisiana, May 30, 1865, copied in Ballinger Diary, TS, p. 79–84.

52 Ibid., 83.

53 Ibid.

54 Ibid.

55 E. D. Etchison to S. A. Hurlbut, New Orleans, Louisiana, February 27, 1865, *OR*, Part 1, 48:1,048–49.

56 Lowell H. Harrison, "Slavery in Kentucky: A Civil War Casualty," *The Kentucky Review* 5, no. 1 (Fall 1983): 39; "Slavery in New Jersey: A Troubled History," an online exhibit by the Durrand-Hedden Hose and Garden Association, Inc., accessed February 15, 2020, *https://www.durandhedden.org/docs/juneteenth-exhibit.pdf.*

57 John B. Magruder to R. W. Johnson, Lewisville, Arkansas, November 5, 1864, *OR*, Part 4, 41:1,030; Randolph B. Campbell, *An Empire for Slavery: The Peculiar Institution in Texas* (Baton Rouge, LA: Louisiana State University Press, 1989), 264–67, Appendix 2; Dale Baum, "Slaves Taken to Texas for Safekeeping during the Civil War," in *The Fate of Texas: The Civil War and the Lone Star State*, Charles D. Grear, ed. (Fayetteville, AR: The University of Arkansas Press, 2008), 83–103; W. Caleb McDaniel, "Involuntary Removals: Refugeed Slaves in Confederate Texas," in *Lone Star Unionism, Dissent and Resistance: Other Sides of Civil War Texas*, Jesús de la Teja, ed. (Norman, OK: University of Oklahoma Press, 2016), 60; W. Caleb McDaniel, "How many slaves were refugeed to Confederate Texas," June 25, 2013, online article, accessed July 22, 2018, *https://wcm1.web.rice.edu/how-many-refugeed-slaves-in-texas.html.*

CHAPTER 17

1 General Orders No. 25, Washington, D.C., May 17, 1865, *The War of the Rebellion: A Compilation of the Official Records of the Union and Confederate Armies*, 128 vols. (Washington, D.C.: Government Printing Office, 1896), Part 2, 48: 475–76 (hereafter cited as *OR*); Ulysses S. Grant to Philip H. Sheridan, Washington, D.C., May 17, 1865, *OR*, Part 2, 48:476.

2 Philip H. Sheridan, *Personal Memoirs of P. H. Sheridan*, 2 vols. (New York: C. L. Webster and Co., 1888), 2:210.

3 Ibid.

4    Ibid.

5    Ulysses S. Grant to Philip H. Sheridan, Washington, D.C., May 17, 1865, *OR*, Part 2, 48:476.

6    Ibid.

7    "Arrival of Gen. Phil Sheridan and Staff," *The Daily Picayune* (New Orleans, LA), June 3, 1865.

8    Philip H. Sheridan to John A. Rawlins, New Orleans, Louisiana, June 2, 1865, *OR*, Part 2, 48:726.

9    Ulysses S. Grant to Philip H. Sheridan, Washington, D.C., May 17, 1865, *OR*, Part 2, 48:476.

10   Thomas North, *Five Years in Texas: or, What You Did Not Hear During the War from January 1861 to January 1866: A Narrative of His Travels, Experiences, and Observations, in Texas and Mexico* (Cincinnati, OH: Elm Street Printing Co., 1871), 104–105.

11   Ibid.

12   Daniel O'Flaherty, *General Jo Shelby: Undefeated Rebel* (Chapel Hill, NC: University of North Carolina Press, 2000), 272–84.

13   Daniel Foxx and Eddy W. Davison, *Rebel Refugees: The Confederate Exodus to Mexico* (Peoria, IL: Draytonville Publications, 2015), 47–50, 54, 69, 72–73.

14   Philip H. Sheridan to John A. Rawlins, New Orleans, Louisiana, June 4, 1865, *OR*, Part 2, 48:767.

15   Ibid.

16   Ibid.

17   M. C. Meigs to Philip H. Sheridan, Washington, D.C., June 17, 1865, *OR*, Part 2, 48:908.

18   Philip H. Sheridan to John A. Rawlins, New Orleans, Louisiana, June 3, 1865, *OR*, Part 2, 48:767.

19   Ibid.; C. G. Sawtelle to Edward R. S. Canby, Mobile, Alabama, May 29, 1865, *OR*, Part 2, 48:648; Edward R. S. Canby to Ulysses S. Grant, New Orleans, Louisiana, May 31, 1865, *OR*, Part 2, 48:691–92.

20   Edward R. S. Canby to Ulysses S. Grant, New Orleans, Louisiana, May 31, 1865, *OR*, Part 2, 48:691–92.

21   A. H. Cañedo to P. J. Osterhaus, Matamoras, Mexico, June 4, 1865, *OR*, Part 2, 48:771.

22   Ibid.

23   Indorsement by Edward R. S. Canby, New Orleans, Louisiana, June 14, 1865, *OR*, Part 2, 48:772.

24   H. K. Thatcher to Edward R. S. Canby, New Orleans, Louisiana, June 1, 1865, *OR*, Part 2, 48:715.

25   Benjamin F. Sands, *From Reefer to Rear-Admiral* (New York: Frederick A. Stokes Co., 1899), 277–78.

26   Message from E. J. Davis quoted in Philip H. Sheridan to John A. Rawlins, New Orleans, Louisiana, June 5, 1865, *OR*, Part 2, 48:775.

27   Philip H. Sheridan to John A. Rawlins, New Orleans, Louisiana, June 5, 1865, *OR*, Part 2, 48:775; C. T. Christensen to S. B. Holabird, New Orleans, Louisiana, June 5, 1865, *OR*, Part 2, 48:776.

28   *The United States Army and Navy Journal and Gazette* 13 (March 11, 1876): 506.

29   William Pitt Ballinger Diary, undated entry that references meeting with Sheridan on June 1 or 2, Typescript, Galveston and Texas History Center, Rosenberg Library, Galveston, Texas, 1865 volume, p. 94 (hereafter cited as TS).

30   Ibid.

31   Ibid.

32   Ulysses S. Grant to Philip H. Sheridan, Washington, D.C., June 15, 1865, *OR*, Part 2, 48:889; Philip H. Sheridan to Gordon Granger, New Orleans, Louisiana, June 16, 1865, *OR*, Part 2, 48:902; Philip H. Sheridan to Ulysses S. Grant, New Orleans, Louisiana, June 8, 1865, *OR*, Part 2, 48:813–14.

33   Gordon Granger to R. H. Jackson, Fort Morgan, Alabama, June 8, 1865, *OR*, Part 2, 48:819; Gordon Granger to Philip H. Sheridan, Fort Morgan, Alabama, June 8, 1865, *OR*, Part 2, 48:819.

34   William L. Richter, "It is Best to Go in Strong-Handed: Army Occupation of Texas, 1865–1866," *Arizona and the West* 27, no. 2 (Summer 1985): 119–20.

35   Philip H. Sheridan to John A. Rawlins, New Orleans, Louisiana, June 13, 1865, *OR*, Part 2, 48:865–66; J. A. Forsyth to G. A. Forsyth, New Orleans, Louisiana, June 13, 1865, *OR*, Part 2, 48:866; Special Orders No. 5, New Orleans, Louisiana, June 9, 1865, *OR*, Part 2, 48:828.

36   Philip H. Sheridan to Gordon Granger, New Orleans, Louisiana, June 29, 1865, *OR*, Part 2, 48:1,026.

37   Philip H. Sheridan to Gordon Granger, New Orleans, Louisiana, July 10, 1865, *OR*, Part 2, 48:1,068.; J. C. Veatch to Frederick W. Emery, Shreveport, Louisiana, July 12, 1865, *OR*, Part 2, 48:1,073; Philip H. Sheridan to Gordon Granger, New Orleans, Louisiana, June 29, 1865, *OR*, Part 2, 48:1,026.

38   Richter, "It is Best to Go in Strong-Handed," 121–23; John M. Carroll, *Custer in Texas: An Interrupted Narrative* (New York: Sol Lewis and Liveright, 1975), 72–73, 104–105.

## CHAPTER 18

1    Ezra J. Warner, *Generals in Blue: Lives of the Union Commanders* (Baton Rouge, LA: Louisiana State University Press, 1964), 181, 184, 437; Joseph H. Parks, *General Edmund Kirby Smith, C.S.A.* (Baton Rouge, LA: Louisiana State University Press, 1954), 35; Robert C. Conner, *General Gordon Granger: The Savior of Chickamauga and the Man Behind Juneteenth* (Havertown, PA: Casemate Publishers, 2013), 18.

2    "In Memoriam," *Society of the Army of the Cumberland Fifteenth Reunion, Cincinnati, Ohio* (Cincinnati, OH: Robert Clarke and Co., 1884), 210–11.

3    Ibid.

4    William F. G. Shanks, *Personal Recollections of Distinguished Generals* (New York: Harper and Bros., 1896), 271.

5    Ibid., 273–74.

6    Conner, *General Gordon Granger*, 20, 29, 200.

7    Shanks, *Personal Recollections*, 273.

8    Marshall P. Thatcher, *A Hundred Battles in the West, St. Louis to Atlanta, 1861–1865, The Second Michigan Cavalry* (Detroit, MI: self-published, 1884), 32.

9    John Pope, *The Military Memoirs of General John Pope*, Peter Cozzens and Robert Girardi, eds. (Chapel Hill, NC: University of North Carolina Press, 1998), 103.

10   Ibid.

11   Conner, *General Gordon Granger*, 24–25.

12  "In Memoriam," *Society of the Army of the Cumberland Fifteenth Reunion*, 213.

13  Ibid.

14  John Corson Smith, *Oration at the Unveiling of the Monument Erected to the Memory of Maj. Gen. James B. Steedman* (Chicago, IL: Knight and Leonard Co., 1887), 15–16.

15  Illinois Infantry, Ninety-Second Regiment, *Ninety-Second Illinois Volunteers* (Freeport, IL: Journal Steam Publishing House and Bookbindery, 1875), 63.

16  Report of S. D. Sturgis, Near Rolla, Missouri, August 20, 1861, *The War of the Rebellion: A Compilation of the Official Records of the Union and Confederate Armies*, 128 vols. (Washington, D.C.: Government Printing Office, 1896), 3:69–70 (hereafter cited as *OR*).

17  Ibid.

18  Warner, *Generals in Blue*, 181.

19  Kristopher A. Teters, *Practical Liberators: Union Officers in the Western Theater during the Civil War* (Chapel Hill, NC: University of North Carolina Press, 2018), 10–11, 55–56.

20  William F. Atkinson, "The Rock of Chickamauga," in *War Papers, being Papers Read before the Commandery of the State of Michigan, Military Order of the Loyal Legion of the United States*, 70 vols. (1898; rpt., Wilmington, NC: Broadfoot Publishing Co., 1993), 51:8.

21  Ibid.

22  J. S. Fullerton, "Reinforcing Thomas at Chickamauga," in *Battles and Leaders of the Civil War: Grant-Lee Edition*, Robert Underwood Johnson and Clarence Clough Buel, eds., 8 vols. (New York: The Century Co., 1887; rpt. Harrisburg, PA: The Archive Society, 1991), 3:666.

23  Ibid.

24  Ibid.

25  Ibid., 667.

26  David S. Stanley, *An American General: The Memoirs of David Sloan Stanley*, Samuel W. Fordyce IV, ed. (Santa Barbara, CA: The Narrative Press, 2003), 150.

27  Conner, *General Gordon Granger*, 98–99; Report of Thomas J. Wood, Chattanooga, Tennessee, September 29, 1863, *OR*, Part 1, 30:638.

28  Address of Gen. Thomas J. Wood, *Seventh Annual Reunion of the Association of the Graduates of the United States Military Academy at West Point, New York* (New York: A. S. Barnes and Co., 1876), 62.

29  Philip H. Sheridan, *Personal Memoirs of P. H. Sheridan*, 2 vols. (New York: C. L. Webster and Co., 1888), 1:170.

30  Ibid., 182.

31  Conner, *General Gordon Granger*, 52.

32  Peter Cozzens, *The Shipwreck of Their Hopes: The Battles for Chattanooga* (Urbana, IL: The University of Illinois Press, 1994), 245.

33  Ibid.; Charles A. Dana, *Recollections of the Civil War; with the Leaders at Washington and in the Field in the Sixties* (New York: D. Appleton and Co., 1902), 149.

34  Joseph S. Fullerton, "The Army of the Cumberland at Chattanooga," in *Battles and Leaders of the Civil War*, 3:725.

35  Ibid.

36  Cozzens, *The Shipwreck of Their Hopes*, 282–86, 349, 386; Conner, *General Gordon Granger*, 123–31; William T. Sherman, *Memoirs of W. T. Sherman* (1875; rpt. New York: Penguin Books, 2000), 395–96.

37  Conner, *General Gordon Granger*, 140–42.

38  Ibid.

39  "The Fourth Army Corps Gen. Granger's Farewell," *New York Times*, April 21, 1864.

40  Conner, *General Gordon Granger*, 150–51.

41  Ibid., 153–57; John C. Waugh, *Last Stand at Mobile* (Abilene, TX: McWhiney Foundation Press, 2001), 62–66; William Dobak, *Freedom by the Sword: The U.S. Colored Troops, 1862–1867* (New York: Skyhorse Publishing, 2013), 140.

42  Henry W. Halleck to Edward R. S. Canby, Washington, D.C., February 28, 1865, *OR*, Part 1, 48:1,001–1,002.

43  Ulysses S. Grant to Henry W. Halleck, City Point, Virginia, March 1, 1865, *OR*, Part 1, 48:1,045; Ulysses S. Grant to Edwin Stanton, City Point, Virginia, March 4, 1865, *OR*, Part 1, 48:1,164.

44  Paul H. Bergeron, ed., *The Papers of Andrew Johnson*, 16 vols. (Knoxville, TN: University of Tennessee Press, 1992), 8:122 (notes 2 and 3).

45  Ibid.

46  Ulysses S. Grant to Edward R. S. Canby, Washington, D.C., May 18, 1865, *OR*, Part 2, 48:486–87.

47  Philip H. Sheridan to John A. Rawlins, New Orleans, Louisiana, June 2, 1865, *OR*, Part 2, 48:726.

48  Philip H. Sheridan to John A. Rawlins, New Orleans, Louisiana, June 4, 1865, *OR*, Part 2, 48:767.

49  Ulysses S. Grant to John A. Rawlins attaching draft telegram to Philip H. Sheridan, Chicago, Illinois, June 10, 1865, *OR*, Part 2, 48:840; Ulysses S. Grant to Philip H. Sheridan, Washington, D.C. June 15, 1865, *OR*, Part 2, 48:889.

50  Philip H. Sheridan to Gordon Granger, New Orleans, Louisiana, June 10, 1865, *OR*, Part 2, 48:841.

5  Bennie Deuson, "Pendleton Murrah," in *Ten Texans in Gray*, W. C. Nunn, ed. (Hillsboro, TX: Hill Junior College Press, 1968), 134.

52  Philip H. Sheridan to John A. Rawlins, New Orleans, Louisiana, June 13, 1865, *OR*, Part 2, 48:865–66.

53  Philip H. Sheridan to Gordon Granger, New Orleans, Louisiana, June 13, 1865, *OR*, Part 2, 48:866–67.

54  *Houston Telegraph*, June 21, 1865.

55  Ibid.

56  Thomas B. Marshall, *History of the Eighty-third Ohio Voluntary Infantry, the Greyhound Regiment* (Cincinnati, OH: The Eighty-third Ohio Volunteer Infantry Association, 1912), 171–72.

57  Ibid.

58  Charles W. Hayes, *History of the Island and the City of Galveston*, 2 vols. (Cincinnati, OH: 1879; rpt. Austin, TX: Jenkins Garrett Press, 1974), 2:643.

59  Ibid.

60  Ibid.

61  Gordon Granger to Philip H. Sheridan, Galveston, Texas, June 19, 1865, *OR*, Part 2, 48:927–28; Carl Adams, *Nance: Trials of the First Slave Freed by Abraham Lincoln* (n.p., 2016); Steve Karnowski, "Sleuths trace fate of 1st black male slave freed by Lincoln," *The Monitor* (McAllen,

TX), July 19, 2015; Phil Luciano, "She was the first Black person freed by Abraham Lincoln, long before his presidency. Her grave was paved over and her story hardly known," *USA Today*, February 6, 2021.

62  "Local activists push for 'absolute equality' with Juneteenth mural in Galveston," *Houston Chronicle*, November 27, 2020.

63  Elizabeth Hayes Turner, "Osterman, Rosanna Dyer," *Handbook of Texas Online*, accessed August 1, 2018, *http://www.tshaonline.org/handbook/online/articles/fos08*; Lilian E. Herz, "Bank Buys Century-Old Building for Patrons' Parking Space," *Galveston Daily News*, August 26, 1951.

64  Hayes, *Island and City of Galveston*, 2:644–45.

65  William P. Craighill, *The 1862 Army Officer's Pocket Companion: A Manual for Staff Officers in the Field* (New York: D. Van Nostrand, 1862; rpt. Mechanicsburg, PA: Stackpole Books, 2002), 61–62.

66  Ibid., 60–62.

67  Ibid.

68  Ibid.

69  General Orders No. 1, Galveston, Texas, June 17, 1865, *OR*, Part 2, 48:910.

70  General Orders No. 2, Galveston, Texas, June 19, 1865, *OR*, Part 2, 48:928.

71  Gordon Granger to Frederick Steele, Galveston, Texas, June 19, 1865, *OR*, Part 2, 48:930.

72  Ibid.

73  General Orders No. 4, Galveston, TX, June 19, 1865, *OR*, Part 2, 48:929.

74  General Orders No. 18, Baton Rouge, Louisiana, May 18, 1865, *OR*, Part 2, 48:437–38.

75  Ulysses S. Grant to Edward R. S. Canby, Washington, D.C., May 28, 1865, *OR*, Part 2, 48:640.

76  General Orders No. 5, Galveston, Texas, June 19, 1865, *OR*, Part 2, 48:929–30.

77  General Orders No. 18, Baton Rouge, Louisiana, May 18, 1865, *OR*, Part 2, 48:437–38; Ulysses S. Grant to Edward R. S. Canby, Washington, D.C., May 28, 1865, *OR*, Part 2, 48:640; Ulysses S. Grant to Philip H. Sheridan, Washington, D.C., May 28, 1865, *OR*, Part 2, 48:639–40; Charles W. Ramsdell, "Texas from the Fall of the Confederacy to the Beginning of Reconstruction," *The Quarterly of the Texas Historical Association* 11, no. 3 (January 1908): 211–12.

78  "The Story of the Seventh Kansas: An address made before the twenty-seventh annual meeting of the Kansas State Historical Society, December 2, 1902, by S. M. Fox, Adjutant General," *Transactions of the Kansas Historical Society: 1903–1904*, George W. Martin, ed., 11 vols. (Topeka, KS: George A. Clark, 1904), 8:26.

79  Ibid.

80  Robert K. Sutton, *Stark Mad Abolitionists: Lawrence, Kansas, and the Battle Over Slavery in the Civil War Era* (New York: Skyhorse Publishing, 2017), 149–50.

81  Ibid.

82  "The Story of the Seventh Kansas," 27.

83  Ibid.

84  General Orders No. 3, Galveston, Texas, June 19, 1865, *OR*, Part 2, 48:929.

85  Emancipation Proclamation, January 1, 1863, in Roy P. Basler, ed., *The Collected Works of Abraham Lincoln*, 9 vols. (New Brunswick, NJ: Rutgers University Press, 1953), 5:30.

86  "From Texas; Important Orders by General Granger," *New York Times*, July 7, 1865.

87  *The Tri-Weekly Telegraph* (Houston, TX), June 21, 1865.

88  *Galveston Daily News*, June 20, 1865.

89  "General Orders Issued Feb.–June 1865," National Archives and Records Administration, Record Group 393, Part II, Entry 5,543; "General Orders and General Field Orders Issued June–July, 1865," National Archives and Records Administration, Record Group 393, Part II, Entry 5,544.

## CHAPTER 19

1  Paul Brueske, *The Last Siege: The Mobile Campaign, Alabama, 1865* (Havertown, PA: Casemate Publishers, 2018), 145–47.

2  This discussion makes extensive use of the introductory comments in Ron C. Tyler and Lawrence R. Murphy, eds., *The Slave Narratives of Texas* (Austin, TX, The Encino Press, 1974), viii–x.

3  Allen C. Guelzo, "How Abraham Lincoln Lost the Black Vote: Lincoln and Emancipation in the African American Mind," *Journal of the Abraham Lincoln Association* 25, no. 1 (Winter 2004): 7.

4  Craig Hlavaty, "Galveston's most historic site, Ashton Villa, celebrates anniversary," *Houston Chronicle*, July 25, 2014; "How Juneteenth turned Texas' Shameful Slave Legacy into an International Celebration of Freedom," *The Dallas Morning News*, June 19, 2018; Reggie Jackson, "The Juneteenth Day Backstory and the Power of Controlling its Narrative," *Milwaukee Independent*, June 18, 2018; Ernest Wallace, *Texas in Turmoil* (Austin, TX: Steck-Vaughn Co., 1965), 146–47.

5  Randolph B. Campbell, *An Empire for Slavery: The Peculiar Institution in Texas, 1821–1865* (Baton Rouge, LA: Louisiana State University Press, 1989), 269.

6  Tyler and Murphy, eds., *The Slave Narratives of Texas*, 113–14.

7  Ibid., 114.

8  Ibid., 125.

9  Ibid.

10  Edmund Birckhead Bensell, Depiction credited to "Phil. Pho. Co." circa 1865, Lot 14022, Gladstone Collection of African American Photographs, Library of Congress.

11  J. Mason Brewer, *Negro Legislators of Texas and their Descendants: A History of the Negro in Politics from Reconstruction to Disfranchisement* (Dallas, TX: Mathis Publishing Co., 1935), 5.

12  Ibid.

13  Account of James Brown, Federal Writers' Project: Slave Narrative Project, Vol. 16, Texas, Part 1, Adams-Duhon, 1936, Manuscript/Mixed Material, Library of Congress, *https://www.loc.gov/item/mesn161/*, 161–62.

14  Account of Isaac Martin, Federal Writers' Project: Slave Narrative Project, Vol. 16, Texas, Part 3, Lewis-Ryles, 1936, Manuscript/Mixed Material, Library of Congress, *https://www.loc.gov/item/mesn163/*, 53.

15  John C. Walker, "Reconstruction in Texas," *Galveston Daily News*, November 15, 1896.

16  Account of Walter Rimm, Federal Writers' Project: Slave Narrative Project, Vol. 16, Texas, Part 3, Lewis-Ryles, 1936, Manuscript/Mixed Material, Library of Congress, accessed March 18, 2018, *https://www.loc.gov/item/mesn163/*, 249.

17  Ibid.

18  Randolph B. Campbell, *A Southern Community in Crisis: Harrison County, Texas, 1850–1880* (Austin, TX: Texas State Historical Association, 2016), 250–51; Thad Sitton and James H.

Conrad, *Freedom Colonies: Independent Black Texans in the Time of Jim Crow* (Austin, TX: University of Texas Press, 2005), 9–10.

19  Tyler and Murphy, eds., *The Slave Narratives of Texas*, 123–24; Claude H. Nolen, *African American Southerners in Slavery, Civil War and Reconstruction* (Jefferson, NC: McFarland and Co., 2001), 139–41.

20  Tyler and Murphy, eds., *The Slave Narratives of Texas*, 123–24.

21  Ibid., 115.

22  Account of Elsie Reece, Federal Writers' Project: Slave Narrative Project, Vol. 16, Texas, Part 3, Lewis-Ryles, 1936, Manuscript/Mixed Material, Library of Congress, *https://www.loc.gov/item /mesn163/*, 234.

23  Ibid., 234–35.

24  Ibid.

25  Account of Laura Cornish, Federal Writers' Project: Slave Narrative Project, Vol. 16, Texas, Part 1, Adams-Duhon, 1936, Manuscript/Mixed Material, Library of Congress, *https://www.loc.gov /item/mesn161/*, 255.

26  *Houston Tri-Weekly Telegraph*, June 28, 1865.

27  Ibid.

28  *Houston Tri-Weekly Telegraph*, June 23, 1865.

29  Ibid.

30  Ibid.

31  *Galveston Daily News*, August 4, 1865.

32  Ibid.

33  *Flake's Daily Bulletin* (Galveston, TX), July 18, 1865.

34  Ibid.

35  General Orders No. 3, Galveston, Texas, June 19, 1865, Part 2, *OR*, 48:929.

36  Tyler and Murphy, eds., *The Slave Narratives of Texas*, 115.

37  Ibid., 116.

38  Account of John James, Federal Writers' Project: Slave Narrative Project, Vol. 16, Texas, Part 2, Easter-King, 1936, Manuscript/Mixed Material, Library of Congress, *https://www.loc.gov/item /mesn162/*, 19.

39  Tyler and Murphy, eds., *The Slave Narratives of Texas*, 123.

40  Account of William Matthews, Federal Writers' Project: Slave Narrative Project, Vol. 16, Texas, Part 3, Lewis-Ryles, 1936, Manuscript/Mixed Material, *https://www.loc.gov/item/mesn163/*, 70.

41  Ibid.

42  Ibid.

43  Tyler and Murphy, eds., *The Slave Narratives*, 121.

44  Ibid.

45  Account of Andrew Goodman, Federal Writers' Project: Slave Narrative Project, Vol. 16, Texas, Part 2, Easter-King, 1936, Manuscript/Mixed Material, *https://www.loc.gov/item/mesn162/*, 79.

46  Ibid.

47  Ibid.

48  Ronald E. Goodwin, "Into Freedom's Abyss: Reflections of Reconstruction Violence in Texas," in Kenneth W. Howell, ed., *Still the Arena of Civil War: Violence and Turmoil in Reconstruction Texas, 1865–1874* (Denton, TX: University of North Texas Press, 2012), 288–303.

CHAPTER 20

[1]  Carl H. Moneyhon, *Texas After the Civil War: The Struggle for Reconstruction* (College Station, TX: Texas A&M University Press, 2004), 19.

[2]  Ibid.

[3]  *Houston Tri-Weekly Telegraph*, June 23, 1865.

[4]  Ibid.

[5]  Ibid.

[6]  Ibid.

[7]  Ibid.

[8]  Randolph Lewis, "Willard Richardson," *The New Handbook of Texas*, Ron Tyler, ed., 6 vols. (Austin, TX: The Texas Historical Association, 1996), 5:572.

[9]  *Galveston Daily News*, June 18, 1865.

[10]  Ibid.

[11]  Ibid.

[12]  *Galveston Weekly News*, June 28, 1865.

[13]  Ibid.

[14]  Ibid.

[15]  *Galveston Daily News*, July 1, 1865.

[16]  Ibid.

[17]  Ibid.

[18]  Ibid.

[19]  Harold Holzer, *Emancipating Lincoln: The Proclamation in Text, Context, and Memory* (Cambridge, MA: Harvard University Press, 2012), 124.

[20]  "Obituary," *Chicago Tribune*, December 7, 1878; "Honors to the Dead," *The Pantagraph* (Bloomington, IL), December 9, 1878; Roger D. Hunt and Jack R. Brown, *Brevet Brigadier Generals in Blue* (Gaithersburg, MD: Olde Soldier Books, Inc., 1997), 347.

[21]  "Editorial Correspondence," *Galveston Weekly News*, June 21, 1865.

[22]  Ibid.

[23]  Ibid.

[24]  Ibid.

[25]  *Galveston Weekly News*, June 28, 1865.

[26]  Ibid.

[27]  Ibid.

[28]  Ibid.

[29]  *Galveston Daily News*, June 24, 1865.

[30]  Ibid.

[31]  *Galveston Weekly News*, June 28, 1865.

[32]  Ibid.

[33]  Ibid.

[34]  Charles W. Hayes, *History of the Island and the City of Galveston*, 2 vols. (Cincinnati, OH: 1879; rpt. Austin, TX: Jenkins Garrett Press, 1974), 2:646; *Galveston Weekly News*, June 28, 1865.

[35]  Hayes, *Island and City of Galveston*, 2:646–47.

[36]  Ibid.

37  Ibid.

38  Ibid.

39  "Editorial Correspondence," *Galveston Daily News*, July 4, 1865.

40  Ibid.

41  Ibid.

42  Ibid.

43  "Negro Peonage," *Galveston Daily News*, July 4, 1865.

44  Ibid.

45  Ibid.

46  *Galveston Daily News*, July 4, 1865.

47  Ibid.

48  *Houston Tri-Weekly Telegraph*, June 30, 1865.

49  *Houston Tri-Weekly Telegraph*, June 29, 1865.

50  Ibid.

51  Ibid.

52  Ibid.

53  *Galveston Daily News*, June 28, 1865.

54  Ibid.

55  *Flake's Daily Bulletin* (Galveston, TX), July 29, 1865.

56  *The Weekly State Gazette* (Austin, TX), July 11, 1865.

57  Ibid.

58  *Galveston News*, July 2, 1865.

59  Ibid.

60  Ibid.

61  Ibid., July 11, 1865; Hayes, *Island and City of Galveston*, 2:649; *Galveston Daily News*, July 9, 1865.

62  Hayes, *Island and City of Galveston*, 2:649; Hunt and Brown, *Brevet Brigadier Generals in Blue*, 425; T. B. Marshall, *History of the Eighty-third Ohio Volunteer Infantry* (Cincinnati, OH: The Eighty-Third Ohio Volunteer Infantry Association, 1912), 26–28.

63  Hayes, *Island and City of Galveston*, 2:649; *Galveston Daily News*, July 23, 1865.

64  Letter from H. Beard to "My Dear Mother," Galveston, Texas, June 25, 1865, Daniel Carter Beard Papers, Box 63, Manuscript/Mixed Material Collections, Library of Congress.

65  Ibid.

66  Letter from H. Beard to "My Dear Mother," Galveston, Texas, July 2, 1865, Daniel Carter Beard Papers, Box 63, Manuscript/Mixed Materials Collections, Library of Congress.

67  Ibid.

68  "The Negro Question in Texas," *New York Times*, July 9, 1865.

69  Ibid.

70  Ibid.

CHAPTER 21

1   Charles W. Hayes, *History of the Island and the City of Galveston*, 2 vols. (Cincinnati, OH: 1879; rpt. Austin, TX: Jenkins Garrett Press, 1974), 2:654.

2   Ibid.

3   "From the Rio Grande and Western Texas," *The Texas Republican* (Marshall, TX), June 30, 1865.

4   "Condition of the City," *The Philadelphia Inquirer*, July 8, 1865.

5   Ibid.

6   Endorsement on Letter of Col. George W. Clark, 34th Iowa Vols. Commanding Post, Houston, Texas, June 29, 1865, by Frederick W. Emery, Headquarters, District of Texas, Galveston, Texas, July 3, 1865, National Archives and Records Administration (hereafter cited as NARA).

7   Ibid.

8   Frederick W. Emery to J. H. Kelly, Headquarters, District of Texas, Galveston, Texas, June 28, 1865, Letters Sent, p. 128–29, NARA.

9   Ibid.

10  Ibid.

11  Ibid.

12  J. A. Callicott to Frederick W. Emery, Headquarters, Post of Millican, Texas, July 14, 1865, Post Reports, District of Texas, NARA.

13  Ibid.

14  Ibid.

15  Ibid.; E. S. Curtis to B. Porter, Headquarters, Post of Millican, Texas, Post Reports, District of Texas, NARA.

16  J. A. Callicott to B. Porter, Headquarters, Post of Millican, Texas, July 17, 1865, Post Reports, District of Texas, NARA.

17  Ibid.; J. A. Callicott to B. Porter, Headquarters, Post of Millican, Texas, July 25, 1865, Post Reports, District of Texas, NARA.

18  E. P. Curtis to B. Porter, Post of Brenham, Texas, July 23, 1865, Post Reports, District of Texas, NARA.

19  Ibid.

20  Ibid.

21  Diane Neal and Thomas W. Kremm, "What shall we do with the Negro? The Freedmen's Bureau in Texas," *East Texas Historical Journal* 27, no. 2 (1989), 23–24.

22  Ezra J. Warner, *Generals in Blue: Lives of the Union Commanders* (Baton Rouge, LA: Louisiana State University Press, 1964), 8–9.

23  "Speech of Brevet Major-General C. C. Andrews at Brenham, Texas, July 20, 1865," *Galveston Weekly News*, July 26, 1865.

24  Ibid.

25  Ibid.

26  Ibid.

27  Ibid.

28  Ibid.

29  Ibid.

30  Ibid.

31   Ibid.

32   Ibid.

33   *Galveston Daily News*, July 25, 1865.

34   *Galveston Daily News*, July 29, 1865.

35   Ibid.

36   *Galveston Daily News*, July 27, 1865.

37   Ibid.

38   Ibid.

39   Philip H. Sheridan to Ulysses S. Grant, New Orleans, Louisiana, July 1, 1865, *The War of the Rebellion: A Compilation of the Official Records of the Union and Confederate Armies*, 128 vols. (Washington, D.C.: Government Printing Office, 1896), Part 2, 48:1,035–36 (hereafter cited as *OR*).

40   Ulysses S. Grant to Philip H. Sheridan, Washington, D.C., July 1, 1865, *OR*, Part 2, 48:1,052.

41   Philip H. Sheridan to Gordon Granger, New Orleans, Louisiana, July 6, 1865, *OR*, Part 2, 48:1,052–53.

42   Ulysses S. Grant to Philip H. Sheridan, Washington, D.C., *OR*, Part 2, 48:1,075.

43   Philip H. Sheridan to Ulysses S. Grant, New Orleans, Louisiana, July 15, 1865, *OR*, Part 2, 48:1,081; Ulysses S. Grant to Philip H. Sheridan, Washington, D.C., *OR*, Part 2, 48:1,081.

44   G. A. Forsyth to Gordon Granger, New Orleans, Louisiana, July 19, 1865, *OR*, Part 2, 48:1,093; Special Orders No. 2, Headquarters, Military Division of the Gulf, New Orleans, Louisiana, July 19, 1865, *OR*, Part 2, 48:1,093; William L. Richter, *The Army in Texas During Reconstruction, 1865–1870* (College Station, TX: Texas A&M University Press, 1987), 19–21.

## CHAPTER 22

1    Mitch Kachun, *Festivals of Freedom: Memory and Meaning in African American Emancipation Celebrations, 1808–1915* (Amherst, MA: University of Massachusetts Press, 2003), 117–18; Elizabeth Hayes Turner, "Juneteenth: Emancipation and Memory," in *Lone Star Pasts: Memory and History in Texas*, Gregg Cantrell and Elizabeth Hayes Turner, eds. (College Station, TX: Texas A&M University Press, 2007), 143–67; William H. Wiggins, Jr., "Juneteenth: A Red Spot Day on the Texas Calendar," in Francis E. Abernathy, Patrick B. Mullen, and Alan B. Govenar, eds., *Juneteenth Texas: Essays in African-American Folklore* (Denton, TX: University of North Texas Press, 1996), 237–39; Afi-Odelia Scruggs, "Five Myths about Juneteenth," *The Washington Post*, June 18, 2020; Candice L. Harrison, "Why Juneteenth isn't a national holiday . . . and should be," *San Francisco Chronicle*, June 19, 2020.

2    Turner, "Juneteenth: Emancipation and Memory," 147.

3    "The Celebration of the Anniversary of their Freedom by the Blacks," *Tri-Weekly Telegraph* (Houston, TX), June 20, 1866.

4    Ibid.

5    "Arrival of Gen. Sheridan at Galveston—The Freedmen's Celebration of Emancipation," *The New York Times*, June 21, 1866.

6    *Tri-Weekly Telegraph* (Houston, TX), June 20, 1866.

7    Ibid.

8   Ibid.

9   *Southern Intelligencer* (Austin, TX), June 21, 1866, quoting undated report from the *San Antonio Herald.*

10  Frank H. Smyrl, "Texans in the Union Army, 1861–1865," *The Southwestern Historical Quarterly* 65, no. 2 (1961): 234–50; C. P. Weaver, ed., *Thank God My Regiment an African One: The Civil War Diary of Colonel Nathan W. Daniels* (Baton Rouge, LA: Louisiana State University Press, 1998), xv; David Work, "United States Colored Troops in Texas during Reconstruction," *The Southwestern Historical Quarterly* 109, no. 3 (January 2006): 339–40.

11  "Observing Emancipation Day Showery," *Galveston Daily News*, June 20, 1879; "Emancipation Day-Eminent Speakers, etc.," *Galveston Daily News*, June 20, 1879.

12  "From an Occasional Correspondent," *Flake's Daily Bulletin* (Galveston, TX), June 19, 1870.

13  "The Celebration," *Austin American-Statesman*, June 20, 1875.

14  From an Occasional Correspondent," *Flake's Daily Bulletin* (Galveston, TX), June 19, 1870.

15  "San Antonio-Emancipation Celebration," *The Galveston Daily News*, June 20, 1883.

16  Carroll Parrott Blue, "Emancipation is a Park," *Houston History* 9, no. 3 (Summer 2012), 15; Teresa Palomo Acosta, "Juneteenth," *Handbook of Texas Online*, accessed July 4, 2018, *http://www.tshaonline.org/handbook/online/articles/lkj01.*

17  Kachun, *Festivals of Freedom*, 118.

18  Bud Kennedy, "Home from 'Walk to DC,' Opal Lee, 90, Sets Sights on Trump," *Star Telegram* (Fort Worth, TX), January 16, 2017.

19  Jamelle Bouie, "The Black American Holiday Everyone Should Celebrate but Doesn't," *Slate* (June 2015), accessed online August 1, 2018, *http://www.slate.com/articles/news_and_politics/politics/2014/06/juneteenth_the_black_american_holiday_everyone_should_celebrate_but_doesn.html.*

20  Annie Dingus, "Independence Day," *Texas Monthly* (June 2001), accessed online August 1, 2018, *https://www.texasmonthly.com/articles/independence-day/.*

21  "Governor, lawmakers hail King's birthday," *Kerrville Daily Times*, June 20, 1991.

22  Ibid.

23  United States Constitution, Article XIII, National Archives and Records Administration; Abraham Lincoln, "Response to a Serenade," in Roy P. Basler, ed., *The Collected Works of Abraham Lincoln*, 9 vols. (New Brunswick, NJ: Rutgers University Press, 1953), 8:255.

24  Michael Vorenberg, *Final Freedom: The Civil War, the Abolition of Slavery, and the Thirteenth Amendment* (Cambridge, UK: Cambridge University Press, 2001), 112, 138, 198–210.

25  Ibid., 222, 232–33.

26  Mason Lowance, *A House Divided: The Antebellum Slavery Debates in America, 1776–1865* (Princeton, NJ: Princeton University Press, 2003), 31; Adam Clark Estes, "Thanks to 'Lincoln,' Mississippi Has Finally, Definitely Ratified the Thirteenth Amendment," *The Atlantic*, February 17, 2013.

27  The Emancipation Proclamation Cases (*Hall v. Keese* and *Dougherty v. Cartwright*), 31 Texas 504, 506 (Texas Supreme Court, 1868). An excellent summary of these cases and their holdings can be found in Randolph B. Campbell, "The End of Slavery in Texas: A Research Note," *The Southwestern Historical Quarterly* 88, no. 1 (July 1984): 71–80.

28  Ibid.

29 Elizabeth Hayes Turner, "Three Cheers to Freedom and Equal Rights to All: Juneteenth and the Meaning of Citizenship," in *Lone Star Unionism, Dissent and Resistance*, Jesús F. de la Teja, ed. (Norman, OK: University of Oklahoma Press, 2016), 202.

30 "Galveston to Receive Juneteenth Statue," *Houston Chronicle*, June 15, 2006.

31 Joe Holley, "Historic Irony in the Preservation of Confederate Veteran's Home," *Houston Chronicle*, November 4, 2016; Samuel Collins, III, "The Rebirth of Stringfellow Orchards," National Trust for Historic Preservation Leadership Forum, accessed online July 6, 2018, *https://forum.savingplaces.org/blogs/special-contributor/2016/05/27/the-rebirth-of-stringfellow-orchards*.

32 "Emancipation National Historic Trail Effort Moves Ahead," *Galveston Daily News*, March 7, 2020.

33 Rob Hodges, "Historical Groups Work Together to Develop THC Marker," *The Medallion* (Fall 2014): 3.

34 Ibid.

# Sources Consulted

MANUSCRIPT COLLECTIONS

**University of Alabama, William Stanley Hoole Special Collections Library, Tuscaloosa, Alabama**
George S. Smith Diary, 1863–1865
**Austin History Center, Austin Public Library**
Early African American Education Research Materials Collection
Pease, Graham, and Niles Families Papers
**Beinecke Rare Book and Manuscript Library, Yale University**
James W. Forsyth Papers
**Chicago Historical Society, Chicago Illinois**
John B. Magruder Papers
**Daughters of the Republic of Texas Library Collection,**
**Alamo Research Center, San Antonio, Texas**
Hanna Family Papers, Labor Contract
**Houston Public Library, Houston Metropolitan Research Center**
Old Vault Collection
**The Huntington Library, San Marino, California**
Abraham Lincoln Papers
**Library of Congress, Manuscript Division, Washington, D.C.**
Abraham Lincoln Papers
Daniel Carter Beard Papers
Ulysses S. Grant Papers
John M. Schofield Papers
Phillip Henry Sheridan Papers
William T. Sherman Papers
Edwin M. Stanton Papers
Works Project Administration, Federal Writers' Project, 1936–1938

**Louisiana State University Library, Baton Rouge, Louisiana**
Louisiana and Lower Mississippi Valley Collection
John Letter Eaton

**Marshall University Special Collections, Morrow Library, Huntington, West Virginia**
Karen N. Cartwright Nance Collection, 1865

**Miami University, Walter Havighurst Special Collections and University Archives, Oxford, Ohio**
Thomas B. Marshall Diary

**National Archives and Records Administration, Washington, D.C.**
Records of the Headquarters, District of Texas (1865)
Letters Received, Adjutant General's Office

**New York Historical Society**
Francis J. Herron Papers
Slavery Collection

**New York State Library**
Abraham Lincoln Papers and Emancipation Proclamation Draft

**Princeton University Library, Manuscripts Division,**
**Department of Special Collections, Princeton, New Jersey**
Andre De Coppet Collection

**Rosenberg Library, Galveston and Texas History Center**
William Pitt Ballinger Diary, Typescript
Sarah M. Barnes Papers
George W. Grover Papers
Juneteenth Celebration Collection
John B. Magruder Letter
Slave Deeds Collection
Ben C. Stuart Papers
United States Bureau of Refugees, Freedmen, and Abandoned Land Records, 1865–1868
C. B. White Letter

**Sam Houston State University, Special Collections and University Archives, Huntsville, Texas**
Texas Slavery and Documents Collection

**Stanford University Library, Special Collections and University Archives**
Frederick Steele Papers

**Texas A&M University, Cushing Memorial Library**
Slavery/Emancipation Documents

**Texas State Library and Archives Commission**
Records of Adjutant General
Andrew Jackson Hamilton Papers
John Hancock Diary
Pendleton Murrah, Records of the Governor

**Dolph Briscoe Center for American History, The University of Texas at Austin**
William Pitt Ballinger Papers
Black History Collection, 1826–1867
Slavery and Abolition Papers

Slavery Scrapbook
Ashbel Smith Papers
**University of Virginia Library, Special Collections, Charlottesville, Virginia**
Edward Jameson Papers

U.S. GOVERNMENT DOCUMENTS

*The Congressional Globe.* John C. Rives, ed. Washington: Congressional Globe Office, 1861.
*The Declaration of Independence,* July 4, 1776.
National Archives and Records Administration, Washington, D.C. Records Group 393, "Records
   of U.S. Army Continental Commands." Part II.
U.S. Naval War Records Office. *Official Records of the Union and Confederate Navies in the War
   of the Rebellion.* 27 vols. Washington, D.C.: Government Printing Office, 1894–1922.
U.S. War Department. *The War of the Rebellion: A Compilation of the Official Records of the Union
   and Confederate Armies.* 128 vols. Washington, D.C.: Government Printing Office, 1880–1901.

NEWSPAPERS AND PERIODICALS

*Austin American-Statesman.* (Austin, Texas).
*The Liberator.* (Boston Massachusetts).
*Brownson's Quarterly Review.* (New York City).
*Chicago Tribune.* (Chicago, Illinois).
*Dallas Morning News.* (Dallas, Texas).
*Douglass Monthly.* (New York City).
*Flake's Daily Bulletin.* (Galveston, Texas).
*Fort Worth Star Telegram.* (Fort Worth, Texas).
*The Daily News.* (Galveston, Texas).
*The Weekly Telegraph and Tri-Weekly Telegraph.* (Houston, Texas).
*Kerrville Daily Times.* (Kerrville, Texas).
*The Texas Republican.* (Marshall, Texas).
*The Monitor.* (McAllen, Texas).
*The Milwaukee Independent.* (Milwaukee, Wisconsin).
*The Daily Picayune.* (New Orleans, Louisiana).
*The New York Herald.* (New York, New York).
*New York Times.* (New York City).
*The Pantagraph.* (Bloomington, Illinois).
*The Philadelphia Inquirer.* (Philadelphia, Pennsylvania).
*The Daily North Carolina Standard.* (Raleigh, North Carolina).
*San Antonio Herald.* (San Antonio, Texas).
*San Francisco Chronicle.* (San Francisco, California).
*Shreveport Semi-Weekly News.* (Shreveport, Louisiana).
*The South-Western.* (Shreveport, Louisiana).
*Slate Magazine.* (New York City).
*The Southern Intelligencer.* (Austin, Texas).

*Texas Monthly Magazine.* (Austin, Texas).

*The United States Army and Navy Journal and Gazette.* (New York City).

*USA Today.* (McLean, VA).

*Washington Post.* (Washington, D.C.).

*The Weekly State Gazette.* (Austin, Texas).


PUBLISHED PRIMARY SOURCES

American Freedmen's Inquiry Commission. *Preliminary Report Touching the Condition and Management of Emancipated Refugees Made to the Secretary of War.* New York: John F. Trow, 1863.

Baker, T. Lindsay and Julie P. Baker, eds. *Till Freedom Cried Out: Memories of Texas Slave Life.* College Station, TX: Texas A&M University Press, 1997.

Bates, David H. *Lincoln in the Telegraph Office: Recollections of the United States Military Telegraph Corps during the Civil War.* New York: The Century Co., 1907.

Bates, Edward. *The Diary of Edward Bates, 1859–1866.* Howard K. Beale, ed. Washington, D.C.: Government Printing Office, 1933.

Bering, John A., and Thomas Montgomery. *History of the Forty-eighth Ohio Vet. Vol. Inf. Giving a Complete Account of the Regiment From Its Organization At Camp Dennison, Ohio, In October, 1861, to the Close of the War, and Its Final Muster-out, May 10, 1866: Embracing Also, an Account of the Escape And Re-capture of Major J. A. Bering and Lieut. W. J. Srofe, And the Closing Events of the War In the Trans-Mississippi Dep't.* Hillsboro, OH: Highland News Office, 1880.

Berlin, Ira, et al., eds. *Freedom: A Documentary History of Emancipation: 1861–1867.* Multiple vols in progress. Cambridge, UK: Cambridge University Press, 1990.

Browning, Oliver Hickman. *The Diary of Orville Hickman Browning.* Theodore C. Pease and James G. Randall, eds. Springfield, IL: Illinois State Historical Library, 1925.

Butler, Benjamin F. *Autobiography and Personal Reminiscences of Major-General Benjamin F. Butler: Butler's Book.* 2 vols. Boston, MA: A. M. Thayer and Co., 1892.

_____. *Private and Official Correspondence of Gen. Benjamin F. Butler.* 5 vols. Norwood, MA: The Plimpton Press, 1917.

Campbell, John A. *Reminiscences and Documents Relating to the Civil War During the Year 1865.* Baltimore, MD: John Murphy and Co., 1887.

Carpenter, Francis Bicknell. *Six Months at the White House with Abraham Lincoln: The Story of a Picture.* New York: Hurd and Houghton, 1866.

Chase, Salmon P. *The Salmon P. Chase Papers.* John Niven, ed. 5 vols. Kent, OH: Kent State University Press, 1993.

Craighill, William P. *The 1862 Army Officer's Pocket Companion: A Manual for Staff Officers in the Field.* New York: D. Van Nostrand, 1862; rpt. Mechanicsburg, PA: Stackpole Books, 2002.

Dana, Charles A. *Recollections of the Civil War; with the Leaders at Washington and in the Field in the Sixties.* New York: D. Appleton and Co., 1902.

Daniels, Nathan W. *Thank God My Regiment an African One: The Civil War Diary of Colonel Nathan W. Daniels.* C. P. Weaver, ed. Baton Rouge, LA: Louisiana State University Press, 1998.

Davis, Jefferson. *The Papers of Jefferson Davis.* Lynda L. Crist, et al., eds. 14 vols. Baton Rouge, LA: Louisiana State University Press, 1971–2015.

Dorsey, Sarah Anne. *Recollections of Henry Watkins Allen, Brigadier-general Confederate States Army, Ex-governor of Louisiana*. New York: M. Doolady, 1866.

Eaton, John. *Grant, Lincoln and the Freedmen: Reminiscences of the Civil War*. London: Longman's, Green and Co., 1907.

Fox, S. M. "The Story of the Seventh Kansas: An address made before the twenty-seventh annual meeting of the Kansas State Historical Society, December 2, 1902, by S. M. Fox, Adjutant General." George W. Martin, ed. *Transactions of the Kansas Historical Society: 1903–1904*. Topeka, KS: George A. Clark, 1904.

Gerard, C. W. *A Diary: The Eighty-third Ohio Vol. Inf. In the War, 1862–1865*. Cincinnati, OH: 1890.

Grant, Ulysses S. *Personal Memoirs of U. S. Grant*. 2 vols. New York: Charles L. Webster and Co., 1885.

_____. *The Papers of Ulysses S. Grant*. John Y. Simon, ed. 31 vols. Carbondale, IL: Southern Illinois University Press, 1967–2009.

Hay, John M. and John G. Nicolay. *Abraham Lincoln: A History*. 10 vols. New York: The Century Co., 1914.

_____. *Inside Lincoln's White House: The Complete Civil War Diary of John Hay*. Michael J. Burlingame and John R. Turner, eds. Carbondale, IL: Southern Illinois University Press, 1997.

Hunter, Robert M. T. "The Peace Commission of 1865." *Southern Historical Society Papers* 3, no. 4 (April 1877): 168–76.

Illinois Infantry. 92nd Regiment. *Ninety-Second Illinois Volunteers*. Freeport, IL: Journal Steam Publishing House and Bookbindery, 1875.

Johnson, Andrew. *The Papers of Andrew Johnson*. Paul H. Bergeron, ed. 16 vols. Knoxville, TN: University of Tennessee Press, 1967–2000.

Johnson, Robert Underwood and Clarence Clough Buel, eds. *Battles and Leaders of the Civil War: Grant-Lee Edition*. 8 vols. New York: The Century Co., 1887; rpt. Harrisburg, PA: The Archive Society, 1991.

Jones, J. William. *Personal Reminiscences, Anecdotes, and Letters of Gen. Robert E. Lee*. New York: D. Appleton and Co., 1875.

Lincoln, Abraham. *The Collected Works of Abraham Lincoln*. Roy P. Basler, ed. 9 vols. New Brunswick, NJ: Rutgers University Press, 1990.

Livermore, Mary A. *My Story of the War: A Woman's Narrative*. Hartford, CT: A. D. Worthington and Co., 1889.

Marshall, T. B. *History of the Eighty-Third Ohio Volunteer Infantry*. Cincinnati, OH: The Eighty-Third Ohio Volunteer Infantry Association, 1912.

Miller, Francis Trevelyan, and Robert S. Lanier. 10 vols. *The Photographic History of the Civil War*. New York: The Review of Reviews Co., 1911.

Military Order of the Loyal Legion of the United States. *War Papers, being Papers Read before the Commandery of the State of Michigan, Military Order of the Loyal Legion of the United States*. 70 vols. 1898; rpt., Wilmington, NC: Broadfoot Publishing Co., 1993.

North, Thomas. *Five Years in Texas: or, What You Did Not Hear During the War from January 1861 to January 1866: A Narrative of His Travels, Experiences, and Observations, in Texas and Mexico*. Cincinnati, OH: Elm Street Printing Co., 1871.

Parton, James. *General Butler in New Orleans: History of the Administration of the Department of the Gulf in the Year 1862.* New York: Mason Brothers, 1864.

Paulus, Carl L. *The Slaveholding Crisis: Fear of Insurrection and the Coming of the Civil War.* Baton Rouge, LA: Louisiana State University Press, 2017.

Pope, John. *The Military Memoirs of General John Pope.* Peter Cozzens and Robert Girardi, eds. Chapel Hill, NC: University of North Carolina Press, 1998.

Rawick, George R., ed. *The American Slave: A Composite Autobiography.* 19 vols. Westport, CT: Greenwood Publishing Co., 1972–1979.

Redkey, Edwin S., ed. *A Grand Army of Black Men: Letters from African-American Soldiers in the United States Army, 1861–1865.* Cambridge, UK: Cambridge University Press, 1992.

Russell, William H. *My Diary North and South.* Fletcher Pratt, ed. 2 vols. New York: Harper and Brothers, 1954.

Sands, Benjamin F. *From Reefer to Rear-Admiral.* New York: Frederick A. Stokes Co., 1899.

Schofield, John M. *Forty-Six Years in the Army.* New York: Century Company, 1897.

Shanks, William F. G. *Personal recollections of Distinguished Generals.* New York: Harper and Bros., 1896.

Sheridan, Philip H. *Personal Memoirs of P. H. Sheridan.* 2 vols. New York: C. L. Webster and Co., 1888.

_____. *Report of Operations of the United States Forces and General Information of the Condition of Affairs in the Military Division of the South-West and Gulf and Department of the Gulf.* New Orleans, LA: n.p., 1866.

Sherman, William T. *Memoirs of W. T. Sherman.* 1875; rpt. New York: Penguin Books, 2000.

_____. *Sherman's Civil War: Selected Correspondence of William T. Sherman, 1860–1865.* Brooks D. Simpson and Jean V. Berlin, eds. Chapel Hill, NC: University of North Carolina Press, 1999.

Smith, John Corson. *Oration at the Unveiling of the Monument Erected to the Memory of Maj. Gen. James B. Steedman.* Chicago, IL: Knight and Leonard Co., 1887.

*Society of the Army of the Cumberland Fifteenth Reunion, Cincinnati, Ohio.* Cincinnati, OH: Robert Clarke and Co., 1884.

Stanley, David S. *An American General: The Memoirs of David Sloan Stanley.* Samuel W. Fordyce IV, ed. Santa Barbara, CA: The Narrative Press, 2003.

Stanyan, John M. *A History of the Eighth Regiment of New Hampshire Volunteers.* Concord, NH: Ira C. Evans, Printer, 1892.

Stephens, Alexander H. *A Constitutional View of the Late War between the States; Its Causes, Character, Conduct and Results, Presented in a Series of Colloquies at Liberty Hall.* 2 vols. Philadelphia, PA: National Publishing Co., 1870.

Stevens, Walter B., ed. *A Reporter's Lincoln.* St. Louis, MO: Missouri Historical Society, 1916.

Swint, Henry L., ed. *Dear Ones at Home: Letters from Contraband Camps.* Nashville, TN: Vanderbilt University Press, 1966.

Taylor, Richard. *Destruction and Reconstruction: Personal Experiences of the Late War.* 1879; rpt. New York: Time-Life Books, 1981.

Thatcher, Marshall P. *A Hundred Battles in the West, St. Louis to Atlanta, 1861–1865, The Second Michigan Cavalry.* Detroit, MI: self-published, 1884.

Tyler, Ron and Lawrence R. Murphy, eds., *The Slave Narratives of Texas.* Austin, TX: The Encino Press, 1974.

Welles, Gideon. *Diary of Gideon Welles: Secretary of the Navy Under Lincoln and Johnson.* 3 vols. Boston, MA: Riverside Press, 1911.

_____. *Civil War and Reconstruction: Selected Essays.* Published in *The Galaxy*, 1871–1873. Rpt. New York: Twayne Publishers, 1959.

Winkler, Ernest W., ed. *Journal of the Secession Convention of Texas: 1861.* Austin, TX: Austin Printing Co., 1912.

Wood, Thomas J. *Seventh Annual Reunion of the Association of the Graduates of the United States Military Academy at West Point, New York.* New York: A. S. Barnes and Co., 1876.

Yetman, Norman R. *Life Under the Peculiar Institution: Selections from the Slave Narrative Collection.* Huntington, NY: Robert E. Krieger Publishing Co., 1976.

_____. *Voices from Slavery: 100 Authentic Slave Narratives.* Mineola, NY: Dover Publications, 2000.

Young, John Russell. *Around the World with General Grant.* Baltimore, MD: The Johns Hopkins University Press, 2002.

## SECONDARY SOURCES

Abernathy, Francis E., Patrick B. Mullen, and Alan B. Govenar, eds. *Juneteenth Texas: Essays in African-American Folklore.* Denton, TX: University of North Texas Press, 1996.

Adams, Carl. *Nance: Trials of the First Slave Freed by Abraham Lincoln.* n.p., 2016.

Adams, Kevin and Leonne M. Hudson, eds. *Democracy and the American Civil War: Race and African Americans in the Nineteenth Century.* Kent, OH: Kent State University Press, 2016.

Angle, Paul M., ed. *Created Equal? The Complete Lincoln-Douglas Debates of 1858.* Chicago, IL: The University of Chicago Press, 1958.

Ballard, Michael B. and Mark R. Cheatem, eds. *Of Times and Race: Essays Inspired by John F. Marszalek.* Jackson, MS: University of Mississippi Press, 2013.

Baptist, Edward E. *The Half Has Never Been Told: Slavery and the Making of American Capitalism.* New York: Basic Books, 2014.

Barr, Alwynn. *Black Texans, A History of Negroes in Texas: 1528–1971.* Austin, TX: Jenkins Publishing Co., 1973.

Bastian, David F. *Grant's Canal: The Union's Attempt to Bypass Vicksburg.* Shippensburg, PA: The Bird Street Press, 1995.

Bean, Christopher B. *Too Great a Burden to Bear: The Struggle and Failure of the Freedmen's Bureau in Texas.* New York: Fordham University Press, 2016.

Beckert, Sven. *Empire of Cotton: A Global History.* New York: Alfred A. Knopf, 2015.

Berlin, Ira. *The Long Emancipation: The Demise of Slavery in the United States.* Cambridge, MA: Harvard University Press, 2015.

_____, Barbara J. Fields, et al. *Slaves No More: Three Essays on Emancipation and the Civil War.* New York: Cambridge University Press, 1992.

_____, Marc Favreau, and Steven F. Miller, eds. *Remembering Slavery: African Americans Talk About Their Personal Experiences of Slavery and Emancipation.* Washington, D.C.: The New Press, 1998.

Blair, William A. and Karen Fisher Younger, eds. *Lincoln's Proclamation: Emancipation Reconsidered.* Chapel Hill, NC: University of North Carolina Press, 2009.

Blake, William O. *The History of Slavery and the Slave Trade, Ancient and Modern.* Columbus, OH: H. Miller, 1860.

Blight, David W. *A Slave No More: Two Men Who Escaped to Freedom*. Orlando, FL: Harcourt, 2007.

_____ and Brooks D. Simpson, eds. *Union and Emancipation: Essays on Politics and Race in the Civil War Era*. Kent, OH: Kent State University Press, 1997.

Blue, Carroll Parrott. "Emancipation is a Park." *Houston History* 9, no. 3 (Summer 2012), 15–19.

Blumenthal, Sidney. *A Self-Made Man: The Political Life of Abraham Lincoln, 1809–1849*. New York: Simon and Schuster, 2016.

Boles, John B. Black. *Southerners, 1619–1869*. Lexington, KY: The University Press of Kentucky, 1984.

Botkin, B. A., ed. *Lay My Burden Down: A Folk History of Slavery*. Chicago, IL: University of Chicago Press, 1945.

Boudreaux, Tommie, and Alice M. Gatson. *African Americans of Galveston*. Charleston, SC: Arcadia Publishing, 2013.

Brasher, Glenn David. *The Peninsula Campaign and the Necessity of Emancipation*. Chapel Hill, NC: University of North Carolina Press, 2012.

Breen, Patrick H. *The Land Shall be Deluged in Blood: A New History of the Nat Turner Revolt*. Oxford: Oxford University Press, 2015.

Brewer, J. Mason. *Negro Legislators of Texas and their Descendants: A History of the Negro in Politics from Reconstruction to Disfranchisement*. Dallas, TX: Mathis Publishing Co., 1935.

Brewster, Todd. *Lincoln's Gamble: The Tumultuous Six Months That Gave America the Emancipation Proclamation and Changed the Course of the Civil War*. New York: Scribner, 2014.

Browning, Robert M., Jr. *Success is All that was Expected: The South Atlantic Blockading Squadron in the Civil War*. Washington, D.C.: Brassey's, Inc., 2002.

Brownstein, Elizabeth Smith. *Lincoln's Other White House: The Untold Story of the Man and his Presidency*. Hoboken, NJ: John Wiley and Sons, 2005.

Brueske, Paul. *The Last Siege: The Mobile Campaign, Alabama, 1865*. Havertown, PA: Casemate Publishers, 2018.

Burlingame, Michael. *Abraham Lincoln: A Life*. 2 vols. Baltimore, MD: John Hopkins University Press, 2008.

Campbell, Randolph B. *An Empire for Slavery: The Peculiar Institution in Texas*. Baton Rouge, LA: Louisiana State University Press, 1989.

_____. *A Southern Community in Crisis: Harrison County, Texas, 1850–1880*. Austin, TX: Texas State Historical Association, 2016.

_____. "The End of Slavery in Texas: A Research Note." *The Southwestern Historical Quarterly* 88, no. 1 (July 1984), 71–80.

Carnahan, Burrus M. *Act of Justice: Lincoln's Emancipation Proclamation and the Law of War*. Lexington, KY: University Press of Kentucky, 2007.

Carroll, John M. *Custer in Texas: An Interrupted Narrative*. New York: Sol Lewis and Liveright, 1975.

Carse, Robert. *Department of the South: Hilton Head Island in the Civil War*. Hilton Head Island, SC: Heritage Library Foundation, 2002.

Carson, Thomas L. *Lincoln's Ethics*. Cambridge, UK: Cambridge University Press, 2015.

Cimbala, Paul A. "The Freedmen's Bureau, the Freedmen, and Sherman's Grant in Reconstruction Georgia, 1865–1867." *The Journal of Southern History* 55, no. 4 (1989): 597–632.

Clark-Lewis, Elizabeth, ed. *First Freed: Washington, D.C. in the Emancipation Era*. Washington, D.C.: Howard University Press, 2002.

Coates, Ta-Nehisi. *We Were Eight Years in Power: An American Tragedy*. New York: One World, 2017.

Coffey, David. *Sheridan's Lieutenants: Phil Sheridan, His Generals, and the Final Year of the Civil War*. Lanham, MD: Rowman and Littlefield Publishers, Inc., 2005.

Collins, Izola Ethel Fedford. *Island of Color: Where Juneteenth Started*. Bloomington, IN: Authorhouse, 2004.

Conner, Robert C. *General Gordon Granger: The Savior of Chickamauga and the Man Behind Juneteenth*. Havertown, PA: Casemate Publishers, 2013.

Conroy, James B. *Lincoln's White House: The People's House in Wartime*. Lanham, MD: Rowman and Littlefield Publishers, Inc., 2017.

_____. *Our One Common Country: Abraham Lincoln and the Hampton Roads Peace Conference of 1865*. Guilford, CT: Lyons Press, 2014.

Cotham, Edward T., Jr. *Battle on the Bay: The Civil War Struggle for Galveston*. Austin, TX: University of Texas Press, 1998.

_____. *Sabine Pass: The Confederacy's Thermopylae*. Austin, TX: University of Texas Press, 2004.

Cozzens, Peter. *The Shipwreck of Their Hopes: The Battles for Chattanooga*. Urbana, IL: The University of Illinois Press, 1994.

Crofts, Daniel W. *Lincoln and the Politics of Slavery: The Other Thirteenth Amendment and the Struggle to Save the Union*. Chapel Hill, NC: University of North Carolina Press, 2016.

Crook, Carland Elaine. "Benjamin Theron and French Designs in Texas during the Civil War." *Southwestern Historical Quarterly* 68 (April 1965), 432–54.

Crouch, Barry A. and Larry Madaras, eds. *The Dance of Freedom: Texas African Americans During Reconstruction*. Austin, TX: University of Texas Press, 1941.

_____. *The Freedmen's Bureau and Black Texans*. Austin, TX: University of Texas Press, 1992.

Damico, John K. "Confederate Soldiers Take Matters into Their Own Hands." *Louisiana History: The Journal of the Louisiana Historical Association* 39, no. 2 (Spring 1998), 189–205.

Dawson, Joseph G., III. "General Phil Sheridan and Military Reconstruction in Louisiana." *Civil War History* 24, no. 2 (1978): 133–51.

de la Teja, Jesús, ed. *Lone Star Unionism, Dissent, and Resistance: Other Sides of Civil War Texas*. Norman, OK: University of Oklahoma Press, 2016.

Deuson, Benny R. "Pendleton Murrah." in *Ten Texans in Gray*. W. C. Nunn, ed. Hillsboro, TX: Hill Junior College Press, 1968.

Dirck, Brian. *Lincoln the Lawyer*. Urbana, IL: University of Illinois Press, 2007.

Dobak, William A. *Freedom by the Sword: The U.S. Colored Troops, 1862–1867*. New York: Skyhorse Publishing, 2013.

Downs, Jim. *Sick from Freedom: African-American Illness and Suffering During the Civil War and Reconstruction*. Oxford: Oxford University Press, 2012.

Drago, Edmund L. "How Sherman's March Through Georgia Affected the Slaves." *Georgia Historical Quarterly* 57, no. 3 (Fall, 1973), 361–75.

Du Bois, W. E. B. *The Souls of Black Folk*. 1903; rpt., New York: Dover Publications, 1994.

Egerton, Douglas R. *Thunder at the Gates: The Black Civil War Regiments that Redeemed America*. New York: Basic Books, 2016.

Ellison, Ralph. *Juneteenth: A Novel*. New York: Random House, 1999.

Engle, Stephen D., ed. *The War Worth Fighting: Abraham Lincoln's Presidency and Civil War America*. Gainesville, FL: University Press of Florida, 2015.

Escott, Paul D. *Lincoln's Dilemma: Blair, Sumner and the Republican Struggle over Racism and Equality in the Civil War Era*. Charlottesville, VA: University of Virginia Press, 2014.

_____. *"What Shall We Do with the Negro?" Lincoln, White Racism and Civil War America*. Charlottesville, VA: University of Virginia Press, 2009.

Everett, Donald E. "Ben Butler and the Louisiana Native Guards, 1861–1862." *The Journal of Southern History* 24, no. 2 (May 1958), 202–217.

Fogel, Robert W. *The Rise and Fall of American Slavery*. New York: W. W. Norton and Co., 1989.

_____ and Stanley L. Engerman. *Time on the Cross: The Economics of American Negro Slavery*. New York: W. W. Norton and Co., 1974.

Foner, Eric. *Forever Free: The Story of Emancipation and Reconstruction*. New York: Vintage Books, 2006.

_____. *Reconstruction: America's Unfinished Revolution*. New York: Harper and Row, 1988.

Foxx, Daniel and Eddy W. Davison. *Rebel Refugees: The Confederate Exodus to Mexico*. Peoria, IL: Draytonville Publications, 2015.

Frazier, Donald S. *Blood on the Bayou: Vicksburg, Port Hudson and the Trans-Mississippi*. Buffalo Gap: McWhiney Foundation Press, 2015.

_____. *Fire in the Cane Field: The Federal Invasion of Louisiana and Texas, January 1861–January 1863*. Buffalo Gap, TX: McWhiney Foundation Press, 2009.

_____. *Thunder Across the Swamp: The Fight for the Lower Mississippi, February–May 1863*. Buffalo Gap, TX: McWhiney Foundation Press, 2011.

_____. *Tempest over Texas: The Fall and Winter Campaigns of 1863-1864*. Kerrville, TX: State House Press, 2020.

Gallagher, Gary W. *The Union War*. Cambridge, MA: Harvard University Press, 2011.

Gates, Henry Louis, Jr. *Stony the Road: Reconstruction, White Supremacy, and the Rise of Jim Crow*. New York: Penguin Press, 2019.

Geise, William R. "Missouri's Confederate Capital in Marshall, Texas." *The Southwestern Historical Quarterly* 66, no. 2 (October 1962), 193–207.

Gerteis, Louis S. *From Contraband to Freedman: Federal Policy Toward Southern Blacks, 1861–1865*. Westport, CT: Greenwood Press, 1973.

Glasrud, Bruce A., ed. *African Americans in South Texas History*. College Station, TX: Texas A&M University Press, 2011.

_____ and Archie P. McDonald, eds. *Blacks in East Texas History: Selections from the East Texas Historical Journal*. College Station, TX: Texas A&M University Press, 2008.

_____ and Deborah M. Liles, eds. *African Americans in Central Texas History: From Slavery to Civil Rights*. College Station, TX: Texas A&M University Press, 2019.

_____ and Milton S. Jordan, eds. *Free Blacks in Antebellum Texas*. Denton, TX: University of North Texas Press, 2015.

Grear, Charles D., ed. *The Fate of Texas: The Civil War and the Lone Star State*. Fayetteville, AR: University of Arkansas Press, 2008.

Grimsley, Mark and Brooks D. Simpson, eds., *The Collapse of the Confederacy*. Lincoln, NE: University of Nebraska Press, 2001.

Guelzo, Allen C. "How Abraham Lincoln Lost the Black Vote: Lincoln and Emancipation in the African American Mind." *Journal of the Abraham Lincoln Association* 25, no. 1 (Winter 2004), 1–22.

_____. *Lincoln's Emancipation Proclamation: The End of Slavery in America*. New York: Simon and Schuster, 2004.

_____. *Redeeming the Great Emancipator*. Cambridge, MA: Harvard University Press, 2016.

Gwynne, S. C. *Hymns of the Republic: The Story of the Final Year of the American Civil War*. New York: Scribner, 2019.

Hahn, Steven. *The Political Worlds of Slavery and Freedom*. Cambridge, MA: Harvard University Press, 2009.

Hall, Andrew W. "Closing Act." *The Civil War Monitor* 5, no. 2 (Summer 2015), 40–51, 72–73.

Hamlin, Charles E. *The Life and Times of Hannibal Hamlin*. Cambridge, MA: Riverside Press, 1899.

Harris, William C. *Lincoln and the Border States: Preserving the Union*. Lawrence, KS: University Press of Kansas, 2011.

_____. "The Hampton Roads Peace Conference: A Final Test of Lincoln's Presidential Leadership." *Journal of the Abraham Lincoln Association*, no. 1 (Winter, 2000), 30–61.

Harrison, Lowell H. "Slavery in Kentucky: A Civil War Casualty." *The Kentucky Review* 5, no. 1 (Fall 1983), 32–41.

Hay, John M. and John G. Nicolay. *Abraham Lincoln: A History*. 10 vols. 1890; rpt. New York: Cosimo Classics, 2009.

Hayes, Charles W. *History of the Island and the City of Galveston*. 2 vols. Cincinnati, OH: 1879; rpt. Austin, TX: Jenkins Garrett Press, 1974.

Heidler, David S. and Jeanne T. Heidler, eds. *Encyclopedia of the American Civil War: A Political, Social, and Military History*. 5 vols. Santa Barbara, CA: ABC-CLIO, 2000.

Hodges, Rob. "Historical Groups Work Together to Develop THC Marker." *The Medallion* (Fall 2014), 3.

Hofstadter, Richard. *The American Political Tradition and the Men Who Made It*. New York: Knopf, 1973.

Hollandsworth, James G., Jr. *The Louisiana Native Guards: The Black Military Experience During the Civil War*. Baton Rouge, LA: Louisiana State University Press, 1998.

Holzer, Harold. *Emancipating Lincoln: The Proclamation in Text, Context, and Memory*. Cambridge, MA: Harvard University Press, 2012.

_____, Craig L. Symonds, and Frank J. Williams, eds. *Exploring Lincoln: Great Historians Reappraise Our Greatest President*. New York: Fordham University Press, 2015.

_____, Edna G. Medford, and Frank J. Williams. *The Emancipation Proclamation: Three Views*. Baton Rouge, LA: Louisiana State University Press, 2006.

_____ and Norton Garfinkle. *A Just and Generous Nation: Abraham Lincoln and the Fight for American Opportunity*. New York: Basic Books, 2015.

_____ and Sara Vaughn Gabbard, eds. *Lincoln and Freedom: Slavery, Emancipation, and the Thirteenth Amendment*. Carbondale, IL: Southern Illinois University Press, 2007.

_____ and Sara Vaughn Gabbard, eds. *1863: Lincoln's Pivotal Year*. Carbondale, IL: Southern Illinois University Press, 2013.

Horowitz, Murray M. "Ben Butler and the Negro: 'Miracles are Occurring.'" *Louisiana History: The Journal of the Louisiana Historical Association* 17, no. 2 (Spring 1976), 159–86.

Howell, Kenneth W., ed. *Still the Arena of Civil War: Violence and Turmoil in Reconstruction Texas, 1865–1874*. Denton, TX: University of North Texas Press, 2012.

_____. *The Seventh Star of the Confederacy: Texas During the Civil War*. Denton, TX: University of North Texas Press, 2009.

Hubbard, Charles M., ed. *Lincoln, the Law, and Presidential Leadership*. Carbondale, IL: Southern Illinois University Press, 2015.

Huff, Sanford W. "Major General F. J. Herron." *The Annals of Iowa* 167, no. 1 (1867), 801–807.

Hunt, Roger D. and Jack R. Brown. *Brevet Brigadier Generals in Blue*. Gaithersburg, MD: Olde Soldier Books, Inc., 1997.

Hurd, Michael. "Let Freedom Ring." *Texas Monthly* 67, no. 6 (June 2020), 54–59.

Huston, James L. "Property Rights in Slavery and the Coming of the Civil War." *The Journal of Southern History* 65, no. 2 (May 1999), 249–86.

Jaffa, Harry H. *A New Birth of Freedom: Abraham Lincoln and the Coming of the Civil War*. Lanham, MD: Rowman and Littlefield Publishers, 2000.

Jones, James P. "General Jeff C. Davis and Sherman's Georgia Campaign." *Georgia Historical Quarterly* 47, no. 3 (September 1963), 231–48.

Kachun, Mitch. *Festivals of Freedom: Memory and Meaning in African American Emancipation Celebrations, 1808–1915*. Amherst, MA: University of Massachusetts Press, 2003.

Kaplan, Fred. *Lincoln and the Abolitionists: John Quincy Adams, Slavery, and the Civil War*. New York: Harper Collins Publishers, 2017.

Kolchin, Peter. *American Slavery: 1619–1877*. New York: Hill and Wang, 1993.

Lang, Andrew F. *In the Wake of War: Military Occupation, Emancipation and Civil War America*. Baton Rouge, LA: Louisiana State University Press, 2017.

Lehman, Donald J. *Lucky Landmark: A Study of a Design and its Survival*. Washington, D.C.: General Services Administration Public Buildings Service, 1973.

Link, William A. and James J. Broomall, eds. *Rethinking American Emancipation: Legacies of Slavery and the Quest for Black Freedom*. Cambridge, UK: Cambridge University Press, 2016.

Long, David. *The Jewel of Liberty: Abraham Lincoln's Re-election and the End of Slavery*. Mechanicsburg, PA: Stackpole Books, 1994.

Lowance, Mason. *A House Divided: The Antebellum Slavery Debates in America, 1776–1865*. Princeton, NJ: Princeton University Press, 2003.

Lupold, Harry F. "A Union Medical Officer Views the 'Texians.'" *Southwestern Historical Quarterly* 77, no. 4 (April 1974): 481–86.

Manning, Chandra. *Troubled Refuge: Struggling for Freedom in the Civil War*. New York: Alfred A. Knopf, 2016.

Marten, James. "Slaves and Rebels: The Peculiar Institution in Texas, 1861–1865." *East Texas Historical Journal* 28, no. 1 (1990), 29–36.

Marszalek, John F. *Lincoln and the Military*. Carbondale, IL: Southern Illinois University Press, 2014.

Masur, Louis P. *Lincoln's Hundred Days: The Emancipation Proclamation and the War for the Union*. Cambridge, MA: Belknap Press, 2012.

_____. *Lincoln's Last Speech: Wartime Reconstruction and the Crisis of Reunion*. Oxford: Oxford University Press, 2015.

McClaughry, John. "John Wolcott Phelps: The Civil War General Who Became a Forgotten Presidential Candidate in 1880." *Vermont History* 38, no. 4 (Autumn 1970), 263–90.

McCrary, Peyton. *Abraham Lincoln and Reconstruction: The Louisiana Experiment*. Princeton, NJ: Princeton University Press, 1978.

McDaniel, W. Caleb. *Sweet Taste of Liberty: A True Story of Slavery and Restitution in America*. Oxford: Oxford University Press, 2019.

McGhee, Fred L. *The Black Crop: Slavery and Slave Trading in Nineteenth Century Texas*. Austin, TX: Fidelitas Publishing, 2016.

McGinty, Brian. *Lincoln and the Court*. Cambridge, MA: Harvard University Press, 2008.

McPherson, James M. *The Negro's Civil War: How American Blacks Felt and Acted During the War for the Union*. New York: Vintage Books, 1965.

_____. *The Struggle for Equality*. Princeton, NJ: Princeton University Press, 1964.

_____. "Who Freed the Slaves?" *Proceedings of the American Philosophical Society* 139, no. 1 (March 1995), 1–10.

Medford, Edna Greene. *Lincoln and Emancipation*. Carbondale, IL: Southern Illinois University Press, 2015.

Messner, William F. *Freedmen and the Ideology of Free Labor: Louisiana, 1862–1865*. Lafayette, LA: University of Southwestern Louisiana, 1978.

Moneyhon, Carl H. *Texas After the Civil War: The Struggle for Reconstruction*. College Station, TX: Texas A&M University Press, 2004.

Moretta, John Anthony. *William Pitt Ballinger: Texas Lawyer, Southern Statesman, 1825–1888*. Austin, TX: Texas State Historical Association, 2000.

Morris, Thomas D. *Southern Slavery and the Law: 1619–1860*. Chapel Hill, NC: University of North Carolina Press, 1996.

Neal, Diane and Thomas W. Kremm. "What shall we do with the Negro? The Freedmen's Bureau in Texas." *East Texas Historical Journal* 27, no. 2 (1989), 23–34.

Neff, Stephen C. *Justice in Blue and Gray: A Legal History of the Civil War*. Cambridge, MA: Harvard University Press, 2010.

Nolen, Claude H. *African American Southerners in Slavery, Civil War and Reconstruction*. Jefferson, NC: McFarland and Co., 2001.

Nunn, W. C., ed. *Ten Texans in Gray*. Hillsboro, TX: Hill Junior College Press, 1968.

Oakes, James. *Freedom National: The Destruction of Slavery in the United States, 1861–1865*. New York: W. W. Norton and Co., 2013.

_____. *The Scorpion's Sting: Antislavery and the Coming of the Civil War*. New York: W. W. Norton and Co., 2014.

Oates, Stephen B. *The Fires of Jubilee: Nat Turner's Fierce Rebellion*. Amherst, MA: University of Massachusetts Press, 1984.

O'Flaherty, Daniel. *General Jo Shelby: Undefeated Rebel*. Chapel Hill, NC: University of North Carolina Press, 2000.

Parker, Foxhall A. *The Battle of Mobile Bay*. Boston, MA: A. Williams and Co., 1878.

Parks, Joseph H. *General Edmund Kirby Smith, C.S.A.* Baton Rouge, LA: Louisiana State University Press, 1954.

Pinsker, Matthew. *Lincoln's Sanctuary: Abraham Lincoln and the Soldier's Home*. New York: Oxford University Press, 2003.

Rae, Noel. *The Great Stain: Witnessing American Slavery*. New York: The Overlook Press, 2018.

Rael, Patrick. *Eighty-Eight Years: The Long Death of Slavery in the United States, 1777–1865*. Athens, GA: University of Georgia Press, 2015.

Ramsdell, Charles W. "Texas from the Fall of the Confederacy to the Beginning of Reconstruction." *The Quarterly of the Texas Historical Association* 11, no. 3 (January 1908), 199–19.

Ransom, Roger L. and Richard Sutch. *One Kind of Freedom: The Economic Consequences of Emancipation*. Cambridge, UK: Cambridge University Press, 2001.

Regosin, Elizabeth A. and Donald R. Shaffer, eds. *Voices of Emancipation: Understanding Slavery, the Civil War, and Reconstruction through the U.S. Pension Bureau Files*. New York: New York University Press, 2008.

Reidy, Joseph P. *Illusions of Emancipation: The Pursuit of Freedom and Equality in the Twilight of Slavery*. Chapel Hill, NC: University of North Carolina Press, 2019.

Reynolds, Donald E. *Texas Terror*. Baton Rouge, LA: Louisiana State University Press, 2007.

Richards, Leonard L. *Who Freed the Slaves? The Fight Over the Thirteenth Amendment*. Chicago, IL: University of Chicago Press, 2015.

Richter, William L. "It is Best to Go in Strong-Handed: Army Occupation of Texas, 1865–1866." *Arizona and the West* 27, no. 2 (Summer 1985), 113–42.

_____. *Overreached on All Sides: The Freedmen's Bureau Administrators in Texas, 1865–1868*. College Station, TX: Texas A&M University Press, 1991.

_____. *The Army in Texas During Reconstruction, 1865–1870*. College Station, TX: Texas A&M University Press, 1987.

Robertson, James. *After the Civil War: The Heroes, Villains, Soldiers, and Civilians who Changed America*. Washington, D.C.: National Geographic, 2015.

Robinson, Armistead L. *Bitter Fruits of Bondage: The Demise of Slavery and the Collapse of the Confederacy, 1861–1865*. Charlottesville, VA: University of Virginia Press, 2005.

Roediger, David. *Seizing Freedom: Slave Emancipation and Liberty for All*. London: Verso, 2014.

Rose, Willie Lee. *Rehearsal for Reconstruction: The Port Royal Experiment*. Athens, GA: University of Georgia Press, 1999.

Ross, D. Reid. *Lincoln's Veteran Volunteers Win the War: The Hudson Valley's Ross Brothers and the Union's Fight for Emancipation*. Albany, NY: State University of New York Press, 2008.

Rozek, Barbara J. "Galveston Slavery." *The Houston Review* 15, no. 2 (1993). 67–101.

Ruane, Michael E. "An original "'Juneteenth' order found in the National Archives." *The Washington Post*. June 18, 2020.

Ruef, Martin. *Between Slavery and Capitalism: The Legacy of Emancipation in the American South*. Princeton, NJ: Princeton University Press, 2014.

Sandburg, Carl. *Abraham Lincoln*. 6 vols. New York: Charles Scribner's Sons, 1942.

Schmidt, James M. *Galveston and the Civil War: An Island City in the Maelstrom*. Charleston, SC: The History Press, 2012.

Silverthorne, Elizabeth. *Ashbel Smith of Texas: Pioneer, Patriot, Statesman, 1805–1886*. College Station, TX: Texas A&M University Press, 1988.

Simon, James F. *Lincoln and Chief Justice Taney: Slavery, Secession, and the President's War Powers*. New York: Simon and Schuster, 2006.

Simpson, Brooks D. *Let Us Have Peace: Ulysses S. Grant and the Politics of War and Reconstruction*. Chapel Hill, NC: University of North Carolina Press, 1991.

Sitton, Thad and James H. Conrad. *Freedom Colonies: Independent Black Texans in the Time of Jim Crow*. Austin, TX: University of Texas Press, 2005.

Smallwood, James M. *Time of Hope, Time of Despair*. Port Washington, NY: Kennikat Press, 1981.

Smith, Thomas T. *The Old Army in Texas: A Research Guide to the U.S. Army in Nineteenth-Century Texas*. Austin, TX: Texas State Historical Association, 2000.

Smyrl, Frank H. "Texans in the Union Army, 1861–1865." *The Southwestern Historical Quarterly* 65, no. 2 (1961), 233–50.

Stampp, Kenneth M. *The Peculiar Institution: Slavery in the Ante-Bellum South*. New York: Vintage Books, 1956.

Stevens, Kenneth R. "William Pitt Ballinger: Galveston's Reluctant Rebel." *East Texas Historical Journal* 40, no. 1 (2002), 37–43.

Striner, Richard. *Father Abraham: Lincoln's Relentless Struggle to End Slavery*. Oxford: Oxford University Press, 2006.

Summers, Mark Wahlgren. *The Ordeal of the Reunion: A New History of Reconstruction*. Chapel Hill, NC: University of North Carolina Press, 2014.

Sutton, Robert K. *Stark Mad Abolitionists: Lawrence, Kansas, and the Battle Over Slavery in the Civil War Era*. New York: Skyhorse Publishing, 2017.

Syrett, John. *The Civil War Confiscation Acts: Failing to Reconstruct the South*. New York: Fordham Univeristy Press, 2005.

Taylor, Amy A. *Embattled Freedom: Journeys through the Civil War's Slave Refugee Camps*. Chapel Hill, NC: University of North Carolina Press, 2018.

Teters, Kristopher A. *Practical Liberators: Union Officers in the Western Theater during the Civil War*. Chapel Hill, NC: University of North Carolina Press, 2018.

Thomas, Hugh. *The Slave Trade: The Story of the Atlantic Slave Trade, 1440–1870*. New York: Simon and Schuster, 1997.

Torget, Andrew J. *Seeds of Empire: Cotton, Slavery, and the Transformation of the Texas Borderlands, 1800–1850*. Chapel Hill, NC: University of North Carolina Press, 2015.

Townsend, Stephen A. *The Yankee Invasion of Texas*. College Station, TX: Texas A&M University Press, 2006.

Tunnell, Ted. *Crucible of Reconstruction: War, Radicalism and Race in Louisiana, 1862–1867*. Baton Rouge, LA: Louisiana State University Press, 1984.

Turner, Elizabeth Hayes. "Juneteenth: Emancipation and Memory." *Lone Star Pasts: Memory and History in Texas*. Gregg Cantrell and Elizabeth Hayes Turner, eds. College Station, TX: Texas A&M University Press, 2007.

_____. "Three Cheers to Freedom and Equal Rights to All: Juneteenth and the Meaning of Citizenship." *Lone Star Unionism, Dissent and Resistance*. Jesús F. de la Teja, ed. Norman, OK: University of Oklahoma Press, 2016.

Tyler, Ron, ed. *The New Handbook of Texas*. 6 vols. Austin, TX: The Texas Historical Association, 1996.

Vorenberg, Michael. *Final Freedom: The Civil War, the Abolition of Slavery, and the Thirteenth Amendment*. Cambridge, UK: Cambridge University Press, 2001.

Wallace, Ernest. *Texas in Turmoil*. Austin, TX: Steck-Vaughn, 1965.

Warner, Ezra J. *Generals in Blue: Lives of the Union Commanders*. Baton Rouge, LA: Louisiana State University Press, 1964.

_____. *Generals in Gray: Lives of the Confederate Commanders*. Baton Rouge, LA: Louisiana State University Press, 1959.

Waugh, John C. *Last Stand at Mobile*. Abilene, TX: McWhiney Foundation Press, 2001.

_____. *Reelecting Lincoln: The Battle for the 1864 Presidency*. New York: Da Capo Press, 2001.

Westwood, Howard C. "Sherman Marched and Proclaimed, 'Land for the Landless.'" *The South Carolina Historical Magazine* 85, no. 1 (January 1984), 33–50.

White, Ronald C., Jr. *A. Lincoln: A Biography*. New York: Random House, 2009.

White, Jonathan W. *Emancipation: The Union Army and the Reelection of Abraham Lincoln*. Baton Rouge, LA: Louisiana State University Press, 2014.

Williams, David. *I Freed Myself: African American Self-Emancipation in the Civil War Era*. New York: Cambridge University Press, 2014.

Willis, Deborah and Barbara Krauthamer. *Envisioning Emancipation: Black Americans and the End of Slavery*. Philadelphia, PA: Temple University Press, 2013.

Winkle, Kenneth J. *Lincoln's Citadel: The Civil War in Washington, D.C.* New York: W. W. Norton and Co., 2013.

Winters, John D. *The Civil War in Louisiana*. Baton Rouge, LA: Louisiana State University Press, 1991.

Wittenberg, Eric J. *Little Phil: A Reassessment of the Civil War Leadership of Gen. Philip H. Sheridan*. Washington, D.C.: Brassey's Inc., 2002.

Wooster, Ralph A. "Texas." *The Confederate Governors*. W. Buck Yearns, ed. Athens, GA: University of Georgia Press, 1985.

_____ and Robert Wooster, eds. *Lone Star Blue and Gray: Essays on Texas and the Civil War*. Austin, TX: Texas State Historical Association, 2015.

Work, David. "United States Colored Troops in Texas during Reconstruction." *The Southwestern Historical Quarterly* 109, no. 3 (January 2006), 337–58.

## DIGITAL SCHOLARSHIP AND ONLINE DATABASES

Federal Writers' Project: Slave Narrative Project, Texas. Retrieved from the Library of Congress. Manuscript/Mixed Material. *https://www.loc.gov*.

"Howstuffworks." *https://history.howstuffworks.com*.

Davis, Kenneth C. "Juneteenth Our Other Independence Day." *Smithsonian Magazine Online*. June 12, 2020. *https://www.smithsonianmag.com/history/juneteenth-our-other-independence-day-16340952/*.

Galveston Historical Foundation. "Juneteenth and General Order No. 3." *https://www.galvestonhistory.org/news/juneteenth-and-general-order-no-3*.

Juneteenth Legacy Project. "The Juneteenth Legacy Project: Absolute Equality for All." *https://www.juneteenthlegacyproject.com/*.

Kenney, Kevin. "Juneteenth Celebrations Past and Present." Galveston and Texas History Center, Rosenberg Library. June 17, 2020. *https://www.galvestonhistorycenter.org/news/juneteenth-celebrations-past-and-present*.

McDaniel, W. Caleb. "How many slaves were refugeed to Confederate Texas." June 25, 2013. *https://wcm1.web.rice.edu/how-many-refugeed-slaves-in-texas.html*.

"National Registry, Juneteenth Organizations and Supporters." *https://www.juneteenth.com/history.htm*.

Robinson, Cliff. "Juneteenth Worldwide Celebration." *http://juneteenth.com.*

"Slavery in New Jersey: A Troubled History." An online exhibit by the Durrand-Hedden Hose and Garden Association, Inc. *https://www.durandhedden.org/docs/juneteenth-exhibit.pdf.*

Texas Historical Commission. "Celebrating Freedom for All: The 150th Anniversary of Juneteenth." May 19, 2015. *https://www.thc.texas.gov/blog/celebrating-freedom-all-150th-anniversary-juneteenth.*

Texas State Historical Association. *The Handbook of Texas Online. http://tshaonline.org/handbook.*

# Index

The letter < *a* > following a page number denotes artwork.
The letter < *i* > following a page number denotes an illustration.
The letter < *p* > following a page number denotes a photograph.
The letter < *t* > following a page number denotes a table.